D1229400

JOURNAL KEEPING

JOURNAL KEEPING

How to Use Reflective Writing for
Effective Learning, Teaching,
Professional Insight, and Positive Change

Dannelle D. Stevens
and Joanne E. Cooper

Sty/us
PUBLISHING, LLC.

STERLING, VIRGINIA

COPYRIGHT © 2009 BY STYLUS PUBLISHING, LLC.

Published by Stylus Publishing, LLC
22883 Quicksilver Drive
Sterling, Virginia 20166-2102

All rights reserved. No part of this book may be reprinted or reproduced in any form or by any electronic, mechanical or other means, now known or hereafter invented, including photocopying, recording and information storage and retrieval, without permission in writing from the publisher.

Library of Congress Cataloging-in-Publication-Data

Stevens, Dannelle D.
    Journal keeping : how to use reflective writing for effective learning, teaching, professional insight, and positive change / Dannelle D. Stevens and Joanne E. Cooper.
        p.   cm.
    Includes bibliographical references and index.
    ISBN 978-1-57922-215-4 (hardcover : alk. paper) — ISBN 978-1-57922-216-1 (pbk. : alk. paper)
    1. English language—Composition and exercises—Study and teaching (Higher)—United States. 2. Diaries—Authorship—Study and teaching (Higher)—United States. 3. English language—Rhetoric—Study and teaching (Higher)—United States. 4. Creative writing (Higher education)—United States. 5. College students—United States—Diaries. I. Cooper, Joanne E. II. Title.
PE1404.S827 2009
808'.0420711—dc22
                                                                                2008055004

13-digit ISBN: 978-1-57922-215-4 (cloth)
13-digit ISBN: 978-1-57922-216-1 (paper)

Printed in the United States of America

All first editions printed on acid free paper
that meets the American National Standards Institute
Z39-48 Standard.

Bulk Purchases

Quantity discounts are available for use in workshops and for staff development.
Call 1-800-232-0223

First Edition, 2009

10   9   8   7   6   5   4   3   2   1

Stylus Publishing, LLC is committed to preserving ancient forests and natural resources. We elected to print this title on 30% post consumer recycled paper, processed chlorine free. As a result, for this printing, we have saved:

13 Trees (40' tall and 6-8" diameter)
4,560 Gallons of Wastewater
9 million BTU's of Total Energy
587 Pounds of Solid Waste
1,104 Pounds of Greenhouse Gases

Stylus Publishing, LLC made this paper choice because our printer, Thomson-Shore, Inc., is a member of Green Press Initiative, a nonprofit program dedicated to supporting authors, publishers, and suppliers in their efforts to reduce their use of fiber obtained from endangered forests.

For more information, visit www.greenpressinitiative.org

Environmental impact estimates were made using the Environmental Defense Paper Calculator. For more information visit: www.papercalculator.org.

To Anita Pearl Friedrich Smith Fitzsimmons
1919–2007, elementary school teacher
my best teacher, my mother

With love, Dannelle

This book is dedicated to a long line of strong women in my life:

To my mother, Marion Elizabeth Beckendorf May, who gave me life,

To my daughters, Kimberly Elizabeth Findling and Katherine Marie Cooper,
who have filled my life with love, and

To my granddaughters, Ruby Heather Cooper-Karl, Elizabeth Mae Findling,
and Maris June Findling, whose lives fill me with hope and joy.

With love, Joanne

CONTENTS

TABLES AND FIGURES

Tables

Figures

ACKNOWLEDGMENTS

WE WOULD LIKE TO ACKNOWLEDGE those who have added to our work. This book about journal keeping is like a community garden. The community owns the land. Anyone with motivation can begin working in and learning about the journal garden by purchasing a blank book or opening a computer document. Yet the quality and enjoyment of the harvest of flowers, fruits, and vegetables is the result of the labor of individuals who seek to invest in health—their own, others', and even the larger community's. Journals, like gardens, have existed for many years in many forms. Our book offers the instructor and the professional seeds of thought and action for growing a healthy garden.

We begin by acknowledging the community who provided rich seeds of thought, our reference list: long and varied and full of the work of others who have studied and productively used journals in their work and lives. We acknowledge the contribution of those who have cared about and studied our ever-so-human processes of reflection, adult development, teaching, and writing: Marcia Baxter-Magolda, Robert Boice, Steven Brookfield, John Dewey, Peter Elbow, Robert Kegan, David Kolb, and Donald Schön. Then we must bow to those who contributed the cases in which they graciously shared the details of how they use journal writing in their classrooms and professional life: E. Kofi Agorsah, L. Rudolph Barton, Micki M. Caskey, Anna Edlund, Phyllis Edmundson, Wayne Iwaoka, Gregg Lizenbery, Laura Lyons, Carol Mack, Barbara Mossberg, Ann Nielsen, M. B. Ogawa, Clara Radcliffe, Gerry Recktenwald, Vicki Reitenauer, Isabelle Soule, and Donald Young.

Our students and colleagues always add to our understanding of how to use journals effectively. Several have given us their journal entries and journal activities that enrich this work: Adriana Burrola, Nicole M. Burton, Sue Butell, Mary Jane Cagle, Darci Denney, Serap Emil, Laura M. Evans, Michael Flower, Dominic Giansante, Drew Holland, Chris Hubley, Kati Hubley, Zafreen Jaffery, Jeff Judd, Kristen Kawczynski, Meg Kilmer, Jolina Kwong Caputo, Sam Leach, Barbara May, Shannan McFadden, Doris Newman, Tobi Page, Elsa Palza-Rink, Susan Reese, Vicki Reitenauer, Janet Sanders, Neil Santiago, Rebecca Lynn Schulte, Joe Scott, Ruth Scovill, Liam Skilling, Maralyn Smart Belgique, Lori Snowbarger-Neely, John C. Stanley, Cary Takara, John W. Vannatta, Alyssa Watanabe, Gayle Weatherson, Greg Wendling, Kathryn Yamamoto, and Chad Yasuda.

We turn to the several others who have contributed to these pages through manuscript reviews: David Kennen, Kathy Lasater, Antonia J. Levi, David Martinez, Judy Rantala, Vicki Reitenauer, Rebecca Schulte, Sally Sorenson, Molly Stevens, Carrol Tama, and Judy Van Zile. Finally, we deeply appreciate John Von Knorring, the publisher, editor, and friend who believed in this book and waited ever so patiently for us to weather the storms in our lives and produce the book you hold in your hands. Truly, this has been a healthy community garden.

PREFACE

GO TO THE BLANK BOOK SECTION OF ANY MEGA-BOOKSTORE and you will see many varieties of blank books for journal keeping: different sizes, shapes, textures, with lines, grids, and unlined pages. There are books dedicated to preserving recipes, documenting travel, listing movies seen, books read, and even golf courses played. This is a surprising phenomenon, given the many other ways to document and reflect on our lives through photos, podcasts, YouTube, computer documents, and scrapbooks. In fact, when we measured the length of all the shelves that contained blank books at our local mega-bookstore, it was 254 feet! Why do people continue to buy journals? Why this need to chronicle our lives? It is as old as the cave paintings of over 5,000 years ago. Document and reflect, stand back and understand, gain perspective and save. Although journals abound in the popular book markets, in academic settings journal keeping is underused and sometimes misunderstood.

This book is about journal keeping in two different contexts: using journal writing in classroom and field settings, and keeping a journal in professional life. We study journal keeping. We seek to inform you about why and how to use journals. Both of us are prodigious journal keepers in our personal and professional lives. We both seek to help our students learn how to use and value reflection and learning through making journal entries. We have taught a course in journal keeping for 10 years and led many faculty development workshops on journals in classrooms and professional life to further the documentation of and reflection on teaching, research, and service.

Until 18 years ago, however, Dannelle was a sporadic journal keeper. To this day, she finds among her things barely filled journals with pretty covers that record her seeking to work out life's problems. These were disaster journals only, recording and trying to make sense of life's challenges. Upon entering academe, she wanted to become a better thinker and writer. She turned to keeping both a professional and personal journal. She writes,

> Learning how to write? I did it myself. All by myself! Yep! I did my academic writing. Yet, my journal was recess where I played with my writing friends—focused freewriting, metaphor, concept mapping, dialogue, listing, and, mostly, freewriting. During recess I could fully express my playful, curious, and contemplative self; I was on an adventure to learn about me and about writing. I became a student of writing. I read about how other people learned to write. I listened when writers spoke of their craft. I thank Peter Elbow and Robert Boice, my guides to authenticity, creativity, and clear thinking. I learned to value the surprises in my writing like "journal writing is like recess."
>
> Back in "class," I wrote research articles, helped to organize an edited volume, and received tenure and promotion. Then I saw other uses for my journal. I began to use my journal to document and organize my professional life.
>
> What is it kids learn at recess? Hmmm, how to explore and play with others. In this metaphor, the others are words on a swing, in the sand box, or on the slide. In class after recess, the words are not as much fun. They are in straight lines and in rows and must be edited so others can understand and access them. Yet I know that to have that elusive quality, voice, to organize my life, to track all my projects and to have new, fresh ideas I need recess, too. I need my journal. Period.

Joanne, who has been keeping a personal journal now for more than 30 years, says,

> I used to write whenever the mood hit me. I already had enough obligation and guilt in my life. Gradually, I developed the habit of writing daily, in the morning right after I woke up as a way to center myself for the day, to record my dreams, and to see what comes up as an important issue for me. I write in longhand in a bound book. I date my entries and record the time of day. I like to use different colored ink each day because the change helps me see where one entry ends and another begins.
>
> I've said for years that writing in my journal "keeps my rudder in the water," helping me sort out what I think and feel amid the competing claims on my life and time. My journal feels like an extension of me now. I never go anywhere without it. I once left one on an airplane and it felt like someone had cut off my arm.
>
> I started keeping a professional journal about 8 years ago because of Dannelle's influence. I had just become the Associate Dean of the College and was attending

meetings almost all day. My professional journal held notes on meetings I attended, phone calls I needed to return, as well as ideas for classes I taught, research projects I was involved in, and freewrites written while I was teaching. It has been so useful when trying to remember what happened the last time a particular committee met or when trying to recall a powerful speaker at a conference or what was decided in the last meeting with one of my doctoral students. This journal, too, goes everywhere with me and has been particularly helpful in planning the contents of our book.

Contents of the Book

This book has three parts. Part one contains the introduction and summary of the book as well as two chapters on how the theories of reflection, adult development, and transformational learning describe and explain the role of journal keeping in learning and adult lives. In part two we show you how to use journals in your teaching and professional life. We cover how to include journals when introducing and structuring your course, to use some basic journal-writing techniques, and to give feedback on journal writing. Part two also includes a chapter on specific ways to use a journal in professional life as well as some considerations when assigning journal writing in the computer age. All of these chapters contain tables that summarize and demonstrate the content. Throughout the book we have peppered our descriptions and explanations with figures and quotations from student, faculty, or administrator journals derived from our classes, our research, and even student comments on our course evaluations. Part three of the book contains 19 case studies over two chapters. These describe how individual faculty, graduate students, and administrators have incorporated journal writing into either their teaching or their professional life.

Audience

We seek to inform a broad audience in education: teachers, faculty, staff, students, and administrators. As our cases indicate, we believe this book will be useful for teachers and faculty across all the disciplines.

JOURNAL KEEPING

Part One

Journal Writing and Its Theoretical Foundations

1 Journal Writing: Definition and Rationale

- What is a journal?
- What is the history of journal keeping?
- What are the key benefits of journal writing for students?
- Is journal writing worth the class time?
- What are the key benefits of journal keeping for faculty and administrators?
- Is keeping a professional journal worth the time?
- What are the ancillary benefits of journal writing?

2 Reflection and Learning From Experience

- What are the three leading theoretical perspectives on reflection and learning from experience?
- How do these theoretical perspectives link to journal writing?

3 Reflection and Adult Developmental Theory

- What is the role of journal writing in adult development?
- How does journal writing further critical reflection and transformational learning?
- How does journal writing foster personal growth and development?

JOURNAL WRITING
Definition and Rationale

The unexamined life is not worth living.
Socrates (470–399 BCE)

MOST PEOPLE WOULD AGREE WITH SOCRATES, whose wisdom still rings true in the 21st century. Yet people today live at such a fast pace that there is little time to examine their lives. Many adults are too busy attending to the ever-present demands of work, home, e-mails, and the phone to really take stock of who they are and where they are going. Life in higher education is, sadly, no exception. Students, faculty, and administrators rush to meet multiple work, family, and personal responsibilities.

If Socrates' words echo anywhere, it should be in the academy—where the central goal is the creation of a thoughtful, educated society. The examined life is a worthwhile goal for all—for students who are tomorrow's citizens; for faculty who must balance the competing expectations of teaching, research, and service; and for administrators who manage and lead. In fact, recent research underscores the value of reflection in academic life. Blackburn and Lawrence (1995) found that self-knowledge appears to be the most powerful influence on productivity for faculty in all of their roles: teaching, research, and service.

Reflection is the path both to self-knowledge and to greater personal efficacy. Although there are many ways to reflect, the journal is concrete evidence of one's evolving thought processes, documenting valuable, often fleeting glimpses of understanding. This ancient tool is central to the pursuit of a more thoughtful life. In short, journal writing is a powerful form of reflection and a time-tested, well-established method for examining our lives.

Reflection is the process whereby we reconstruct and make meaning of our experience. Philosopher John Dewey described reflection as the "reconstruction and reorganization of experience which adds meaning to that experience" (1938, p. 6). Harvard developmental psychologist Robert Kegan (1982, 1994) sees making meaning as the central task of all adults. The well-known educator and lifelong journal keeper Madeleine Grumet argues that ". . . any writing and reading of our lives presents us with a challenge that is at the heart of every educational experience: making sense of our lives in the world" (1990, p. 3).

The journal in its many forms has been around for a long time. From the early archived Chinese historical documents in 56 AD (Lowenstein, 1987), to *The Pillow Book of Sei Shonagon* in the 10th century (translated by Morris, 1967), to *The Diary of Anne Frank* (Frank, 1952), to the postings of today's multitudinous bloggers, journals offer a means by which people chronicle their lives, not simply to document events and ideas that are important to them, but also to foster deeper reflection on those events and ideas.

For all its long and distinguished history in providing a locus for reflection and for furthering learning in many cultures, journal writing in classroom instruction or in the day-to-day work of faculty and administrators in higher education is not as widely used as it could be (English & Gillen, 2001). This book describes journal-writing strategies used both by students in college classrooms and by professionals in higher education. We also share detailed case studies of how journal writing is used across a wide range of academic disciplines and professional contexts. In this chapter we examine the following key questions:

- What is a journal?
- What is the history of journal keeping?
- What are the key benefits of journal writing for students?
- Is journal writing worth the class time?
- What are the key benefits of journal keeping for faculty and administrators?
- Is keeping a journal in professional life worth the time?
- What are the ancillary benefits of journal writing?

The purpose of this chapter is to provide the reader with our working definition of a journal and set it in its historical context. In addition, we describe both the benefits and the reasons for engaging in journal writing in the classroom and in professional life.

What Is a Journal?

We define a journal as a sequential, dated chronicle of events and ideas, which includes the personal responses and reflections of the writer (or writers) on those events and ideas. Scholars use various words to describe such collections of reflective writing: *journal, log, diary, dialectical notebook,* and *workbook* (Mallon, 1984; Moon, 1999a). Keeping a journal can also be described as *journaling, journal keeping,* or *journal writing.*

Our definition of a journal is intentionally flexible, but also at times arbitrarily restrictive given the purpose of this book: to describe the potential variety of uses of journal writing in academe. Although we recognize that uncollected writings, letters, business card collections, or other documents that are later compiled into a volume can be considered journals in some contexts, we do not consider them such in this book. Likewise, photo albums, scrapbooks, sketchbooks, and most audiovisual recordings, although they may contain journal elements, are not classified as journals according to our definition.

A journal has six defining attributes: It is written, dated, informal, flexible, private, and archival.

- **Written.** The primary form of expression in journals is the written word. Pencils, pens, typewriters, and computers are the tools for transferring and organizing information, ideas, thoughts, and questions on blank pages. Expressing thoughts or ideas on paper within a bound book or in a text file can be replaced in some cases by words spoken into a recorder. Ideas, observations, thoughts, and musings can be shown through visual images as well, particularly in art, science, or architecture classes. Even video journals, Facebook, and YouTube could be considered "written," personal expression.

- **Dated.** Journal entries are dated so that both the sequential order and the context of each entry are clear. Ideally, the date (and time in some cases) should precede the entry. Careful dating is important not only to chronicle actual events, but also to reveal the evolution of the journal keeper's own ideas and understandings. In the case of classroom or field settings, the evolution of ideas is usually the more important consideration. Students may or may not need to know exactly when an entry was made, but they do need to be able to chart and compare the course of their own learning and perceptions over time. In professional settings, dated entries allow faculty or administrators to easily track meetings, notes, phone calls, professional contacts, and a variety of other professional activities, as well as the development of their research ideas, observations, reflections, and insights (Cooper & Stevens, 2006; Stevens & Cooper, 2002).

- **Informal.** Journal writing is usually informal or almost conversational in tone (Fulwiler, 1987). Indeed, many journal keepers regard the journal as a way of conversing with the self (Cooper & Dunlap, 1991; Durgahee, 2002; Grumet, 1990; Ostermann & Kottkamp, 1993; Stevens & Cooper, 2002). Journals are among the few places in academe where the conventions of writing have very little importance. Student journals may or may not follow the usual writing conventions: Some may contain many drawings or even doodles, whereas others that are produced on the computer may look more conventional. Because one of the main purposes of classroom journal writing is to enhance learning without the constraints of formal written or oral presentation expectations, instructors usually do not demand conventional grammar or spelling (Crème, 2005; Fenwick, 2001; Hampton & Morrow, 2003; Murray, 1984). In many classroom journal-writing activities, spelling, grammar, paragraph construction, and even overall organization take a back seat to ideas, especially ideas in progress. A good journal entry is judged more by its willingness to take risks, to voice confusions, to explore undeveloped ideas (or even projects), and the degree to which it furthers the development of voice and the ability to take the perspective of others than by its adherence to writing conventions of correct grammar, spelling, and organization (Boud, 2001; Dickerson, 1987; Durgahee, 1998; Fulwiler, 1987).
- **Flexible.** From the type of entries, formatting of pages, purposes for journal keeping, audience for whom it is intended, and benefits that accrue from keeping them, journals can vary tremendously, one from another and even internally. This flexibility is a central characteristic of a journal. Virginia Woolf (1954) described such flexibility:

What sort of diary should I like mine to be? Something loose knit and yet not slovenly, so elastic that it will enhance anything, solemn, slight or beautiful that comes to mind. I should like it to resemble some deep old desk, or capacious hold-all, in which one flings a mass of odds and ends without looking them through. (April 20, 1919)

- **Private.** Journals are typically intended for private use, not public distribution. In educational settings, the audience can vary depending on the use of the journal. If the audience is the self, journaling is essentially a private act. In classrooms instructors have to decide and inform students about how "private" the student journal writing will be. Some of today's journaling practices, such as blogs (computer weblogs), can include a larger audience. Bloggers can send their entries to themselves, selected friends, or even to the World Wide Web (Suzuki, 2004). Some faculty require students to post (and more than likely polish) their papers on a blog for other students to read and react to. Chapter 8 elaborates on the opportunities and challenges of journaling on a computer.
- **Archival.** After completion, a journal may or may not be saved by students or faculty members. However, because of the authentic observations of the writer, the chronological nature of the entries, and the bound format of many journals, the journal can become an archival document. Its usefulness depends on the journal keeper and the reader. Historically, journals have been quite important in understanding and examining daily life (Lowenstein, 1987; Mallon, 1984).

In light of this list of defining attributes, we now examine how this form of human expression has appeared throughout history.

The History of Journal Keeping

In the past, the diary or journal was a handwritten "book" that described the daily activities, interests, observations, problems, and insights of the journal keeper (Lowenstein, 1987). One of the early examples of journal keeping dates to 10th-century Japan where Heian court ladies kept "pillow books" inside their stone pillows or in the drawers of wooden pillows. *The Pillow Book of Sei Shonagon* (Shonagon, 1967), a journal of a lady in waiting to Empress Sadako during 995–1010 AD, offers a valuable glimpse into the intrigues, daily activities, and interests of Japanese court life over 10 years. One remarkable feature of Shonagon's books is their 164 lists, such as "Elegant things" and "Things that cannot be compared."

During the 1600s in London Samuel Pepys began keeping a journal to track his financial progress, but, as his career progressed, it grew to encompass every aspect of his life, from dalliances to matters of state. His diary covered events such as his appointment as Chief Secretary to the Admiralty and his account of the Great Fire of London. After his death, his journal was one of the first diaries to be published and widely distributed. Today it offers a vivid glimpse into many aspects of life in 17th-century London.

In the United States the Puritans recorded their spiritual goals and growth in journals, and women pioneers wrote serial letters to their families back home about life on the western frontier (Lowenstein, 1987). Culley states, "Women diarists in particular wrote as family and community historians. They recorded in exquisite detail the births, deaths, illnesses, visits, travel, marriages, work, and unusual occurrences that made up the fabric of their lives" (1985, p. 4). The creators of these 18th- and 19th-century semi-public diaries intended them to be read. It is only more recently that journals have come to be perceived as a record of private thoughts and feelings (Culley, 1985).

Today journals perform a wide array of functions in a variety of educational settings. In the higher education classroom, Hiemstra (2001) describes nine types of journals or journal formats: (1) learning journals; (2) diaries; (3) dream books or logs; (4) autobiographies, life stories, or memoirs; (5) spiritual journals; (6) professional journals; (7) interactive reading logs; (8) theory logs; and (9) electronic journals. Besides different types of journals, students may keep journals in various learning contexts such as classrooms, labs, and field and clinical sites (Fulwiler, 1987; Hiemstra, 2001; Kerka, 2002; Stevens, Cooper, & Lasater, 2006). Yet Hiemstra notes that despite more than three decades of using journal writing with students in colleges and universities across America, this practice "remains underused as a teaching or learning tool" (2001, p. 19).

Those in the academy use journals in their roles as instructors, faculty members, researchers, and administrators. From our research we found that academics used journals in four ways: to hold conversations with themselves about work and life, to organize their work, to experiment with a variety of strategies to meet different work demands, and to reflect on their professional lives (Cooper & Stevens, 2006). In the next sections we discuss the benefits and time-worthy reasons to use journal writing, both in classrooms and in professional life.

Key Benefits of Journal Writing for Students

Research has shown that requiring students to keep a journal is an effective way of accomplishing key learning objectives (Boud, 2001; Fulwiler, 1987; Moon, 2006). The type of student journal entries faculty assign can range from the methodical and mundane (e.g., laboratory notes or a research log) to the esoteric and highly educative (e.g., creative responses to text or examination of underlying personally held assumptions about readings and field observations). Tables 1.1 and 1.2 summarize the key benefits of journal writing and list some of the research evidence related to those benefits.

• By writing in a journal students can integrate and apply course content, practice skills, and develop insights and new perspectives.

As summarized in Tables 1.1 and 1.2, research indicates that journal writing can play a central role in classroom learning. Yet even with this good news about all the different objectives that can be accomplished with journal-writing assignments, instructors need to consider whether journal writing is really worth taking valuable class time.

Is Journal Writing Worth the Class Time?

Whether or not journals are worth the class time depends on how assigned journal writing supports, reinforces, and helps you accomplish your course objectives. Success also depends on your spending time introducing, explaining, and giving feedback on journal writing. Therefore, it is important to understand the benefits of assigned journal writing and relate those to your objectives. The following set of questions will help you identify some of the objectives that can be efficiently and effectively addressed with classroom journal use.

1. Are my students completing the class readings? Participating in class discussions?
2. Did my students accomplish course objectives the last time I taught the course?
3. Are my students connecting course concepts and material to their own life experiences?
4. Do my students struggle with writing and generating ideas for writing?
5. Are my students participating fully in non-classroom activities like service learning experiences, laboratory work, clinical observations, or group work?
6. Are my students willing to examine the hidden personal assumptions that influence their responses and actions?
7. Are my students reflecting critically about their readings and experiences?
8. Do I encourage creative and "out-of-comfort-zone" thinking?

Each of these questions is related to overall course objectives. For example, look at the question, "Are my students doing the class readings?" In a research methods course,

Table 1.1
Classroom Journal Writing

Objective I: Integrate and Apply Course Content

Student Learning Objectives	References
Keep a dated log of progress on a project.	Loo, 2002.
Practice, learn, and connect course content to one's life.	Fenwick, 2001; Fisher, 1990; Fulwiler, 1987; Hampton & Morrow, 2003; Klein & Boals, 2001; Koirala, 2002; Moon, 2006; Park, 2003; Stork & Sisson, 2005; Thorpe, 2004.
Collect, document, and analyze field and clinical observations to develop and hone observation skills.	Craft, 2005; Durgahee, 1997; Eyler, 2002; Krmpotic, 2003; Nicassio, 1992.
Reflect critically on issues addressed in class.	Fisher, 1990; Kerka, 2002; Hampton & Morrow, 2003.
Reflect on deeply held assumptions and beliefs.	Brookfield, 1990, 1991; Durgahee, 1997, 1998; Gil-Garcia & Cintron, 2002; Hoban, 2000; Tsang, 2003.

Table 1.2
Classroom Journal Writing

Objective II: Practice Skills, Develop Insights, and Expand Perspectives

Student Learning Objectives	References
Become better writers and clearer thinkers.	Dickerson, 1987; Elbow, 1973; Kerka, 2002.
Develop voice; discover, examine, and affirm beliefs and insights.	Boyd & Fales, 1983; Hatcher & Bringle, 1997; Holt, 1994.
Improve problem identification and problem-solving ability.	Durgahee, 1998; Hatcher & Bringle, 1997; O'Hanlon, 1997.
Develop professional identity in professional preparation programs.	Boud, 2001; Penney & Warelow, 1999; Spalding& Wilson, 2002; Tsang, 2003.
Understand others' perspectives, reduce stress, and improve health.	DeSalvo, 1999; Hubbs & Brand, 2005; Kalb, 1999; Pennebaker, 1990, 2000, 2004.

your course objective might be: "Through reading course material, students will be able to describe and critique the major research paradigms." To accomplish this objective, of course, students have to do the course readings. Yet during classroom discussion of the reading, you observe that only two or three students are participating.

What are the silent ones doing? Have they completed the readings, or are they just shy? From a large body of research (Fulwiler, 1987; Kerka, 2002; Moon, 1999b), we know that when students respond in writing to readings outside of class, usually in a "learning journal," they retain more and are more active during class discussion. Thus, having students keep learning journals addresses your concern that students are not doing the course readings (Brost & Bradley, 2006). As Darci noted in a reflection written after one of our classes,

> This semester I approached journal keeping from a whole new perspective. From day one, I forced myself to get into the habit of writing journal reflections after each class. Instead of having a separate notebook of various sheets of folder paper filled with notes from class discussions and assigned readings, I decided to keep everything in one journal. I found this technique to be very useful. Finding notes from a certain class discussion or readings has been much easier because everything is in one place, my journal. I also found that writing reflections after each class helps a lot because it helped me remember what we discussed in each class. Writing reflections each time I read has also been helpful because, when we were asked to write about what we learned from the readings, I was able to refer back to my journal. (personal communication, May 12, 2008)

One of the key objectives of this book is to give you enough information about the various ways that journals can be used in different educational settings so that you can make an informed decision about their value in relation not only to class objectives but also to the limited time you have with students. Faculty can learn about journal writing by using it in their classrooms, and they can also use it in their professional lives.

Key Benefits of Journal Keeping for Faculty and Administrators

Faculty and administrators in academic settings lead multifaceted lives (Boice, 1990, 2000; Kegan, 1994). A typical faculty member must learn how to effectively coordinate grading papers, teaching classes, developing a research agenda, managing programs, working on committees, and providing leadership on campus and in the community. A seasoned academic administrator grapples with organizing projects and program development, managing staff, keeping track of meetings, and setting strategic planning goals. To become skilled at managing these many and varied expectations requires numerous iterations of organizational systems. Calendar organizers, personal digital assistants (PDAs), academic plan books, sticky notes stashed in different places, or our own paperless memory are popular organizational options. Some faculty members and administrators have found that the very best organizational tool is a journal. To assist in making a decision about keeping a journal in your professional life, we encourage you to ask yourself the following questions:

1. Do I spend a good deal of time searching for the notes from committee meetings?
2. When I update my curriculum vita or prepare for promotion, am I frustrated because my materials are scattered in different files and binders?
3. Do I have a system for keeping track of phone calls and correspondence?
4. Do I have one place to document and keep track of my observations, my teaching, and my research?
5. Do I want to capture insights and ideas while they are still fresh in my mind?
6. Do I want to write with a clearer voice?
7. Would I like to find a way to improve my writing and productivity?
8. Do I need a place to clarify, plan, and review my current and future research agenda?
9. Do I want to gain a clearer perspective on challenging communication problems in my department or program?
10. Do I want to think more deeply about issues in teaching as well as about my role in departmental and community leadership?
11. Do I want to expand my creative expression and playfulness with fresh ideas?

These questions encompass common faculty concerns. If you answered "yes" to any of these questions, keeping a journal in professional life may be for you. For example, the first question deals with having notes available from meeting to meeting. By keeping a journal that has all ongoing activities and meeting notes in chronological order, you will have all notes from the prior meetings at your fingertips. You can easily retrieve them, especially if the pages are numbered and you have a table of contents. A growing body of research has shown that keeping a journal in professional life addresses all of the issues embedded in these questions (Cooper & Dunlap, 1991; Cooper & Stevens, 2006; Gee, 2004; Holly, 1989; Miller, 2003; Stevens & Cooper, 2002).

The journal in professional life is certainly not imposed from outside like a classroom assignment, but rather is a self-generated solution to meeting the many expectations of academic life. Barbara, a lifelong journal keeper, professor, college president emerita, and program director, stated,

> My journal is the key to my resilience and my intellectual growth. Through all my years in the academy, I have kept a journal. Even when I became a college president, I never stopped journaling, never stopped publishing articles or going to conferences, writing poetry, and certainly never stopped writing in my journal. (personal communication, November 19, 2006)

Tables 1.3 and 1.4 summarize the typical objectives of keeping journals in professional life in the first column, and the references in which this objective was discussed in the second column.

In Tables 1.3 and 1.4 you can see that journals are used to accomplish two major professional objectives: managing day-to-day and long-term work expectations, and developing skills and insights. Keeping a journal organizes, simplifies, clarifies, and develops the kind of skills, thinking, and spontaneous creativity expected in academic work. Yet it takes time, precious time, that many of us feel we just don't have.

Is Keeping a Professional Journal Worth the Time?

How you manage your time is a critical factor in achieving success in the academy. Academic work is one career in which you have to learn how to balance the number and variety of opportunities as well as develop your own unique contribution (Boice, 2000). To create time to use a journal in professional life and to make keeping a journal worth the time, faculty carry the journal with them all day long, through classes, meetings, and office hours, and then take it home to reflect on their day. Micki, a newly tenured faculty member, takes her journal to all meetings because not only does she have the notes from the last meeting in her journal, but she is also ready to create a to-do list in her journal during the meeting. She states,

> My journal helps balance so many things. As an academic, I have many things going on at the same time. The only way to keep it all straight is to journal. It is like I have all these plates spinning in the air—some have chips because they have fallen or collided with one another. They collide less often when I have a journal. (personal communication, November 15, 2006)

Table 1.3
Journal Writing for the Professional

Objective I: Manage Day-to-Day and Long-Term Work Expectations

Journal Objective	References
Record committee activities and decisions.	Cooper & Stevens, 2006; Holly, 1989; Miller, 2003.
Keep a dated log of professional activities for promotion and peer review.	Stevens & Cooper, 2002.
Develop and organize research activities.	Hickman, 1987; Jones, Torres, & Arminio, 2006; Stevens, Cooper, & Lasater, 2006.
Reflect on and address problems and issues in the work setting.	Bryan, Cameron, & Allen, 1988; Gee, 2004; Progoff, 1992; Shepherd, 2004.

Table 1.4
Journal Writing for the Professional

Objective II: Develop Skills and Foster Insights

Journal Objective	References
Converse with the self.	Cooper & Dunlap, 1991; Durgahee, 2002; Glaze, 2002; Grumet, 1990.
Foster better writing and clarity of thought.	Boice, 1990, 2000; Elbow, 1973; Klein & Boals, 2001.
Reflect critically on teaching and professional expertise.	Bryan, Cameron, & Allen, 1998; Gee, 2004; Glaze, 2001, 2002; Grumet, 1990; Kerka, 2002.
Develop professional identity.	Durgahee, 2002; Penney & Warelow, 1999; Valli, 1997.
Examine deeply held assumptions.	Boud, 2001; Brookfield, 2006; Kegan & Lahey, 2001; Wallace & Oliver, 2003.
Reduce stress and improve health.	DeSalvo, 1999; Kalb, 1999; Lepore, 1997; Pennebaker, 2004; Pennebaker, Mayne, & Francis, 1997.

Micki is not alone. Those who consistently use a journal have found that, ironically, it takes time and it also saves time. As Skip, the director of a university research center, stated, "This [pointing to his journal]? This is my life!" (personal communication, April 3, 2005).

So far, we have described how the journal can forward classroom instructional goals as well as help faculty meet demands in their professional lives. Yet there are other benefits that are often not acknowledged or even well known.

What Are the Ancillary Benefits of Journal Writing?

The first ancillary benefit of journal keeping is better health through stress reduction; the second is clearer thinking and, ultimately, better writing. When faculty assign journal writing in their classes or begin to keep a journal in their professional lives, the intended objective may not be better health nor improved thinking and writing. Yet both of these ancillary benefits are research-validated outcomes of the kind of reflective writing that a journal contains.

Better Health Through Stress Reduction

The first ancillary benefit of journal keeping is that reflective writing decreases stress and improves health. There is solid scientific evidence that journal writing improves both emotional and physical health with benefits accruing to both healthy and unhealthy individuals who write regularly about troubling or traumatic events in their lives (De Salvo, 1999; Pennebaker, 1990, 2000, 2004; Smyth, 1998).

Much of this evidence comes from the work of James Pennebaker (1990, 2004), who conducted 10 years of research on the relationship between telling personal stories and health. For example, Pennebaker (2004) found a significant drop (50%) in visits to the health center for those who wrote about both traumatic events and feelings as compared with those who wrote about trivial things or those who simply described traumatic events without relating their feelings. These writers often reported feeling a greater sense of well-being when they began to write. They felt calmer, more able to cope with stress, and more serene as they faced life's challenges. After writing for 15 minutes a day over a 4-day period, this improvement tended to last for 6 weeks.

Other studies indicate that people who write about their problems demonstrate positive behavior changes, such as being absent from work less often, improving grades, finding a new job more quickly, improving relationships, and increasing appreciation for life ("Journaling After Trauma," 2002). After students were asked to write their deepest thoughts and feelings about an upcoming exam, one study found a significant decline in depressive symptoms from 1 month to 3 days before the exam (Lepore, 1997). Thus journal writing can help the writer cope with future as well as past stressful events. Research indicates that healthy students who write about problems or issues, versus those writing about trivial or positive events, experience an increase in memory capacity as well (Smyth, Stone, Hurewitz, & Kaell, 1999). Smyth conducted a review of literature that found that "written emotional expression produces significant health benefits in healthy participants" (1998, p. 179).

How does writing about traumas produce these results? According to Pennebaker, Mayne, and Francis (1997), writing about traumatic events helps writers convert memories into an organized, linguistic format. Originally, these memories may not be in a form that appears organized or understandable. By writing about the event, writers can distance themselves from the event and identify the feelings that accompany the event. Writing organizes their thoughts and facilitates better psychological and physiological well-being. These researchers explain that inhibiting traumatic events and feelings over time acts as an ongoing stressor, gradually undermining the body's defenses. De Salvo states,

> . . . when we deal with unassimilated events, when we tell our stories and describe our feelings and integrate them into our sense of self, we no longer must actively work at inhibition. This alleviates the stress of holding back our stories and repressing or hiding our emotions, and so our health improves. (1999, p. 24)

DeSalvo also recommends writing about illness through the use of "wounded body narratives" (1999, p. 184). These writings help the journal keeper to feel "more composed (calmed, quieted, settled, soothed)" (1999, p. 184). A randomized study of clinically ill patients who wrote about stressful experiences found clinically relevant improvements in health status after 4 months (Smyth, Stone, Hurewitz, & Kaell, 1999). There are journal-keeping workbooks for healing available (Adams, 1998). Written narratives, whether the writers have asthma, multiple sclerosis, or AIDS, help them to make sense of life and their illness, provide safe places to express their feelings of helplessness and rage, and share important information with others about their illness and ways to survive it.

Improved Thinking and Writing Skills

A second ancillary benefit of regular journal writing is the improvement of both thinking and writing skills. Regular writing practice leads to an abundance of new ideas and increased fluency (Boice, 1990). Faculty who require their students to practice certain writing techniques, such as freewriting, know this (Cooper, Stevens, & Chock, 2006). Students report that they learn to write more fluently and easily. For example, one of our returning students reported that her journal-writing experience in our class bolstered her feelings about herself as a writer to the point that she had the courage to enter and complete a doctoral program.

Peter Elbow (1973, 1981) has been a major proponent of freewriting as a means to clearer, better writing for students. Freewriting involves writing steadily for 5 minutes or more without stopping to edit what you've written. This is essentially the kind of writing that many veteran journal keepers use. It is a way to see what is on your mind. In his research on faculty productivity, Boice (1990, 2000) also recommends a kind of freewriting called "spontaneous writing" to enhance momentum and to generate ideas for articles and research. Boice's research on new faculty describes freewriting or spontaneous writing as a "momentum-inducing strategy" (2000, p. 45). Compared with those who write in binges, the faculty who have writing momentum use brief, daily writing sessions and produce more written pages per week, write more hours per week, and have more manuscripts submitted and accepted for publication (Boice, 2000). Cameron (1992), in the highly regarded book *The Artist's Way,* also recommends regular journal writing to enhance creativity. In a sequel to *The Artist's Way,* Bryan, Cameron, and Allen (1998) discuss journal writing in the workplace. By writing at least three pages each morning in a journal, they claim artists, writers, and others can enhance their creativity and become more productive.

Of course freewriting and regular writing do not have to take place in a journal. Yet, because the writer can find ideas generated in the past and can feel free to write any small snippet of thought in this highly flexible format, the journal is particularly conducive to writing and thinking improvement. In fact, Boice's (2000) suggestions for spontaneous writing with daily entries and informal style fit well with the way a journal works. Dated journal entries allow writers to review previous thoughts and insights over time. The journal's flexibility, informality, and privacy encourage risk-taking and the creation of new ideas while at the same time encouraging connections across the ideas. The journal's privacy and potential for playfulness engenders voice. Journals can be the location of notes from conferences and conversations with colleagues working on similar projects. Journal entries can, then, become the foundation for future publications, grants, research projects, and so on. Entries become the "seeds" to future projects. For students, writing regularly can improve their writing and thinking (Moon, 2006). For faculty, writing regularly can enhance their ability to maintain a steady output of manuscripts and subsequently produce enough publications to earn tenure and promotion (Silvia, 2007).

In sum, although those who assign classroom journal writing or keep a journal in their professional lives are often aware of the immediate purposes and benefits, they may be unaware of the ancillary benefits to health and writing productivity. Those who write about traumatic events in their lives are often healthier both psychologically and physically. Those who write in a journal regularly are more creative and clearer thinkers, as well as more fluent writers. These ancillary benefits can be powerful motivating factors in building the habit of reflective journal writing both for our students and in our own professional lives.

Conclusion

In this first chapter, we define a journal, share its history, and describe its value as a classroom activity and in the lives of faculty. Keeping a journal in higher education holds many obvious as well as hidden benefits. We, Dannelle and Joanne, have kept personal and professional journals for a combined total of more than 60 years. In addition, both of us have used journals in our university classrooms for a combined total of more than 30 years. Our experience has taught us the enduring value of journal keeping in our own personal and professional lives. We know that journal writing helps students learn more, become clearer thinkers and writers, and develop the habit of using reflective writing in their future lives.

This chapter presents the characteristics, history, and some of the benefits of journal writing. In chapters 2 and 3, we present the powerful theoretical frameworks that explain the value of journal keeping. Chapters 4 to 8 present the more practical side of teaching and keeping a journal. In the last two chapters, we share the stories of faculty who use journals in their classrooms and their professional life.

2

REFLECTION AND LEARNING FROM EXPERIENCE

My journal has become a symbol of independence. It allows me the luxury of time to myself.
The journal requirement for this class gave me permission to stop and spend some time on
my thoughts. My family would consider journal writing self-absorbent, selfish and a waste
of time. I had to overcome and reframe this mindset that has influenced me throughout my
life. It was a slow process for me to change my attitude about the importance and utility of
the journaling activity. I found that writing in my journal gave me justification to spend
time focusing, venting or thinking metacognitively about different aspects of the semester.
The professor said it well when she said, "writing is thinking."

Laura, returning graduate student

BEFORE COMPLETING CLASS ASSIGNMENTS IN HER JOURNAL, Laura viewed journal keeping as "self-absorbent." She has modified her prior assumption and now knows the power of journal writing. She connects writing, learning, and reflection. The theoretical foundation for journal writing lies in learning models that place reflection as a centerpiece in learning. Because of the connection between reflection, writing, and learning, we use the work of three well-known learning theorists: John Dewey, David Kolb, and Donald Schön, who all emphasize that reflection is a fundamental component in human learning and development.

Reflection is more than merely thinking or musing (Boud, 2001; Dewey, 1933). Reflection is a complex and intentional intellectual activity that generates learning from experience (Boyd & Fales, 1983). What kind of learning results from reflection? Dewey (1933), a prominent 20th-century educational philosopher, argues that reflective thinking builds the foundation for the furtherance of democratic principles.

Kolb (1984) and Schön (1983) assert that reflection helps adults cope with and learn from ill-structured, complex problems in social settings and the workplace. If the potential results of reflective thinking are that adults develop positive democratic attitudes and practices and are more able to address problems in their social and professional lives, then as educators it is important for us to find ways to foster reflection. Journals promote reflection on and learning from experience (Boud, 2001; English & Gillen, 2001; Fulwiler, 1987; Moon, 1999a, 1999b, 2006).

This chapter addresses the following key questions:

- What are the three leading theoretical perspectives on reflection and learning from experience?
- How do these theoretical perspectives link to journal writing?

The purpose of this chapter is to describe and explain how three well-known and respected theorists use reflection in their explorations of human learning and how those theories support the use of journal-writing activities in classroom learning and in professional life.

Three Leading Theoretical Perspectives on Reflection and Learning From Experience

John Dewey (1859–1952): Experience, Reflection, and Learning

As the father of the 20th-century progressive movement in education and an eminent philosopher, John Dewey's work is particularly helpful in defining and describing the relationships among experience, reflection, and learning. Because faculty expect students to learn, especially the knowledge within their respective disciplines, reflection on course readings and field experiences is essential. Across a variety of disciplines, journals are a well-established way to record, reflect, and continue to learn from experience. John Dewey has defined what experiences are educative, how learning proceeds, and what role reflection plays in learning.

Dewey (1933) states that an *experience* is an interaction between the individual and the environment. An experience first includes more than participation in activities; experience could be reading a book, taking lecture notes, or talking with others.

Secondly, an experience contains what Dewey referred to as *continuity,* a continuous flow of knowledge from previous experiences. Dewey writes:

> What [a person] has learned in the way of knowledge and skill in one situation becomes an instrument of understanding and dealing effectively with the situations that follow. The process goes on as long as life and learning continue. (1938, p. 44)

Learning, therefore, is a continuous and cumulative process. Prior learning becomes the fodder for further understanding and insight.

In his 1933 work, *How We Think,* Dewey distinguishes between four different modes of thinking: imagination, belief, stream of consciousness, and reflection. Dewey acknowledges that imagination, belief, and stream of consciousness are certainly part of our thinking activities, yet they do not necessarily contribute to learning and even less to lifelong learning. Reflection, however, plays a different role. Dewey defines reflection as the:

> . . . active, persistent and careful consideration of any belief or supposed form of knowledge in light of the grounds that support it and the further conclusions to which it tends. (1933, p. 9)

Reflection is active. When we reflect we examine prior beliefs and assumptions and their implications. Reflection is an intentional action. A "demand for a solution of a perplexity is the steadying, guiding factor in the entire process of reflection" (Dewey, 1933, p. 14). Dewey adds

> The function of reflective thought is, therefore, to transform a situation in which there is experienced obscurity, doubt, conflict, disturbance of some sort into a situation that is clear, coherent, settled, harmonious. (1933, p. 100)

Reflection starts with discomfort during an experience and leads a person to a balanced state. It takes time and focus to reach clarity of thought.

Dewey writes that reflection "gives an individual an increased power of control" (Dewey, 1933, p. 21). It "emancipates us from merely impulsive and merely routine activity. . . . It converts action that is merely appetitive, blind and impulsive into intelligent action" (1933, p. 17). It is not enough just to have an experience. Reflection directs that experience to learning and deeper insights. Many of the journal writers we have interviewed highly value the role of the journal in their thinking and learning. Barbara, professor and college president emerita, describes her journal as a place

> . . . where I can be most fully conscious. I trust that process. My journal is where I am consciously conscious of what it means to be a human being on this earth. It is where I listen to myself. (personal communication, November 19, 2006)

Reflective thinking takes time and requires one to engage in several different "phases" or "aspects" of reflective thought:

1. *Perplexity:* responding to suggestions and ideas that appear when confronted with a problem
2. *Elaboration:* referring to past experiences that are similar
3. *Hypotheses:* developing several potential hypotheses
4. *Comparing hypotheses:* finding some coherence within these hypotheses
5. *Taking action:* experiencing "mastery, satisfaction, enjoyment" when selecting and then acting on these hypotheses (Dewey, 1933, pp. 106–115)

Dewey asserts that these are not steps but aspects of reflective activity. An individual may stop at some point and find it necessary to go back and, for example, collect more experiences.

A key point is that informed action follows this reflective thinking process and leads to more ideas and therefore generates more experience on which to reflect. "Reflective thinking impels to inquiry" (Dewey, 1933, p. 7). Journal writing is particularly helpful in this recursive process of examining and generating ideas to address problems or confusions (Boud & Walker, 1998; English & Gillen, 2001; Kerka, 2002).

In fact, to Dewey, reflective thinking fosters the development of three attitudes that further the "habit of thinking in a reflective way." These three attitudes are:

- Openmindedness (freedom from prejudice)
- Wholeheartedness or absorbed interest
- Responsibility in facing consequences (Dewey, 1933, p. 33)

These dispositions are the foundation for education that gives people "a personal interest in social relationships and control and the habits of mind that secures social changes without introducing disorder" (Dewey, 1944, p. 99).

As in Laura and Barbara's reflections, journal writing gives journal keepers the tools to examine and learn from the life events that swirl around them. Research in a variety of disciplines underscores the powerful role reflective journal writing can play in the adult life. Durgahee (1997) found that when nursing students kept a journal, they continually reflected on the social and personal meanings of inter-actions in clinical settings. Rodriquez and Sjostrom (1997) helped their student teach-ers examine their preconceived notions about students of color through a series of journal-keeping activities followed by class discussions. Faculty who assign journals in their classrooms believe that journals help students develop ways to understand their motives, thoughts, and learning, as well as to grapple with many personal dilemmas (Stevens, Cooper, & Lasater, 2006).

Faculty and administrators who keep a journal at work often cite addressing prob-lems as one of its key benefits. They use the journal not only to document and organ-ize the continuous work flow but also to converse with themselves about problems and issues in the workplace (Cooper & Stevens, 2006). Cooper and Dunlap (1991) found that administrators used their journals to examine and reexamine the complex problems in their work settings and to develop deeper understandings. Through written docu-mentation of observations, responses, and insights, adults create fuel for current reflec-tions and for even deeper and broader connections and informed actions in the future.

Dewey's work has been cited in numerous studies as the theoretical ground for re-flective journal writing (English & Gillen, 2001; Kerka, 2002). Two other theorists who use reflection in their work, David Kolb (1984) and Donald Schön (1983, 1987), also add to our understanding of the role of reflection in human learning. Kolb describes the elements in the cycle of learning from experience; Schön focuses on the role of reflection in professional practice settings such as education and medicine.

David Kolb (1939–   ):
Reflection and an Experiential Learning Model

David Kolb's (1984) theory of experiential learning elaborates the process by which adults learn from their experience. "The significance of his work may be that he sets experience in a context in learning. He sees it as a reflective process that develops con-cepts from the medium of experience" (Moon, 1999a, p. 24). Kolb's model (1984) (Figure 2.1) illustrates the four stages of learning from experience: concrete experience, reflective observation, abstract conceptualization, and active experimentation.

Figure 2.1
Kolb's Theory of Experiential Learning

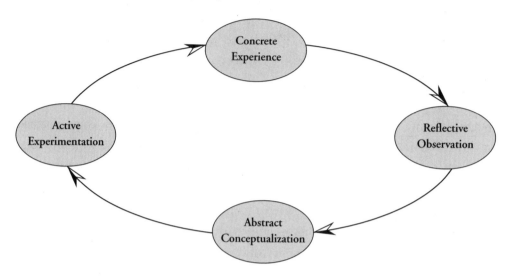

The first phase in the Kolb cycle—concrete, "real world" experience—means direct, practical experience that results in "knowledge by acquaintance" as opposed to "knowledge about" something. Concrete experience precedes reflective observation of that experience. The next phase, reflective observation, involves focusing on what that experience means and its connotations in light of past learning. In the third phase, abstract conceptualization, learners relate their reflective observations to what they already know: extant theories, preconceived notions, and embedded assumptions. During active experimentation, the last phase before the cycle begins again, the learner applies new concepts and theories to the real world.

For Kolb (1984), learning is a cycle that perpetuates more learning. "The learner moves 'from actor to observer' from 'specific involvement to general analytic detachment,' creating a new form of experience on which to reflect. The quality of reflection is crucial in ensuring that the learner does progress in [his or her] learning" (Moon, 1999b, p. 25). Reflection is the engine that moves the learning cycle along its path to further learning, action, and more reflection. Without it, the learner is "stuck" in the experience without gaining any new understanding.

Kolb did not address journal writing per se as a reflective tool. Yet the journal offers a unique opportunity to chronicle and examine more closely and carefully our concrete experiences, and then to ask the hard questions about how these experiences relate to what is already known. When students or faculty keep a journal, they are capturing a concrete experience in a written form. During writing, journal writers can readily examine their concrete experiences, and even step back and reflect on how those observations might relate to other experiences. To extend the learning further, during abstract conceptualization the writing can be reread and analyzed for underlying assumptions and beliefs that contribute to positive outcomes (Boud, 2001; Brookfield, 1995; Hatcher & Bringle, 1997). According to Kolb's theory, then, journal writers can actively experiment with the ideas that motivate their actions and thus approach new experiences with fresh insights and the possibility for new learning.

Faculty who require students to complete service learning projects often have students record their observations in a log or a journal that is used for class discussion and reflection (Eyler, 2002; Hatcher & Bringle, 1997). "Service learning extends the classroom into the community, and students frequently encounter unfamiliar situations that challenge and contradict their perspectives" (Hatcher & Bringle, 1997, p. 154). Using Kolb's model and a written "values clarification" activity, Hatcher and Bringle helped students express and analyze their perspectives during a service learning assignment.

When students are involved in a service learning activity at a homeless shelter, for example, an instructor might assign the students to list the words or phrases that describe their senses, feelings, and actions in this site. These are their reflective observations. Then, after this brainstorming activity, they might write about their overall impressions and thoughts about the homeless as well as identify the contradictions and challenges to their prior assumptions. These activities encourage students to unlock and examine their abstract conceptualizations that were closely held assumptions about the homeless. Using these journal entries in small-group or whole-class discussion informs the students' future active experimentation on these ideas at the homeless shelter service site.

Many examples of the use of journals in field settings appear in the nursing education literature. Research on preservice nurses who journal during their initial service learning and clinical experience has shown that their written observations of concrete experience are a critical underpinning for reflective observations of all the experience and knowledge they bring to the clinical setting (Craft, 2005; Durgahee, 1998; Eyler, 2002). To move students to a deeper examination of course content, as well as to persuade students to grapple with their preexisting beliefs and unexamined assumptions, faculty often make comments in the margins of student journals. By asking questions and linking student journal reflections to course material, faculty can begin a written conversation with the student (Durgahee, 2002; Shuttloffel, 2005; Stevens, Cooper, & Lasater, 2006).

In summary, these service learning and clinical setting examples highlight the fact that merely exposing students to a new off-campus experience is not enough. For students to uproot and dissect their prior knowledge and preconceived notions, to foster integration of new insights, and to boost the overall effects of clinical experience, service learning, and community projects, faculty must guide their students through a reflective activity. A journal is an appropriate location for documenting experience, generating reflections, and examining assumptions. Boyd and Fales further argue that reflective learning is the

> . . . core difference between whether a person repeats the same experience several times, becoming highly proficient at one behavior, or learns from experience in such a way that he or she is cognitively or effectively changed. Such a change involves essentially changing his or her meaning structures. (1983, p. 100)

Kolb's work elaborates a cycle of learning that leads to informed future action. Another theorist, Donald Schön, describes the power of two different kinds of reflection to develop expertise in professional practice fields such as education and medicine.

D. A. Schön (1930–1997):
Reflection and Professional Practice

Schön (1983, 1987) was interested in how and when professionals use reflection to build professional knowledge and expertise. Schön's work appeals to professionals who teach professionals because he distinguishes between the static knowledge found in textbooks and the dynamic, adaptive knowledge that the expert uses in clinical and professional settings. To bridge this gap, preservice professionals need guided practice. Given the dynamic, complex, and unstructured settings in which professionals work, developing reflective capacity is essential.

Schön's initial work (1983) was geared toward those who educate professionals. He asserts that in the past, professional practice programs have delineated the profession's "espoused theories" to novices. Yet these theories may make sense in the textbooks but may not actually be applied in daily practice. The theories that guide daily decision making, the "theories-in-use," are contextually specific, idiosyncratic, and often not mentioned in textbooks of professional practice. Over and over again the theories-in-use are tested and developed to become proven, sometimes even unconscious, ways of performing. One of Schön's central concerns is how to help novices learn the theories used by experts in real life settings.

Schön describes two processes that contribute to the development of expertise: reflection-in-action and reflection-on-action. Professionals reflect while they are engaged in an experience (reflection-in-action) and after an experience (reflection-on-action). In this process of reflection, novice professionals develop the theories-in-use that underlie competent, expert decision making.

Research indicates that the nursing and education fields have frequently used reflective journal writing to help professionals develop theories-in-use (Boud & Walker, 1998; Brookfield, 1995; Craft, 2005; Durgahee, 1998). Gil-Garcia and Cintron (2002) analyzed the journals of 35 teachers and administrators over 2 years for their value as a reflective tool. The predominant topics of reflective journaling were analysis of teaching actions, introspection of the teaching or administrating decisions, and testing of ways to adapt and modify lessons. The participants in the study concluded that their journals were beneficial. As one participant noted, "I will continue to keep a journal where I can review my classroom activities and my students' reactions because that helps me keep in touch with what I am doing and keep an eye on improving my teaching" (Gil-Garcia & Cintron, 2002, p. 7).

For most professionals, the journal is a reflection-on-action zone allowing them to slow down the constant array of demands, scrutinize their actions, and determine whether their present activities contribute in the long run to their goals and desires. Thus the journal can become a place where professionals can develop the ability to identify tacit, unspoken knowledge that is not typically taught. Many professional preparation programs have relied on Schön's work to guide their use of journal-writing activities.

How These Theoretical Perspectives Link to Journal Writing

Through the reflective activity of journal writing, the writer records, examines, and learns from experience. Reflection is a critical and central construct in Dewey, Kolb, and Schön's theories. Analysis and comparison of their theories leads to the following themes.

- Reflection occurs in a cycle of action–reflection–action.
- Reflection contributes to the development of valued human capabilities.

How Does Reflection Occur? The Action–Reflection–Action Cycle

Reflection occurs in a cycle of action, reflection, and action. Dewey, Kolb, and Schön included reflection in at least one step in their theories on learning from experience. For all three, reflection is not isolated from experience; it is part of a cycle of learning and experiencing. Dewey described "aspects" of reflection. Kolb described "phases." Schön divided reflection into two parts: reflection "in" and "on" action. All include experience followed by reflection and the generation of hypotheses or experimental conclusions that are applied to further experience. For each, learning from experience requires shuttling back and forth from observations, to examination and reflection on those observations, and then acting on those conclusions. The more people reflect on action, the better they get at reflecting and the more they can learn about themselves (Boyd & Fales, 1983; Fulwiler, 1987; Rainer, 1978; Valli, 1993).

Journal writing promotes a cycle of reflection, experience, reflection, and ultimately learning through observation of the self in action. When faculty ask students to summarize and respond to a class reading in their journals, several things happen. First, students have to review, select, and organize what they have read and then put their reactions into their own words. This should be an engaging and active learning activity. In one of our surveys of student response to journal writing, we found that 94% of students felt that journal writing helped them to track their learning, and 98% considered writing a reflection on all their journal entries at the end of the term to be a valuable activity as well (Stevens & Cooper, 2007). Because the entries are dated, journal writers can track the development of their thinking and insights over time. Journal entries can be reread, reviewed, and reexamined at different times. Reflecting on past journal entries affirms that one can learn from experience and can allow the journal writer to witness a developing self.

Why Is Reflection Worthwhile?
Development of Valued Human Capabilities

Through the development of reflective capacity and the habit of reflective thinking the student or professional achieves certain broader, more lasting outcomes as well. Dewey (1933) asserts that reflection is the foundation for democracy through developing the capacity for openmindedness, wholeheartedness, and responsibility. Kolb's (1984) theory shows how important it is to assess our basic beliefs that may blind us to new knowledge. Finally, Schön's model (1987) leads the professional to becoming an expert.

Journal writing over time can lead to the development of these valued outcomes. Written reflections are more than a mirror of experience. Because perceptions and insights based on reflections can be distorted by prior knowledge and beliefs, writing these reflections down and reviewing them allows the journal writer to scrutinize assumptions and beliefs and glean a deeper understanding of the assumptions that underlie their decision making. Learning how to learn, how to examine assumptions, how to abstract key ideas from experience, and how to feed those ideas back into our next experience are valued human activities that may lead to those qualities that Dewey propounds: openness, absorbed interest, and responsibility. Journal-writing activities document the thinking and observations of writers, allow writers to go back and review their thinking, acknowledge their own misconceptions, and adjust their thinking accordingly.

Conclusion

Journal writing can be justified from a variety of theoretical perspectives. This chapter introduces three theories that can be used to justify journal keeping as a reflective activity. Three classic theorists, Dewey, Kolb, and Schön, use reflection as the engine that drives their theories of human learning. Journal writing has a place in each one of these theories because it reinforces and boosts learning whether it is in the context of social settings, service learning sites, or professional practice programs. In the next chapter we explore another set of theories that interface well with journal writing, those associated with adult development, transformational learning, and personal development.

Table 2.1 summarizes this chapter's key themes and shows how these themes are manifested in classrooms and in professional life. In the last column on the right, we have added some specific assignments that demonstrate how this theme might be realized in classroom journal-writing assignments.

Table 2.1
Theories of Reflection and Classroom Journal-Writing Assignments

Reflection Theme	Journal Writing: Demonstrating the Theme	Discipline-Specific Classroom Assignments
Reflection occurs in a cycle of action–reflection–action.	Document observations and insights. Encourage review, application, and reexamination of ideas.	NURSING: After writing your reflections on your clinical experience today, list two key assumptions about the power dynamics at the nurses' station: Who makes decisions? Who is supervising? How do things function? When we visit next week, check whether your assumptions (theories) are accurate.
Reflection contributes to the development of valued human capabilities.	Write about and examine personally held assumptions about social problems to develop democratic dispositions, to act with insight, and to develop tacit knowledge in professional settings.	EDUCATION: When we visit the school in which 75% of the children participate in free and reduced lunch programs, note how the school compares with the school you attended. What implications do these differences or similarities have for teaching and learning? Write out what you think a teacher needs to know to be successful at this school in this context.

3

REFLECTION AND
ADULT DEVELOPMENTAL THEORY

Journal keeping has helped me to spill out what is in my brain. My brain is like a treasure chest filled with gold and silver and the way to get it is by unlocking the lock. The key to opening the chest is the journal.

Cary, a graduate student

CARY DESCRIBES HIS BRAIN AS A VERITABLE "TREASURE CHEST." By examining the treasures of thought in his journal, he begins to understand what he knows. A large body of research over the last 25 years has deepened our understanding of how adults learn and develop (Baxter Magolda, 1998; Brookfield, 1990; Drago-Severson, 2004; Kegan, 1982, 1994; Kegan & Lahey, 2001; Merriam & Caffarella, 1999). Reflecting critically on the assumptions that underlie beliefs and behavior energizes adult development. Journal writing is a powerful tool for adults who seek to make meaning and to critically reflect on their lives (Brookfield, 1995).

Journal writing can lead to adult learning and even development. Journals are used for many different reasons that include capturing an experience, recording an event, exploring feelings, or making sense of what we know (Boud, 2001). The audience can be the self or others. Journal writing is "as varied as those who engage in it" (Boud, 2001, p. 9). Chiefly, however, journal writing enhances reflective thinking; it is "a device for working with events and experiences in order to extract meaning from them" (Boud, 2001, p. 9). As Cary affirmed with his treasure-chest metaphor, journals help us to make "sense of the world and how we operate within it" (Boud, 2001, p. 9). As another student commented, "This class encourages me to be a reflective professional.

33

Reflection improves my understanding of my own life and actions. It keeps me centered and aware. This is crucial."

Using the theoretical perspectives of those who study adult development, this chapter considers how journal writing facilitates adult learning and development in classrooms, professional life, and personal life. We address three key questions:

- What is the role of journal writing in adult development?
- How does journal writing further critical reflection and transformational learning?
- How does journal writing foster personal growth and development?

The purpose of this chapter is to explore how journal writing interacts with four key perspectives that describe and explain how and in what ways adults develop: adult developmental theory, critical reflection, transformational learning, and personal growth theory.

The Role of Journal Writing in Adult Development

A central assumption of adult development is that development does not stop at childhood's end, but continues throughout the lifetime (Kegan, 1982, 1994; Drago-Severson, 2004). By *development* we mean a progression from a simpler or lower stage to a more mature, complex, or advanced stage. Adult development involves cognition and emotion, resulting in a relatively permanent change in behavior or understanding (Kegan & Lahey, 2001).

Adults develop in a variety of ways, including biological and psychological development, sociocultural development, and cognitive development (Merriam & Caffarella, 1999). At any given moment these types of development are in a process of continuous, reciprocal interaction and are influenced by the context in which adults find themselves (Magnusson, 1995).

Adults actively construct their own reality. One sign of development is a growing ability to reflect on experience and to construct a new kind of self that better responds to and meets the demands of adulthood. This involves becoming more self-directed as well as moving from one order of consciousness to another, so that adults are able to distinguish what they really feel, want, and need, as opposed to what others believe they should feel, want, and need. The voices of others recede as adults begin to identify their own feelings, desires, and thoughts. However, this development is not easy because adults have meaning-making systems that prevent, resist, and even circumvent change (Kegan & Lahey, 2001). The challenge for professionals who work with adults is to provide them with the tools to continue to develop and to examine the thought systems that resist change. Journal keeping is one such tool.

To answer some of adulthood's central questions and to continue to learn, adults construct meaning through conversations with the self and others. For novice and experienced journal writers, the journal is a tool for having this conversation. If the self is central to knowledge construction, as so many theorists claim (Baxter Magolda, 2001; Belenky, Clinchy, Goldberger, & Tarule, 1986; hooks, 1994; Kegan, 1982; Noddings, 1984), then conversations with the self are important elements in adult development. Journals facilitate these conversations (Cooper & Stevens, 2006). Hopkins claims that "Our narratives are the means through which we imagine ourselves into the persons we become" (1994, p. xvii).

One of the journal-writing techniques that furthers that conversation is the practice of writing a dialogue between parts of the self. As Zafreen, a novice journal writer in one of our classes, wrote in her reflective piece about the value of journal keeping,

> The most intriguing part of journal keeping is interactive dialogues. Sometimes I write dialogues with myself and get answers from my subconscious mind. That phenomenon is particularly fascinating to me. When I talk to myself in the journal, I find concrete, valid answers to the problems and troubles that exist within me. It enables me to solve a conflict or a problem. (personal communication, May 15, 2006)

Kegan's (1982) constructive-developmental theory involves two basic tenets: People construct reality by making meaning of their experience, and adults evolve through qualitatively different ways of dealing with the world characterized by periods of stability and transition. Thus, personality development is seen as a spiral progression of balances between subject and object or self and other. Kegan asserts that cognition and emotion are inextricably tied to each other, and when there is developmental change there is tension and frustration. Kegan's theory ties the individual to the social and it is the balance of the two that constitutes the self. Journal writing assists adults in identifying these two parts as well as seeking balance and handling the tensions inherent in development (Bryan, Cameron, & Allen, 1998; Cameron, 1992).

As an extension of Kegan's work, Baxter Magolda (1998, 1999b) examines the attainment of "self-authorship" in college students. "The early years of the journey into adult life are particularly difficult because they are marked by transformation from reliance on external authority to taking ownership and responsibility for one's life" (Baxter Magolda, 2002, p. 3). Self-authorship involves the ability to balance one's own perspectives against the claims of others, which, for college students, includes peers, parents, and scholars. Keeping a journal is one way for students to clarify their individual perspectives (O'Hanlon, 1997).

Self-authorship involves complex assumptions about the nature and construction of knowledge, the ability to evaluate evidence in deciding what to believe, and a sense of identity through which individuals perceive themselves as capable of knowledge construction. College programs need to promote student self-authorship by emphasizing how to construct one's perspective and how to balance it with external forces, and by providing experiences that strengthen confidence and internal identity (Baxter Magolda, 2002). Journal writing in the classroom or field setting is an ideal vehicle for the construction of students' own perspectives, as well as a place to consider how to balance that perspective against the claims of others (Lankard, 1996).

From her 16-year longitudinal study of young adults, ages 18 to 34, Baxter Magolda (2004) created a model of epistemological reflection that portrays individual meaning-making as socially constructed and context-bound. She believes that "people actively construct or make meaning of their experience—they interpret what happens to them, evaluate it using their current perspective, and draw conclusions about what experiences mean to them" (2004, p. 31). In this model, developmental transformation stems from the interaction of internal and external factors, namely assumptions and experiences. Personal epistemology is thus "intertwined with other dimensions of development, namely identity and relationships" (2004, p. 31). One example of this is a "learning partnerships" model in which young adults partner with peers or professors to transform their thinking (Baxter Magolda, 2001; King & Baxter Magolda, 2005). Although some participants in her study experienced learning partnerships in college, many more experienced them after college. These post-college experiences offered "substantial challenge," and were accompanied by "substantial support" (Baxter Magolda, 2004). Baxter Magolda states,

> Challenge came in the form of three core assumptions inherent in contexts participants viewed as growth producing: knowledge is complex and socially constructed; self is central to knowledge construction; authority and expertise are shared in mutual knowledge construction among peers. (2004, p. 41)

Her participants' experiences demonstrated three principles essential to the development of self-authorship: Learners need to be validated as knowing something, learning needs to take place based on and within the learner's experience, and learning itself is not the sole property of one person but is mutually constructed. Applying these principles in classrooms, in what she calls "learning-centered practice," furthers young adult development (Baxter Magolda, 1999a).

Journal writing provides a window into how young adults address these epistemological questions by offering concrete evidence of their meaning-making to themselves and their instructors. By putting thoughts on paper, the journal writer makes explicit and visible that which is often fleeting and difficult to capture. In light of Baxter Magolda's (1999a) learning-centered practice, journal writing can make concrete what the writer already knows, as well as generate new ideas. In a journal, writers can mine their own experiences to learn more. By voluntarily sharing journal entries or even writing dialogues with the self or imagined others, the writer is co-constructing meaning. As a student, Maralyn, notes, "My journal contains the hard stuff, the good things in life and just the 'everyday' things. By writing about them, it helps me. It gives me a place to *put* things. My journal gives me a place to look at things I do and make better decisions in the future" (personal communication, January 24, 2006).

Whether they are students in a college classroom, faculty struggling with tenure, or administrators trying to lead their organizations, many adults use journals to further their meaning-making. Barbara, an experienced journal writer, noted,

> When I want to know what I really think, I write in my journal. It is more than a mirror: it does not reflect me. It is an evolving me; it is an organic process; it is discovery work. Writing in my journal changes me. I am growing and I am evolving as I write. (personal communication, November 19, 2006)

The journal is a reflective tool that allows adults to make long-term, relatively permanent changes in cognition and behavior.

Furthering Critical Reflection and Transformational Learning

According to developmental psychologists Kegan (1994) and Drago-Severson (2004), there are two basic types of learning: informational learning and transformational learning. *Informational learning* involves the acquisition of skills or knowledge, whereas *transformational learning* involves critical reflection on one's assumptions or "a 'leading out' from an established habit of mind" (Kegan, 1994, p. 232). Both of these types of learning are used in classrooms and in professional life. Informational learning occurs, for example, when adults learn new information or connect course content with their previous experience in their journal. Transformational learning, on the other hand, occurs when adults question assumptions that underlie their beliefs and actions in the world. Journal-writing assignments based on service-learning activities, clinical nursing experiences, and teacher education field placements are often focused on transformational rather than informational learning. Students are encouraged to examine their entering beliefs and assumptions, and then reflect on how these shape and even limit their responses and perceptions in field and clinical settings. These reflections further their development as professionals (Craft, 2005; Durgahee, 1997; Glaze, 2002; Hatcher & Bringle, 1997; Krmpotic, 2003; Tsang, 2003).

Reflection on experience, whether verbal or written, forms the basis for both informational and transformational learning (Mezirow & Associates, 2000). Although informational learning is common and useful, transformational learning builds the foundation for adult development and allows for growth and development from one stage to another. Mezirow defines transformation as "a movement through time or reformulation of reified structures of meaning by reconstructing dominant narratives" (2000, p. 19). The narratives can be the stories we tell ourselves that explain our observations. If transformational learning involves the reconstruction of narratives (explanations of the world, points of view or habits of mind), then the journal, as a repository of these narratives, becomes a natural support for reflection and transformational learning.

To transform one's narratives (i.e., assumptions or established habits of mind), adults must first examine these critically. Critical reflection or "assumption hunting" is the first step in the process of transforming beliefs (Brookfield, 1990, 1995). Certainly critical reflection can take place in conversation with others (such as in a university class) or in conversation with the self (such as in a journal). Even though keeping a journal is only one way of examining one's operating assumptions about the world and the self, many have found that the privacy and informal nature of journal writing fosters a closer and deeper awareness of the self. Rainer notes,

> Four 20th-century pioneers of psychology and literature played major roles in conceptualizing the principles of modern journal writing: Carl Jung, Marion Milner, Ira Progoff, Anais Nin. Each of them, in an individual way, pointed out how the diary permits its writer to tap valuable inner resources. And they developed techniques that

aid in this process. Jung emphasized the importance of recording dreams and inner imagery; Milner, the usefulness of intuitive writing and drawing; Progoff popularized techniques for uncovering an inner destiny; and Anais Nin demonstrated the creative fulfillment achieved through listening for and valuing one's feelings. All of them recognized a need in the modern world to reflect calmly upon knowledge that comes from within. (1978, p. 21)

Written reflection upon knowledge that comes from within can take the form of student responses to assigned readings in a particular course, faculty deliberations on what they know about creating team learning in their classrooms, or administrator insights about how to engage in strategic planning for their organizations. These types of journal entries are not, by definition, transformative. Yet, they can become the seeds for further reflections that can lead to the examination of internal, closely held assumptions and beliefs.

In Joanne's qualitative research methods class, she used several journal-writing activities to help students examine their beliefs and assumptions that serve as a foundation for research. "Deepening self-awareness helps to sharpen one's reflection, writing, thinking, and ability to communicate. Thus, for the qualitative researcher, the meditative focus of journal writing can only help to refine the researcher as research instrument" (Janesick, 2004, p. 95). As Kathryn, one of our graduate students, wrote,

> Throughout the journal, I noticed that I was constantly going back and forth between what was going on outside (my interaction with the world) and inside (my feelings or ruminations about it) in a dialectical evolution of new understandings. I would go to class and then reflect. From re-reading the journal, I was constantly capturing a new piece of the puzzle of my research interest. The journal kept me focused and probing more deeply in my investigative inquiry. (personal communication, May 7, 2007)

Reflection becomes critical, and therefore capable of getting past adherence to established ways of thinking, when it has two distinct purposes: to understand how considerations of power undergird, frame, and distort perceptions; and to question the assumptions and practices that may seem to make adult lives easier but actually work against their best long-term interests (Brookfield, 1995).

Assumptions are "the taken-for-granted beliefs about the world and our place within it that seem so obvious to us as not to need stating explicitly" (Brookfield, 1995, p. 2). These assumptions are often termed *hegemonic,* that is, assumptions that appear to the majority of people as "wholly natural, preordained, and working for their own good, when in fact they are constructed and transmitted by powerful minority interests to protect the status quo that serves those interests" (Brookfield, 1995, p. 15). Here is an example of a student reflection on one of her journal entries. It illustrates how a seemingly offhand journal entry contained the seeds of deeper awareness of power imbalances in her work life:

> I read a bumper sticker on the way to class that day when I wrote this freewrite. It really affected me. The bumper sticker read, "Women are men without ambition." This bumper sticker struck me so strongly that I knew there had to be some reason why. As I started writing the freewrite in class, the words came quickly and by the end of the freewrite, I was surprised by the feelings that I had revealed. Both the quote and freewrite raised issues I am grappling with professionally. . . . I was not expecting that this simple bumper sticker would evoke such personal concern about gender inequity among my colleagues. I found that the more I wrote, the more bitter I became. I realize now I have a real issue with how women are treated in my school district. (Jennifer, personal communication, May 15, 2006)

The awareness of power imbalances is an important part of reflection and critical thinking that enable us to develop as adults.

Students must have the freedom and safety to respond honestly and openly in their journals to identify their assumptions and question the power dynamics in their lives. As one student said in one of our research surveys, "In this course I learned that leadership, management and communication are embedded within and are not just perfunctory qualities" (personal communication, December 16, 2006).

Through critical reflection faculty can also learn and grow. Faculty can explore the assumptions that underlie the objectives, assignments, and outcomes of their teaching practices. In addition, they can examine the assumptions they hold about what they want their lives in the university to be like. Conscientiously conducted, this written examination of core assumptions in a journal can lead to a positive transformation in teaching, service, and research (Boice, 2000; Cooper & Stevens, 2006).

Richard, a graduate student, used his journal to examine his place in his doctoral program. He spent some time at the beginning of his program doubting his place in the program. Through his journal he came to the conclusion that we all have special talents and that his fellow students had expertise in areas that were different from his, but that he belonged in the doctoral program. He states, "Keeping a journal has taught me a lot about myself. My professional decisions are now based on good evidence, the evidence that comes from my journal. The process has been empowering" (personal communication, October 17, 2006). Examining assumptions allowed Richard to reflect on and reassess previous thoughts and actions that may have been problematic and to decide on his place among his fellow students.

Another lens by which some writers think about adult development is that of "personal development." The focus in the next section is on the use of narrative or story as a guide to personal growth and development.

Fostering Personal Growth and Development

In the more popular literature, journal writing is consistently related to personal growth and development. It is a way to discover who we are and why we are living our lives in a particular way. Pipher states, "Growing our souls could be defined as the steady accretion of empathy, clarity, and passion for the good. . . . Our lives are journeys toward a certain kind of wisdom. . ." (2006, p. 58). We can see this growth in Richard's journey, described previously.

Underscoring the importance of narrative, Pipher asserts, "We all have stories to tell. However, we do not necessarily know what they are and why they are important. Writing can help us see why our stories matter, and why we feel a sense of urgency to tell them" (2006, p. 40). Whether we are students reflecting on our lives and our learning, faculty sorting through a research agenda, or administrators planning a new program, our stories creep into our writings, coloring the way we live our lives. It is important to understand those stories and the ways in which they influence us. As Pipher states, "You have your own set of life themes, habits and ways of organizing yourself into a coherent 'I.' . . . All of this individuality that is you, properly understood and clearly presented, is a tremendous gift to the world" (2006, p. 41). Note that Pipher says "properly understood and clearly presented"; these are not easy tasks. To create the "coherent I," journal keepers must reflect on their own unique and disparate set of experiences and then choose actions based on that understanding. As one student said in an anonymous survey from our research, "What I learned in this class is that just understanding that encountering differences (different people, different ideas) is almost always a good thing because of the invaluable lessons that can be learned" (Stevens & Cooper, 2007).

This journey toward a certain kind of wisdom embodies the experience of personal growth and development that can be enhanced by journal writing. Hiemstra points out that journal writing is "an investment in self through a growing awareness of personal thoughts and feelings" (2001, p. 24). Berman would agree; he states, "introspective classroom diary writing is therapeutic, not because it causes our problems to disappear magically, never to return, but because it heightens our understanding of those problems and helps us find ways to live with them" (1994, p. 38). Writing about one's problems helps students (or professionals) to reframe those problems in more positive ways. Berman asserts, ". . . by changing our stories of ourselves, we change our lives" (1994, p. 40).

Many scholars recommend journal writing as a tool for learning and growing (Brookfield, 1995; Drago-Severson, 2004). Ruderman and Ohlott (2002), for example, recommend journal writing for the development of women as leaders. Scholars such as English and Gillen claim that journal writing "is central to the reflective practice approach of adult education and a good way of keeping track of the development of ideas and of monitoring works in progress" (2001, p. 89). Our research on keeping a professional journal also supports the use of journals as an essential support to growth and development (Cooper & Stevens, 2006). The flexible format of the journal allows for conversation with the self, with another person, or even with an imagined person. These conversations facilitate evolving insights that are enhanced by successive entries. These entries can be read and reread, allowing for "a progressive clarification of insights" (Hiemstra, 2001, p. 20). Thus the journal is a depository for the stories of adult lives, for successive layers of those stories that can lead to new insights, and for the rethinking of operating assumptions that can energize personal growth and development.

Conclusion

Development does not stop at the end of childhood but continues throughout adulthood. Central to that development is meaning-making—in other words, constructing meaning around one's life experiences. Two important elements in meaning-making are conversations with the self and with others. Journal writing can be an important tool in facilitating conversations with the self and furthers a deeper understanding of our values and beliefs, as students Cary and Richard describe. It can even serve as a private place to sort out beliefs and to craft an identity that balances the demands of others and the self. In the journal adults can draw conclusions about their experiences, as well as make decisions about next steps.

Journals support both informational and transformational learning. Students who use journals in their classes to connect course material to their own experience are more involved in informational learning, the acquisition of new knowledge. Yet when instructors use journal-writing techniques and incorporate the journal into their class structure, students have the opportunity to engage in transformational learning as well, hopefully critically examining the very foundation of their beliefs.

Faculty members who use journals to examine long-held assumptions about the meaning of their work and to rethink those assumptions are also involved in transformational learning. Critical reflection is the tool adults use to root out and examine their daily operating assumptions and to rethink the efficacy of those assumptions as they move through adulthood. This process is not easy. Brookfield states, "becoming aware of the implicit assumptions that frame how we think and act is one of the most challenging intellectual puzzles we face in our lives. It is also something we instinctively resist, for fear of what we might discover" (1995, p. 2). Discovering that the assumptions we have based our lives and our work on do not make sense any more can be painful, yet ultimately fulfilling. The journal is a private place to expose and examine the very ground we are walking on, as well as to try new paths.

Part Two

USING JOURNALS IN CLASSROOMS AND PROFESSIONAL LIFE

4 Introducing and Structuring Classroom Journal Writing

- What are several basic writing principles that support journal writing?
- In what ways can journal-writing expectations be communicated?
- What are the different ways to format classroom journal writing?

5 Classroom Journal-Writing Techniques

- What are eight useful classroom journal-writing techniques?
- What techniques encourage students to read the course material?
- What techniques improve student writing and thinking?
- What techniques foster engagement in service-learning projects?

6 Grading Classroom Journal Writing

- What role does feedback play in fostering classroom journal writing?
- What are the different ways to give feedback on journal writing?
- How can faculty handle the volume of student journals?

- What about privacy and the ethics of reading student journal writing?

7 Journal Writing in Professional Life

- What are the uses of journal writing in professional life?
- What techniques are used when keeping a journal in professional life?
- What formats work well for keeping a journal in professional life?
- How can the journal be used to improve writing skills and productivity?
- How can the journal be used to develop research focus and topics?
- How can the journal be used to reflect on and improve teaching?

8 Journal Writing in the Computer Age

- In what ways is journal writing different when typed on the computer?
- How can you incorporate the computer into classroom journal-writing assignments?
- How can you use blogs and the Internet to facilitate classroom journal writing?

4

INTRODUCING AND STRUCTURING CLASSROOM JOURNAL WRITING

I don't do journaling.
Terry, response at beginning of the term

At first I was a little apprehensive about journaling. I prefer to keep it all bottled up.
After this last term with classroom journal assignments, I am sold on using a journal.
Sometimes I want to tell life to slow down so that I can think and take it all in.
I hope I maintain the self discipline to journal so that I don't miss the journey.
Shannan, reflection at the end of the term

TERRY AND SHANNAN ILLUSTRATE THE RANGE OF STUDENT RESPONSES to classroom journal writing. Terry made this statement in the first class of the term. Shannan, on the other hand, wrote this reflection at the end of the term after she had used a journal in one of our classes. What is it about journal writing that makes it seem appropriate for a student to say, "I don't do journaling"? Would students say, "I don't do term papers"? Hardly, for they risk a low grade by not completing an assignment. Is there something unique about journal writing that signals the "I don't do journaling" response? Yes, there is.

Typical academic work and journal writing are not the same thing. An academic term paper usually includes references to outside sources. On the other hand, journal writers are the sole source of the text. In addition, the type of writing in a journal may challenge students' preconceived notions of what is acceptable quality for course work.

In a journal entry no one closely scrutinizes and gives feedback on the conventions of writing such as grammar, punctuation, and sentence structure. Nor do students usually receive feedback on the validity of their ideas, a certainty that many seek in college, depending on their developmental level (Kitchener & King, 1994; Perry, 1999). Unlike other products in a course, the journal-writing text might not be graded.

Even though the basic nature of journaling will not change, how instructors introduce and structure the use of the journal can be changed to produce a more positive student response. For most instructors journal writing is only 10% to 30% and usually only 20% of the final grade. To be successful with journal writing and to learn to value it, students must see the use of journals not as an add-on, but rather as an essential part of the course. By being clear about journal-writing expectations in the syllabus and demonstrating expectations through the use of the journal during lectures and discussions, instructors can ensure that students attend to assignments, learn course content, and build a repertoire of journal-writing strategies. Similarly, by practicing different ways to use a journal in professional life, faculty and administrators can find that the journal fosters organization and furthers long-range professional goals. This chapter focuses on the use of classroom-assigned journal writing and suggests ways to structure and place the journal within your curriculum. Chapters 5 and 6 focus on specific writing and assessment techniques for classroom journal-writing assignments; chapter 7 shows how faculty and administrators can effectively integrate the journal into their professional lives.

Derived from research and our own experience, this chapter provides an array of choices that you can make to integrate and structure the use of classroom journals. At the end of this chapter, we have created a checklist for quick reference to all the topics covered.

The key questions that guide this chapter are:

- What are basic writing principles that support journal writing?
- In what ways can journal-writing expectations be communicated?
- What are the different ways to format classroom journal writing?

The purpose of this chapter is to guide instructors toward the successful use of classroom journal writing. First, we lay out several basic writing principles that undergird our work with journals. Then we show different ways to communicate journal-writing expectations through the course objectives, syllabus, assignments, and in-class and out-of-class activities. Finally, we share descriptions of the variety of ways that a classroom or field-based journal can be formatted.

Basic Writing Principles That Support Journal Writing

There are three basic writing principles for any classroom that undergird our work:

- Writing is thinking.
- Practice builds fluency in writing and the motivation to write.
- Students value journal writing when it is fully integrated into the course objectives and structure.

When engaging in an instructional practice like journal writing and teaching it to students, it is important to understand your own assumptions and values about writing. Because these are our basic beliefs about writing in general and its role in student learning, these principles inform our teaching and our expectations for and interactions with students. Because we believe these principles, we incorporate journal writing in all of our classes and show students how to use their journals to learn and become better writers and thinkers.

Writing Is Thinking

Central to our understanding of the writing process and teaching students about journal writing is the idea that writing is thinking on paper. We have found that many students believe that writing is what happens *after* they have all their thoughts organized in their mind. Then, students believe, all they have to do is sit down and transfer those thoughts to paper.

There are several problems with this mindset. First, it means students do not commit pen to paper, or words to a word processing document, until they are "ready." Students do not write papers as "drafts," but just "produce" the papers in their heads and put the ideas down on the page, often at the last minute. Second, given all the thinking it took to produce the ideas in the first place, the problem is that there is little room for adaptation or change. They have applied a rigid, preconceived structure to the text. Instructors usually have no idea how a term paper or other class assignment was developed. Receiving a passing grade on work produced this way does little to persuade students that there is a better way to write.

Journal-writing techniques can show students how to brainstorm and cluster thoughts in the early stages of writing a paper. The journal can become the writing "sketchpad" for thoughts, insights, quotations from references, and background knowledge sources. Showing students how their journal can be a container in which they can observe, sift, sort, and grab onto ideas (often fresh ones) can do much to alter their beliefs about writing and improve their final product. Through intentional practice in the journal, students can begin to change their methods of producing writing and can experience that writing *is* thinking, not something that is done after thinking. Our research (Stevens & Cooper, 2007) on student responses to journal writing in our classes indicates that students begin to understand that "writing is thinking" and that they find themselves producing more and writing with more enthusiasm. In our research, 90% (54 out of 60) of our students believed that "Writing in a journal is thinking on paper."

Practice Builds Fluency and the Motivation to Write

The second writing principle that we espouse is that directed and sustained practice helps students be more motivated to write, and builds writing fluency—that is, the ability to simply get words down on the page without editing. While completing a journal-writing assignment on developing a term paper topic, they may end up writing more about it than they realized they knew. They may uncover some strong feelings that they did not know were there. They may recognize some connections between ideas that they did not appreciate before. These discoveries often surprise them and, of course, encourage them to continue their exploration and clarification of their thinking through writing.

Peter Elbow (1973) states that, if it weren't for the "surprises," no one would be motivated to write. Surprises are the "A-ha!" moments when writers look at what they've written and say to themselves, "Oh! So that's what was on my mind!" Writers might find themselves also saying, "I never thought of that before. Hmm, I do already know something about this topic. Maybe I can use that in my paper." Journal writing is a perfect way to introduce students to the "surprises" that motivate good writers to write more, develop greater fluency in writing, and therefore produce more material that can be edited later.

Any one of the activities in this book encourages students to write in a new direction and to be "surprised" by what they have written. Whether students are brainstorming for a term paper, responding to class readings, organizing their field project, or exploring their basic assumptions about being professionals, approaching the writing project with commitment, motivation, and enthusiasm generates more ideas, develops voice, and builds a foundation of confidence in their own viewpoints. Journal writing helps students internalize the concept "writing is thinking," and then be motivated to write to find breadth, depth, and creativity embedded in their thinking.

Students Value Journal Writing When It Is Fully Integrated Into Course Objectives and Structure

Our third basic assumption is that when writing assignments are integrated into the class structure—that is, introduced at the beginning of the course, included in the syllabus, used in class, and assessed appropriately—the contribution of journal writing to students' learning becomes clear. When journal writing is not integrated, students are more likely to see journal writing as a "busy work" activity and carry around the "I don't do journaling" attitude.

One of our students described how journal writing was used in her high school. Students were required to reach a certain word count. Therefore, on the day before their journals were due, many students could be found in the cafeteria furiously scribbling nonsense. This kind of journal-writing assignment that is not integrated into the course content and structure is useless at best and destructive at worst.

How to Communicate Journal-Writing Expectations

There are several ways that journal-writing expectations can be clearly introduced, structured, and communicated to students:

- Write about journal-writing expectations in the course syllabus.
- Introduce and discuss the role of journal writing in the first class.
- Use the journal during class.

Write About Journal-Writing Expectations in the Syllabus

How a course syllabus is constructed can have a positive effect on teaching and learning in any course. A course syllabus is a contract between the student and the instructor wherein the instructor promises to deliver course content and indicates how students will be required to demonstrate their learning of that content in a variety of ways (Slattery & Carlson, 2005; Thompson, 2007). The syllabus serves several purposes: It is "motivational, structural and evidentiary" (Slattery & Carlson, 2005, p. 157). Because students receive the syllabus in the first class, the written syllabus conveys the overall tone of the class, which can affect student motivation throughout the course. In addition, the syllabus lays out the course structure to which students can continually refer. Because it is written, the syllabus contains legal evidence of course expectations. Thompson (2007) found that presentation of the syllabus in the first class was an important element in communicating course expectations, setting the tone for the class, and motivating students to complete the work.

The course syllabus also signals students how journal writing fits into the class objectives and the overall structure. There are a number of different specific decisions to make about the journal and how it fits into your overall expectations for what students will learn. A syllabus description might include the following:

- How the journal is formatted
- How journal writing reinforces other learning activities or readings
- Whether students should bring their journals to class
- How journals will be used in class
- Who will be reading it
- When it will be collected
- How it will be graded

A written description can distinguish the journal from other types of academic writing. In Table 4.1 we have several examples of the ways faculty have written about the journal requirement in their syllabi.

Besides a written description of journal writing in the syllabus, you can show how specific course objectives are accomplished through journal writing. Research has shown that clearly stated course objectives promote goal-directed action, produce persistent on-task behavior, and encourage students to resume tasks even when they are attracted to other alternatives (Bargh, Gollwitzer, Lee-Chai, Barndollar, & Trotschel, 2001). These findings provide powerful reasons to find ways to explicitly match overall stated class objectives to the practice of journal writing. For example, look at the overall learning objectives across three courses in Table 4.2 and see how specific journal-writing assignments meet these objectives.

Table 4.1
Description of Journal Writing in Course Syllabi

Discipline	Level and Course	Journal Assignment Description
Architecture	Undergraduate level: Arch 100: Introduction to Architecture	Architectural Journal: One of the major requirements for this course consists of developing and maintaining an architectural journal that demonstrates your individual participation and personal engagement with the class. For this assignment, the journal is *not* a collection of notes from class lectures. It is an opportunity to help you "think with yourself" through the course topics and discuss personal reactions and questions about the subject matter of architecture. This assignment will be evaluated both on the quality and quantity of entries. There are no easy answers as to length or quantity of pages; however, about 5 pages per week could generally be considered "satisfactory." Your journal should be used for a variety of entries that will demonstrate your level of interest in the subject matter. The following is a list of potential activities you may consider when starting and developing your journal. • Observing architecture • Making judgments about architecture • Analyzing images of architecture (20% of grade) (Rudy Barton, personal communication, June 12, 2007)
Higher Education	Graduate level: Advanced Qualitative Research	Qualitative Research Course Journal: Students will be expected to keep a journal that contains critical reviews and interpretations of course readings, connects course material to your own experience, and examines problems you have encountered in your own research process. These journals will be used in three ways: a. They will be turned in to your instructor twice during the semester. Sign up for a time most convenient for you during the semester. Journals are due as noted on the schedule. b. They will be used to support and enrich class discussions on the course readings. Please bring your journal with you when you come to class.

(continues)

Table 4.1 (continued)

Discipline	Level and Course	Journal Assignment Description
		c. Journal entries can be used to support your thinking for Comparison & Critique assignments. You may quote from your journal in writing that assignment. Please cite yourself, giving the date of entry when doing so.
		You will not be graded on the quality of the writing in your journal (e.g., spelling, grammar, punctuation, etc.), but will be expected to demonstrate reflective and critical thinking. (25% of total grade)
Political Anthropology	Undergraduate survey course with reading assignments	Study Journal: The record of study is a summary of the reading and other research you have carried out in the course along with notes on your views of the material you have encountered in the reading, seminars, and lectures. It is a kind of history of the work you have done on the course and a record of what you have read and how your ideas have changed. . . . It is designed to encourage reflexivity about your own learning. (Crème, 2005, p. 288)

Certainly, the objectives in Table 4.2 could be met through a short paper handed in for comment and grading. However, the journal can be a crucible for developing ideas; creating drafts; and generally unearthing, dusting off, and sorting through concepts and experiences before they are submitted in a more finished and formal paper.

Instructors often make the mistake of thinking that because the journal can be loose and elastic, the assigning of the journal can be the same. The exact opposite is true. If you are assigning something that can take various forms and is focused more on process (reflection on course readings) rather than product (a polished research paper), it is even easier for students to get lost. The more open-ended the assignment, the more important it is for students to understand its purpose and parameters. By making an explicit link between the course objectives and journal writing, the instructor shows the importance of the journal in the overall scheme of the class.

The written statements in the syllabus are students' first clue that journal writing is valued and important to the learning of course content. The second clue is how the instructor discusses journal writing in the first class.

Table 4.2
Course Objectives Linked to Journal-Writing Assignments

Course	Course Objective	Class Journal Writing Assignments
Teacher Education Graduate Level: Action Research	Students will be able to reflect on, identify, and describe key teaching challenges suitable for an action research project.	Focused freewrite List Metaphor
Black Studies Undergraduate Level: Field Studies	Students will create an organized record of their field observations in a journal. Students will be able to distinguish observations from inferences in their field notes.	Focused freewrites Log entries *Two-column method:* Column 1: Observations Column 2: Inferences
University Studies Undergraduate Level: Senior Capstone	Students will be able to write about and understand the perspective of our community partners as they seek to address the community partners' problem. Students will demonstrate their ability to work effectively with a multidisciplinary team.	Dialogue with community partner. Write about challenges and opportunities that teamwork presents.

Introduce and Discuss
Journal Writing in the First Class

The second way to communicate journal-writing expectations is through an introduction and discussion in the first class. Students' prior journal-writing experience can enhance or detract from their reaction to keeping a journal for class. Opening a class discussion about their prior experience gives students an opportunity to share as well as ask about journal writing. You will learn about their attitudes and motivations toward journal writing. You can distinguish, on one hand, journal writing from diary writing and, on the other, journal writing from traditional academic writing. In addition, to overcome the "I don't do journaling" mentality, you can establish that journal writing is not only required but essential to learning course material. Over time and with the proper guidance, students begin to see its powerful contribution to their learning. Some even add it to their repertoire of successful ways to learn and continue to use it in other classes. As Alyssa noted in one of our classes,

Journaling throughout my course work has become part of the learning process. I feel much more connected to the material, more focused in class discussions, and have a better understanding of myself and how I learn. Because of this increased awareness, I always see myself keeping a journal in my academic endeavors. (personal communication, May 12, 2008)

Student background knowledge and experience influence student responses to journal keeping. A university studies instructor, Vicki (see her case in chapter 9), who assigns a journal in her senior capstone class, stated that her journal assignment is ". . . weighted heavily. In some ways my job is to deconstruct what journaling means to students due to their previous class experiences with journaling for other professors" (personal communication, October 31, 2007).

In other situations, students' own particular learning styles may cause them to harbor doubts about journal writing. One math major, Katie, wrote about her resistance to journal writing and what she had learned during one of our courses:

The journal helped me find insight into myself that I likely otherwise never would have found. In general I do not enjoy writing; I prefer to focus my thinking and energy on math, logic, and reasoning. When I write I feel the need to be somewhat of a perfectionist, which becomes tiresome for me. In journaling, though, I found a new freedom and joy that writing had not given me in a long time. I was able to move away from grammar rules and sentence structure and instead get in touch with the thoughts trapped deep inside my head. (personal communication, July 7, 2007)

Chad, a doctoral student in a qualitative research class, also noted his initial resistance to journal writing:

Although I did dread writing my first couple of entries in my journal, I reflected on the reading and about how I felt about the class. After a couple of weeks of giving the journal a second chance, I surprisingly discovered how valuable my journal became in enhancing my learning abilities toward the class. While writing, I was able to remember things from the readings a lot better. . . . Once I got the hang of writing a journal, I noticed how it especially helped me understand the class after feeling as though everything went over my head. Putting my thoughts into words helped me realize how much I actually need this journal for my benefit. Writing about what I read, even though it may not have been discussed during class, helped my learning in the long run. (personal communication, May 1, 2008)

In your first class, you also can share the intended outcomes and broader benefits of journal keeping. The literature on effective feedback demonstrates that students have two main questions early in the term: "Where am I going?" and "Why am I going there?" (Hattie & Timperley, 2007). In other words, effective instructors *tell* students exactly where to direct their attention and why it is important to do that. Discussing the general outcomes and benefits of journal writing helps students be open to learning through journal writing. For example, in the Black Studies course described in Table 4.2, Kofi's objective for journal writing is to help students become aware of their biases and to learn how to be more objective observers of human interactions (see chapter 9). Rudy, an architecture professor, tells students that keeping a journal "is not just about looking, but also about seeing. Journals are a path where you talk to yourself about what you see" (see chapter 9). The drawing (Figure 4.1) shows what one of Rudy's students wrote in his architectural journal about looking and seeing. Making this journal entry allowed this student to document his thinking and even later to revisit the core course outcome of developing the ability to not just look at architecture but to really see it.

The third and final clue to students that journal writing is valuable in this class is how the instructor uses the journal during class.

Figure 4.1
Student Journal Entry: Observations About Looking and Seeing in Architecture

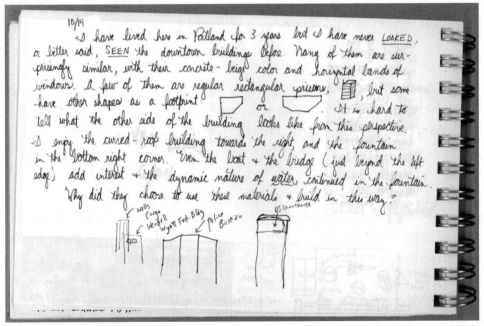

Art/text by Daniel Whitehead from journal in the collection of Rudy Barton.
Reproduced by permission.

Use the Journal During Class

After introducing the journal in the syllabus, discussing its role, eliciting student background knowledge, and conveying the benefits of journal writing, it is especially important to encourage the use of the journal as frequently as possible during class. The next chapter presents some specific journal-writing techniques. In the following section, we describe six different teaching strategies that can underscore and integrate journal writing into classroom lessons.

Tell Students to Bring the Journal to Class

Even though students may be writing journal entries at home, to convey the message that you are serious about journal writing and to show students the utility of keeping a journal, tell them to bring it to class, and then use it in class. In fact, we often have in-class journal-writing activities, although some are very brief.

Provide Sample Journal Entries

One of the most influential ways to show students how to write their journal entries is to provide students with models, or sample journal entries. Rebecca, a teacher educator, requires students to keep a "learning journal" on the course readings. Rather than a long list of preset criteria for the journal entries, she writes her own journal reflections on the readings for that class, and then reads her reflections to the class before they begin class discussion. This method clearly demonstrates how to write journal entries that respond appropriately to course readings.

Write in Your Journal When Students Write in Theirs

As Bandura (1975) finds, modeling is one of the most powerful teaching strategies. When you assign journal-writing activities to be completed in class, you can write in your journal when students write in theirs, clearly modeling the value of journal writing in your life.

Use Quick-Write Lecture and Discussion Reflections

Another way to promote practice and reflection during class time is quick-write lecture and discussion reflections. This relatively simple activity involves asking a question that requires deeper thinking or critical analysis. Instead of opening it to class discussion, students first write out the answer to the question in their journals. We have used writing prompts like the following:

- How does this topic relate to your own life experiences?
- Draw a quick sketch of how the ideas in this lecture relate to one another.
- What is the most important thing you learned in the last 15 minutes of lecture and why is it important?
- What was the most confusing part of the lecture today?
- What questions do you still have about this topic?

For nonnative English speakers, writing responses to class discussion questions and lecture topics is a way to practice ideas in English before expressing them publicly during class discussions (Stevens, Emil, & Yamashita, 2007). In addition, those who are more introverted are given a chance to rehearse what they want to say before sharing with the whole class. The journal serves as a rehearsal stage for students with varying learning styles who may not be accustomed or comfortable with dynamic, interactive classroom discussions.

Use Write–Pair–Share

When you ask a question and a student answers (called classroom recitation), you can only be sure that this one person is reflecting on the course content. The others may be listening or look like they are listening, but you really do not know for sure. Write–pair–share is a valuable classroom activity that expands the opportunities for all students to think and talk about course content with another student.

During class, direct all the students to write a brief reflection on course content, either from their reading or from the lecture, and then turn to a person next to them and share their ideas on the topic. Write–pair–share ensures that all students are actively engaged through writing and then talking. Because all students have practiced their ideas in writing and then spoken about them with another person, more students will be prepared to participate in a whole-class discussion. This activity is particularly effective in diverse classes in which some students may be reluctant to participate.

Assign Peer-to-Peer Dialogue Journal Entries

Another form of interaction that allows students to reflect and fosters the responses of other students is the peer-to-peer dialogue journal. Students respond to each other by writing in each other's journal. Of course you need to warn students ahead of time that classmates will be reading and writing responses in their journals.

Before reading the course material outside of class, tell students to divide their journal page into four columns. They complete the first two columns before class with reflections on the readings or field observations. When class begins, have the students divide into pairs and exchange journals and write a response to their partner's reflections in their partner's journal. The journal format is illustrated in Table 4.3.

After reflecting in writing on what their fellow student has written, students talk to each other about their responses. Students seem to really enjoy getting another student's viewpoint and, in our experience, the energy level of the conversation during this activity is very high. Because students do not wish to be embarrassed in front of their peers by not having done the readings, peer-to-peer dialogue journal entries encourage students to complete the readings, as well as to be more thoughtful in their reflections about the material.

In addition to structuring, introducing, and using the journal in class, the format of the journal needs to be considered. The following section offers a potpourri of choices.

Different Ways to Format Classroom Journal Writing

A written journal or a computer file is the container for the journal entries. A journal "format" includes how the pages are bound or brought together and how the journal

Table 4.3
Peer-to-Peer Dialogue Journal Example

Column 1	Column 2	Column 3	Column 4
The journal writer (Student A) writes out the facts from assigned readings.	Student A writes her reflections on the facts from Column 1 here.	Student B writes responses or reflections in this column.	Questions from either student are noted here.
Following the chapter reading, Student A wrote in her journal: Brookfield (1991) states that adult learners have a wealth of experience to connect to what they are learning.	*Student A then wrote her response to this idea from her reading:* This is true for me. I find that in class I can draw on my experiences to help me understand the literature on adult learning.	*In class, Student A handed her journal entry to Student B, who wrote:* Sometimes as an older student I feel less able to make connections to the course material because I am less confident of my ability to understand.	*Student A then wrote this response in her journal:* I wonder what Brookfield says about the role of confidence in adult learning.

writing is "laid out" on the inside of the journal. Some instructors are not concerned about the container—whether the journal is written in a book or on the computer, how the pages are laid out, or what the journal cover looks like. These instructors leave all those decisions up to the students. For those who are concerned about the format of the journal both inside and outside, there is an array of possibilities.

This section addresses journal formatting on the outside and on the inside. Our discussion of outside formatting considers the choices you can make for the type of journal you want students to purchase or where you want students to collect their entries, whereas the discussion of inside formatting addresses the organization and layout of the pages within the journal pages themselves.

Journal Format: Outside

The selection of a journal can be left to the student, or you can specify the kind of journal students should use. To fully appreciate the variety of choices for journals, browse through the blank-book section of your local bookstore. There are almost a dizzying number of journals available to students, from bound blank books to spiral bound books of any size; from small, index-card–size books to large portfolio size. There are a large variety of preformatted journals for trips taken, books read, recipes tried, and dreams experienced. Then there are blogs and electronic journals produced on a computer. There are computer programs for journaling like One Note, Scrivener, and MacJournal.

Faculty often match the format of the journal with their view of how students should approach their journal entries. One architecture instructor, Rudy, has students use 5" × 8" journals bound with large spirals. Before the journal is turned in at the end of the term, however, the journal pages are disassembled and reordered to cluster similar projects together. In one assignment, for example, students are required to observe and document a building that is being constructed over the 10-week term. At the end of the term they cluster these drawings and journal entries together and write a reflection on their observations. Dannelle believes that the typical college notebook, with college-ruled lines and small metal spirals holding it together, connotes school. Therefore, she requires that students use a journal in which the pages are glued or sewn together. With this type of bound journal, she hopes that students feel that they are creating a book, a book of their professional life. She says to students,

> This is your first book, a journal about your school work, your life, and how you organize and think about what you do. I encourage you to not only use this journal for

this class but use it everyday: to note meetings you attend, groups you work with, etc. You do not have to limit your entries to this class. Perhaps you will find ways to include other parts of your life as well. Remember journals can be archival, too. My grandmother was a high school mathematics teacher in the 1890s. I would love to have her journal today. Perhaps your future grandchildren will feel the same way.

Joanne lets students select whatever format they are comfortable and familiar with. She notes, "I believe students are more likely to write in a journal of their own selection, using a format they are most comfortable with, whether that be a bound book or a computer file."

How the journal is formatted on the outside may not be of interest to you. Yet we have found that students will ask if you have a preference. There may be some advantages for your students to have a prescribed format. One of our students, Ruth, wrote about it like this:

> I had an experience Fall Quarter where I was keeping a journal in an Action Research Education class and doing similar exercises in an English class where no formal journal was kept. I quickly found that having the exercises together in the formal journal gave them more weight than when my English teacher said, "Take out a sheet of paper." This seemed to demote the project to scrap paper instead of making it a future resource for writing. This was interesting since I liked the directed freewriting exercises in the English class better than the undirected freewrites in the Education class. My personal solution was to keep all the exercises in my journal. I also tried to make myself a list of prompts in the front of my journal to help me focus and give myself some direction for the undirected freewrites in the Education class. (personal communication, April 27, 2007)

Here are some of the choices you can make about the outside format of the journal:

Bound Book or Spiral Rings

Journals today come in many different formats. By formats, we mean the way the pages are put together. They could be sewn together with a cardboard or heavyweight cover. They could be bound with wire rings, large or small. The type of binding depends on your preferences, or you may wish to let students use any binding they want. If you are so inclined, you can have students construct their own journals, choosing the paper and type of binding. Books such as *The Decorated Page* (Diehn, 2003) provide instructions on how to bind your own books, the quality of various papers, and many examples of decorated pages.

Loose-Leaf Pages in a Binder

Some instructors have students use a loose-leaf binder to collect their journal entries. The advantage of this is that the pages can be pulled out easily and handouts can be easily integrated. Pages can be written elsewhere and added to the journal. The journal does not have to be carried around all the time. Students can easily add lecture notes and field notes and can turn in the finished project in a complete binder. A loose-leaf binder has the added advantage of allowing students to keep making journal entries while the instructor is reading or grading the other parts of their journal.

Electronic Journal

Students can keep their journals on the computer in a computer file. Chapter 8 elaborates on electronic journals. Some students may be much more used to composing on the keyboard, and others may find it useful because of a physical disability. Lori, one of our students, wrote:

> Journal writing has been a struggle for me. Especially handwritten journaling. Due to a stroke I suffered a number of years ago, my right hand is very weak and therefore handwriting is not easy nor is it fun. Yes, I do and can write on a daily basis, but my thoughts go so much faster than my hand and I become very frustrated. The end result is that I usually do not write as much or as in-depth as I would like. Last year my professional goal was reflection and journal keeping. My journal was done on the computer. This was a huge help. (personal communication, July 15, 2006)

Given the availability of computers and the prevalence of computer use by students today, instructors need to consider the value of keeping a journal on a computer in terms of their overall objectives.

Journal Format: Inside

We now address the formatting of what is inside the journal—the journal pages. We are not talking about what students write but rather how the entries are laid out on the page. Once again, you may not be interested in having a special format for the inside of the journal. Both Dannelle and Joanne have experimented with various formats for classroom journal entries. We have come up with some ideas that seem to work for students and offer you some choices about formatting.

Table of Contents

Before students start writing their first entry in the journal, Dannelle has students set aside a page or two at the beginning of their journal for a table of contents. The table of contents helps students find their entries and may actually help them begin to view their journal as a "book" of reflections because some books, of course, have tables of contents. As one of our students wrote in our research survey, "I feel like the table of contents made the material accessible and gave it a feeling of something to come back to." Figure 4.2 is an example of a table of contents from a student journal. Adriana photocopied her table of contents and mounted it on another paper so that it could be graded. To increase accountability, we often have students photocopy their journal table of contents and turn it in at the end of the course.

In our research (Stevens & Cooper, 2007), we found that 67% of the students found that creating a table of contents was valuable. When students have to make a table of contents with the date, title of entry, and page number, they become more conscious of what they have experienced and learned over time. Reviewing these dated entries encourages reflection on changes in thinking and learning. The meta-reflection assignment described in chapter 5 encourages writers to go back and reread, revisit, and review their previous journal entries.

Numbered Pages

Numbered pages facilitate the creation of a table of contents at the end of the semester and connote the fact that this volume is a book. In his first class, Kofi, a faculty member in Black Studies, has students number their journal pages even before they start their field study in Ghana. For the students, numbering pages is part of their preparation for the trip. For Kofi, numbering pages assures him that they do not tear out any pages while they are in Ghana. He wants to know how and what they are thinking about their experience day by day. This helps him evaluate student work and informs him about what he needs to improve for the trip next year.

Double-Column Method

The double-column method is a page-formatting method in which the journal writer draws a 1" to 1.5" column down the side the page. The column has many purposes:

Figure 4.2
Table of Contents: Photocopied Pages From Adriana's Student Journal

PSU Graduate School of Education
CI 560: Action Research
Adriana Burrola

TABLE OF CONTENTS
PROFESSIONAL JOURNAL

TABLE OF CONTENTS

PAGE	CONCEPT/TITLE	DATE
1	Class notes What is Action Research?	06/29/07
2	Examples of research questions.	06/29/07
3	Class notes Characteristics of research questions. The question funnel	07/06/07
4	Class notes Research literature	07/06/07
5	APA style references.	07/06/07
6	5 parts of a research project	07/06/07
6,7	How to do my literature review? 2 methods	07/06/07
8	Individual methods	07/06/07
8,9	Triangulation	07/06/07
9	Sociogram	07/06/07
10	Methods	07/06/07
11	Final project	07/13/07
12	Action research timeline	07/13/07
13	Presentation standards - how to be a good speaker	07/13/07

TABLE OF CONTENTS
FREEWRITING

TABLE OF CONTENTS

PAGE	TITLE	DATE
1,2	First freewriting in class: Choosing a topic for my action research project.	06/29/2007
2	How do I feel when freewriting?	06/29/2007
3	Focus freewriting (Everything related to a topic)	06/29/2007
4,5	Second freewriting in class	07/06/2007
5,6	Reflections on group methods presentations	07/06/2007
7,8	Freewriting at home and reflections on literature review	07/10/2007
9	Third freewriting in class	07/13/2007
9,10	Reflections on group methods presentations	07/13/2007

to record the date, to record the participants of a meeting, to make a to-do list that results from the meeting, and to jot down key ideas from the information in the larger column. Hughes and others (1997) describe a variation of this method, dialogic reflection, for students to use when taking notes in class, while reading, and when working in small groups. Figure 4.3 describes some uses of the two columns.

Dividing the journal page into two columns echoes the "Cornell Note-Taking System" (Figure 4.4), which is a classic way to take lecture notes using one column for notes and the second column to review the notes.

Students do not necessarily know how to take lecture notes (Bligh, 2000). Using the Cornell system in their journals, however, can help them learn this skill. The student writes the lecture notes in the larger column and reviews and summarizes the notes in the smaller column. The Cornell method of lecture note taking has been shown to be very helpful for retention of lecture content. You might suggest that students use their journal for lecture notes in this way. In addition, the two-column method is also useful for review, reflection, and action. Figure 4.5 is a photocopy of

Figure 4.3
Two-column Method: Hand-out for Students

How to keep a journal in your professional life

Dannelle D. Stevens, Ph.D.
Portland State University, Graduate School of Education
stevensd@pdx.edu, 503-725-4679

Joanne E. Cooper, Ph.D.
College of Education, University of Hawaii
jcooper@hawaii.edu, 808-956-8085

A journal for your professional life has several key components ========➜ to log and record professional activities
  ========➜ to collect notes from meetings, conferences, reflections

DIMENSION	JOURNAL FORMAT SMALL COLUMN (1.5"-2") "Bank of the river"	JOURNAL FORMAT LARGE COLUMN "River of experience"

CONTENTS
Dated
Pages numbered
Bound journal
Table of Contents
Option: Personal side separate from professional side
	Narrower than large column
	Put in date of entry
	Meetings: List names of those present
	Note ideas that are
	    Interesting
	    Link to other activities
	    Spark your imagination
	    Require more work
	Write out comments, reflections & responses
	"To do" list
	Grocery list (to get it off your mind)
		Wider than small column
		Notes on the activity (minutes, agenda, key topics covered, etc.)
		Diagrams, concept maps that summarize thinking
		Narratives from freewriting (or turn journal over and write from the back for the more personal reflections)
		Quotations from participants at the meetings
		Glue in agendas, Power-point miniature slides from handouts, business cards
		Notes from conference presentations attended that can be used for ideas for future research
		Rough drafts of writing and research ideas
		Notes from research collaborations with colleagues
		Resources found: Web sites, books read, references
		** Often useful to photocopy key pages and use for discussion & reflection

BENEFITS	Written reflections over time: trail of dates & ideas "To do" list to follow up on commitments Confusions to track later Easy to find when pages numbered and table of contents used	Actual record of what happened, what was said and by whom Quotations from participants allow you to reflect on other perspectives Track dates and activities as evidence for promotion Opportunity to reflect on activity after the event No fumbling for folders and notes from previous meetings Way to pull together ideas for future projects (photocopy relevant pages) © D. D. Stevens, 2008

Figure 4.4
Cornell Note-Taking System

Cornell Note-Taking System

Recall Column
------2 1/2"-------- ----------------6"--------------------

Reduce ideas and facts to
concise jottings and
summaries as cues for   Record the lecture as fully and as
Reciting, Reviewing,   meaningfully as possible.
and Reflecting.

The format provides the perfect opportunity for following through with the 5 R's of note-taking. Here they are:

1. Record. During the lecture, record in the main column as many meaningful facts and ideas as you can. Write legibly.

2. Reduce. As soon after as possible, summarize these ideas and facts concisely in the Recall Column. Summarizing clarifies meanings and relationships, reinforces continuity, and strengthens memory. Also, it is a way of preparing for examinations gradually and well ahead of time.

3. Recite. Now cover the column, using only your jottings in the Recall Column as cues or "flags" to help you recall, say over facts and ideas of the lecture as fully as you can, not mechanically, but in your own words and with as much appreciation of the meaning as you can. Then, uncovering your notes, verify what you have said. This procedure helps to transfer the facts and ideas of your long term memory.

4. Reflect. Reflective students distill their opinions from their notes. They make such opinions the starting point for their own musings upon the subjects they are studying. Such musings aid them in making sense out of their courses and academic experiences by finding relationships among them. Reflective students continually label and index their experiences and ideas, put them into structures, outlines, summaries, and frames of reference. They rearrange and file them. Best of all, they have an eye for the vital-for the essential. Unless ideas are placed in categories, unless they are taken up from time to time for re-examination, they will become inert and soon forgotten.

5. Review. If you will spend 10 minutes every week or so in a quick review of these notes, you will retain most of what you have learned, and you will be able to use your knowledge currently to greater and greater effectiveness.

© Academic Skills Center, Dartmouth College 2001

Figure 4.5
Two-Column Method: Sam's Student Journal

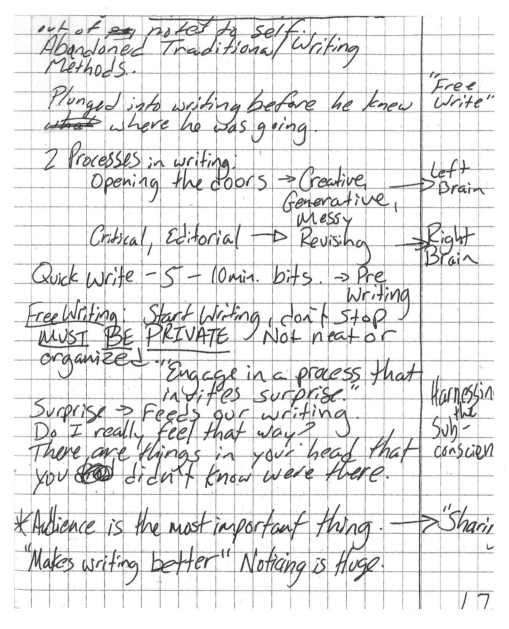

a student journal using the two-column method. These were Sam's notes from watching a Peter Elbow video on writing. You can see how he added his own connections in the smaller column: "opening the doors" (video) to "left brain" (Sam), and "critical, editorial" (video) to "right brain" (Sam). He knows how to link what he is learning to his prior knowledge and cement the connection through writing about it in his journal.

Pages: Grids, Lines, or Blank

There are many choices for the pages themselves: lines, grids, or blank pages. Most instructors leave the choice up to the student. Some students find the grid lines are helpful because they feel freer to write in all directions and to put in charts and diagrams. Others like the structure of a lined page and the guidance in making sure their writing is straight on the page. Before they purchase a journal, students can be alerted to these choices just in case they want to try out different page formats.

Professional Side and Personal Side

One method of organizing the journal involves dividing the journal into two sections. The first section is the professional side and might include class notes, field notes, research notes, group meeting minutes, and so on. When students turn the journal over and open the back cover, they can write from the back forward. The back section becomes a second section in which they can put their more personal writing, leaving the front of the journal for more "public" things. Adriana's table of contents (see Figure 4.2) shows how she sectioned off her journal into the classroom side and the freewriting, more personal side, and had a table of contents for each.

The "Decorated Page"

In addition to the various structural ways in which students might format pages of their journal, there are endless possibilities for decorating the pages of a journal. Students might, for example, customize a blank book; modify the cover; paint; paste photos or drawings; or create designs, grids, mandalas, organic shapes, cut-outs, or add-ons as demonstrated in *The Decorated Page* (Diehn, 2003) or *Making Journals by Hand* (Thompson, 2000). In today's world of scrapbooking, students may want to experiment with how to make a journal distinctly theirs. They might include drawings, pictures, or "found words" cut from magazines and pasted into their journals.

Joanne likes to create word collages, such as the one in Figure 4.6 that illustrated the front of her personal journal in the summer of 2007. The front of the journal serves as a summary entry for the time covered in the journal itself.

The collage symbolizes many of the events of that summer. Joanne also jotted down quotes describing the events that are depicted on this page. Many of these word collages and decorated pages are playful, "spontaneous and unedited, fresh and

Figure 4.6
Collage of Found Words: Joanne's Journal

in bold color" (Woods & Dinino, 2006, p. 7). In essence this is another way for students to express their individuality, to bring their creativity to the page not only in words but in images. Various disciplines, such as architecture, encourage students to use photographs and drawings to express their unique responses to what they are learning. Figure 4.7 shows a page from one architecture student's journal in which photos, pencil drawings, and words were added to the journal entry.

Botany and biology are disciplines in which students are often asked to keep field journals that include drawings of various animals or plants they observe in the natural world. Figure 4.8 shows a page from a botany student's journal, in this case a drawing of an okra plant. Taking the time to draw and then label their drawings allows students to observe more carefully and closely than they might otherwise. It also creates a vivid record of what has been observed that cannot be replicated with words only.

Figure 4.7
Collage of Photos, Drawings, and Writings: Architecture Student Journal

Art/text by Grace Lubke from journal in the collection of Rudy Barton.
Reproduced by permission.

Figure 4.8
Botany: Nicole's Student Journal

In this section we have discussed the decisions that instructors have to make about the outside and inside formatting of the journal. These elements can be incorporated into course assignments or left to the discretion of the individual student.

Another key element in the successful introduction of journal keeping is telling students how you will give feedback and assess their journals. Those who are successful with journal writing give students some form of feedback on their entries (Stevens, Cooper, & Lasater, 2006). Of course students attend to what is assessed: how they are going to be graded and what you expect them to do to accomplish the course objectives, especially regarding journal keeping. Journal-writing assessment is so important in communicating faculty expectations and getting student "buy-in" that we have devoted all of chapter 6 to this topic.

Conclusion

The purpose of this chapter is to give some specific ideas for introducing and structuring classroom journal writing. Providing clear guidelines and expectations serves as the foundation for journal writing in any class and builds a positive attitude toward the journal. As John S., one of our students, stated, ". . . the class journal has helped me to develop many personal insights, but also in getting the creative juices flowing and overcoming bouts of writer's block as I begin writing the different papers for class" (personal communication, December 3, 2007). By using these methods students see the journal as an integrated part of the course, useful both in and out of the classroom and as a sketchpad for ideas in the future. Through these methods we seek to have students learn course content as well as develop the habit of reflective writing, a potentially powerful tool in their adult life. To summarize this chapter, we have created a checklist in Table 4.4.

Table 4.4

Checklist for Introducing and Structuring Assigned Journal Writing

The following checklist should provide the basic framework for introducing and including journal-writing assignments within your course structure.

Main Topic	Subtopics
Describe journal-keeping expectations in writing in syllabus.	• Write out journal-keeping expectations clearly and specifically. • Show how journal writing helps students accomplish course objectives in syllabus.
Introduce and discuss journal writing in first class.	• Distinguish journal writing from other academic writing • Ask about student background knowledge and experience with journal writing. • Discuss the short- and long-term benefits of journal keeping.
Use journal during class.	• Tell students to bring the journal to class. • Provide examples of journal entries. • Write in your journal when students write in theirs. • Use quick-write lecture/discussion reflections. • Use write–pair–share activities. • Assign peer-to-peer dialogue journal entries.
Decide on a format.	Choices for the outside of the journal: • Bound book: hardcover or paperback • Spiral rings • Loose-leaf pages in a binder • Electronic • Students select own cover Choices for the inside of the journal: • Double-column method • Cornell method of notetaking • Pages: grids, lines, or blanks • Table of contents and numbered pages • Divided into professional side and personal side • Use inside pages of journal cover
Decide how you will give feedback	See chapter 6 for details on feedback and assessment of journal entries.

5

CLASSROOM JOURNAL-WRITING TECHNIQUES

Having a broad range of diary devices permits the writer to select a special way
of proceeding when expressing an event, feeling, or thought. . . .
Tristine Rainer (1978, p. 72)

ALYSSA, A GRADUATE STUDENT, credits her use of classroom journals as "a saving grace to my feelings of anxiety and lack of motivation toward graduate school." On the verge of taking a leave, Alyssa was required to keep a journal in one of her graduate classes and soon had developed a method for using journals in all of her classes to "build competence and self-confidence." She keeps a journal for each course she takes, reflecting on readings, recording particularly salient quotes, writing questions that arise, or jotting down topics she would like to explore. Alyssa states,

> using my journal in this reflective manner has revolutionized the way I make meaning of course material. . . . I feel more prepared for class and more willing to share my thoughts on a topic. I used to have a lot of anxiety when speaking in front of my peers, but now my thoughts are already gathered so I am more self-assured and I articulate my ideas more effectively than ever. . . . Keeping a journal has rejuvenated my spirit and enthusiasm for graduate school. (personal communication, December 10, 2007)

She states, "In the future, I plan to continue keeping a journal. I have already started one to organize myself for writing my master's thesis."

Although faculty cannot expect all their students to be this enthusiastic, Alyssa's experience is powerful testimony to the variety of ways in which journal keeping can enhance learning and build self-confidence. The purpose of this chapter is to describe a number of journal-writing techniques that support classroom learning. Our research indicates that students value practicing and using different journal-writing techniques (Stevens, Cooper, & Lasater, 2006). As one student commented, "One of the most important things I learned this term is that different methods of journal keeping work better for different events—dialogues, unsent letters, lists, guided free-writes. I like the variety."

We offer these for you to try out and decide which work best for your particular purposes. As Fulwiler noted in a landmark book on reflective journal writing, when faculty use different techniques that match their classroom learning objectives, they help students use their journals to "seek, discover, speculate and figure things out" (1987, p. 9).

The key questions for this chapter are:

• What are eight useful classroom journal-writing techniques?
• What techniques encourage students to read the course material?
• What techniques improve student writing and thinking?
• What techniques foster engagement in service-learning projects?

This chapter provides you with a set of time-tested journal-keeping techniques that allow you to pick and choose those that match your intended course objectives. In addition, we have three sections in which we highlight three typical classroom objectives that can be met through journal keeping: reading and reflecting on course material, improving writing, and engaging in service learning projects.

Eight Useful Classroom Journal-Writing Techniques

Although there are many other useful journal-writing techniques, the eight basic techniques in this section provide a good foundation for using journals in your classroom. Chapter 7 discusses the application of these techniques to professional life. The value of these is continually reinforced in our own classrooms and in the research literature (Boice, 1990, 2000; Elbow, 1973; Fulwiler, 1987; Progoff, 1992; Rainer, 1978). Figure 5.1 summarizes the eight techniques.

Figure 5.1
Eight Basic Journal-Writing Techniques

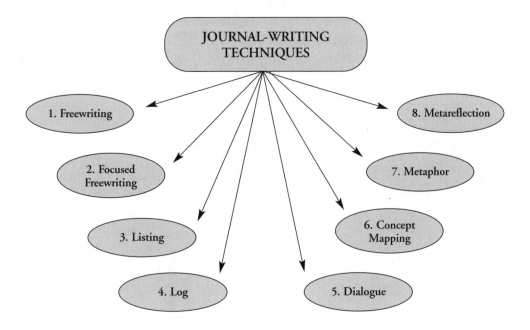

Tables 5.1 and 5.2 suggest how the student learning objective on the left can be accomplished using the classroom journal-writing technique listed on the right. Each technique is described in this section.

In our discussion of each technique, we first define it and then provide support for its use from the literature. Next, we describe several ways the technique can be used in class. Look for charts that summarize each technique in Appendix A, in which we lay out the key elements to consider when implementing the technique: definition, learning objectives, procedures for use, and a short example.

Freewriting

Freewriting is one of the most powerful activities that faculty can teach their students. The only rule in freewriting is that the pen hits the page, produces words, and does not come up for a set period, say 5 to 10 minutes when first introduced (Elbow, 1973). Writing conventions like using proper punctuation, writing complete sentences, spelling correctly, or even sticking to one topic are thrown out the window in favor of

Table 5.1
Overall Classroom Journal-Writing

Objective I: Integrate and Apply Course Content

Student Learning Objective	Journal-Writing Technique
Keep a dated log of progress on a project.	Log, list
Practice, learn, and connect course content to one's life.	List, focused freewrite, concept map
Collect, document, and analyze field and clinical observations to develop and hone observation skills.	Log, list, metareflection
Reflect critically on issues addressed in class.	Focused freewrite
Reflect on deeply held assumptions and beliefs.	Focused freewrite, dialogue, metaphor

Table 5.2
Overall Classroom Journal Writing

Objective II: Practice Skills, Develop Insights, and Expand Perspectives

Student Learning Objective	Journal-Writing Technique
Become better writers and clearer thinkers.	Freewrite, focused freewrite, dialogue, metaphor, concept maps
Develop voice; discover, examine, and affirm beliefs and insights.	Freewrite, focused freewrite, dialogue, metareflections
Improve problem identification and problem-solving ability.	Focused freewrite, dialogue, metaphor
Develop professional identity in professional preparation programs.	Guiding questions, dialogue, metaphor, metareflections
Take the perspective of others, reduce stress, and improve health.	Dialogue, metareflections, metaphor

getting words, any words that come to mind, on the page. Students may find it easier to approach this by writing, "I don't know what to write, I don't know what to write . . ." until they gradually discover that, indeed, they do have something to write.

For many students freewriting does not make sense at first. It seems to be "garbage" and certainly does not meet their internalized standards of acceptable academic work.

Students have to complete several freewrites to begin to see its benefits. For students who have never done a freewrite before, it is helpful to say "suspend your disbelief; just follow the directions and see what happens." After students have completed their first freewrite, you can discuss the process, asking questions like, "Let's talk about the process, not the product. How did that work for you? Did you find anything that was particularly interesting in what you wrote? Any surprises?"

If you want to talk to students about the product, the actual writing, be sure to ask for volunteers. Freewriting is not designed to be shared with others. If you insist or imply that freewriting must be shared with others, its value and concomitant student motivation to do it will diminish quickly. Still, if you want to provide some models of freewriting that encourage students, you can read your own freewrites or ask for volunteers to read what they wrote.

Researchers on writing, such as Elbow (1973) and Boice (1990, 2000), agree that some form of spontaneous writing contributes to at least three aspects of the writer's craft: idea generation, voice, and fluency. Although it may produce writing that the student might call messy and off-topic, freewriting also "produces bits of writing that are genuinely better than usual: less random, more coherent, more highly organized" (Elbow, 1973, p. 8). In addition, it builds fluency through the practice of not editing while generating ideas in their raw, undeveloped form. Freewriting also develops a student's unique voice and can be the source of fresh and often surprising ideas. The poet William Stafford has stated, "A writer is not so much someone who has something to say as he is someone who has found a process that will bring about new things he would not have thought of if he had not started to say them" (Stafford, 1964, pp. 14–15). Here is an example of a freewrite that illustrates how Janet, a master's student, uses the freewrite at the beginning of class to decompress.

> I am soooo tired. I didn't go to bed last night because I still hadn't finished either of my two BIG important portions of my paper—the methods (which I know I wrote poorly) and the literature review. I rode my bike to Conestoga and Schols Ferry and boarded, the 62 instead of the 92 ☹!! I need to take up the new adage, "look twice, board once!" (personal communication, July 20, 2007)

What did the student have the opportunity to learn here? Certainly that her writing has voice and that she can produce words—fluency. Her humor shines through as well. In her reflection on this writing, she noted, "Why am I always so hard on myself? I got my papers back Monday and they were FINE." In addition, she may have learned to quiet her inner critic and just start writing and producing words and ideas.

It is essential that freewriting not be evaluated for content or adherence to writing conventions. Otherwise, writers can end up trying to edit as they write. Elbow believes "it's an unnecessary burden to try to think of words and also worry at the same time whether they're the right words" (1973, p. 5). The power of freewriting lies in putting words, any words, on the page without criticism. Fresh, original ideas are often hard to find; yet freewriting, with its lack of constraints, encourages, supports, and even cheers the production of words in whatever form. Accomplished writers have deep respect for the enduring value of this kind of expressive writing. We believe it is important for students to experience freewriting and begin to acknowledge its benefits so that it will be a resource for them in the future.

Admittedly some of our students have great difficulty with freewriting because we have not given them a topic to write about. For these students we suggest that they keep a list of topics in the front of their journals. In this way, they assign themselves their own topics for freewrites. In the next example of freewriting, the student assigned himself the topic of a sentence completion. The sentence was "A phrase came to me the other day. . . ."

> A phrase came to me the other day that I have seen many times in my life . . . "live today as if it was going to be your last." I like the premise of this phrase, but I find it pretty ironic the places that I read this phrase. I have nothing against books (in fact I love them), but honestly, would you really be living by this motto, if you were writing this quote in a book? . . .
>
> If a person were really living by this quote, then I would expect to see it written on a bull's forehead in Pamplona and the person reading the quote would be right in front of the stampeding bull running for his life. I would expect to see that quote written in the sand so big that you could see it if you were falling to earth, hoping that your parachute is going to open. It would make sense if it was written on a blackjack table at Caesar's or drawn in the snow atop the Swiss Alps. But seeing this quote in Section D of the newspaper? That just doesn't make sense. Because I bet that if you were honest with yourself, reading a newspaper would be the last thing you would be spending your time doing if it was the last day of your life. (Drew, personal communication, July 9, 2008)

There are a variety of ways to use freewrites for classroom learning.

Freewriting at the Beginning of Class

Start the class with 5 to 10 minutes of freewriting to build fluency and "wash off the dust of the road." This is a significant amount of class time; however, because many of our students come to class after a full day in their professional settings, freewriting not only teaches students that they can write but helps them be more "present" when the class begins.

Freewriting at the End of Class

Without telling students that they need to write about any class topic, the class can be ended with a short freewrite (3 to 5 minutes). Some students may find this an important time to integrate course content, get ready for their next class, or just let some other ideas and experiences emerge.

Freewriting as Homework

Students can practice doing the freewrites at home. Faculty have sometimes required students to complete three 10-minute freewrites at home during the week. This builds fluency and helps students generate ideas.

Focused Freewriting

A *focused freewrite* has the basic characteristics of a freewrite. There are no grammar rules, punctuation rules, or sentence rules about what kind of writing ends up on the page. However, the focused freewrite is different because the topic is selected before the students start to write. To begin a focused freewrite, ask students to write a guiding question or a topic on the top of the page. For example, "What do I need to know to write this term paper on the architecture of Spain?" Or it could be just a key word; for example, a freewrite in a psychology class might use the word *motivation*. As in freewrites, students should not edit or monitor the ideas that bubble up. They should push themselves to generate as many ideas, questions, concerns, insights, and words as they can about the topic. Students should not be constrained in their thinking by demanding that they have to organize these ideas.

The journal pages generated during a focused freewrite are usually full of questions, key terms, contact names, prior knowledge, concerns, plans, and unknown topics placed on the page in any order. Thus, there should not be too much twiddling of the pen while thinking but just writing as much as possible. A faculty member who uses this regularly calls this a "knowledge dump." It helps students "dump" onto the page what they already know about the topic as well as find the areas in which they need to do more work. In reflecting on the power of focused freewrites in developing his research project, Chris wrote:

> This focused free-write served as the first formalizations of the ideas I was having concerning my research project. Not only did it get me thinking about the actual strategies I was going to use, it made me think about the complexity of what I was after. My ideas kept leading to other things that I had not thought about yet. I am a high school math teacher. I hate having unorganized notes with arrows to other comments and things written sideways on the page. In this entry I kept thinking of new things, and I was forced to write them in the margins and on the next page. It still bugs me to look at it, but those ideas ended up adding to my project. (personal communication, July 9, 2007)

Chris was able to give himself permission to write out ideas as quickly as he thought of them, and then loosen up his notion that writing must proceed logically and neatly. And, as he noted, this process added value to his final project.

There are a variety of ways to use a focused freewrite for classroom learning.

Focused Freewrite to Develop a Term Paper Topic

To introduce students to a focused freewrite for developing a paper topic, students read the assignment description in the syllabus. Direct them to just jump in and consider several topics. Select one and write it at the top of a journal page. Do a focused freewrite and see where their thinking leads them. Sometimes we write some questions that students can consider as they write the focused freewrite:

- What questions do I have about this topic?
- What resources are available?
- What do I already know about this?
- How does my own previous experience add to this topic?
- Why do I care about this topic?
- Why should others care about it?
- What do I need to do to get more information on this topic?
- Whom do I talk to? Are there experts that I can talk to about it?
- When can I start this project?
- Do I need to go to the library or can I access material online?

• What problems will I have in getting it done?
• What else is competing for my time?

A follow-up from the focused freewrite might be to have students read what they have written; select various tidbits of information, questions, and so on; and arrange them into a to-do list or a concept map on another journal page.

Focused Freewrite Before a Classroom Lecture

Before the lecture, have the students write the lecture title at the top of the page and write down all they know about this topic, including questions that the topic inspires. Students often find they already have some background knowledge, and this activity can guide them to gathering further knowledge and maybe even transforming their prior learning during the lecture. In addition, the activity can keep them motivated and engaged during the lecture as they see familiar topics presented and, perhaps, have some of their questions answered.

Focused Freewrite Following a Classroom Lecture

After students have listened to a lecture or watched a classroom video, they can spend 2 or 3 minutes writing a focused freewrite on the topic or experience. If you have them write one freewrite at the beginning of the lecture and another at the end of the lecture, students can compare what they knew and wanted to know in the beginning of class with what they learned during the lecture.

Focused Freewrite Following a Prompt

One of the prompts that we often use at the beginning of class is for students to focus on "Being here." It is an easy prompt for students to use and can generate many different types of responses.

Figure 5.2 is a student response to the focused freewrite journal prompt, "Being here." Generally this student responds with drawings and words in his journal. Obviously, he is quite comfortable drawing. To improve his reflection through writing, we suggested that he draw, then write.

Lists

Lists as a classroom journal-writing technique are exactly what they sound like. They are lists of words that are connected conceptually in some way. They are not paragraphs

Figure 5.2
Focused Freewrite: Dom's Student Journal (Response to Prompt "Being Here")

nor charts. As Tristine Rainer writes, a list "can enumerate feelings, sense impressions, intuitions, or thoughts without using complete sentences. Lists are time-savers and time-condensers" (1978, pp. 72–73).

People in today's society are well-practiced list makers. If you ask your students what kind of lists they make, they will generate a number of ways that they frequently make lists, including grocery lists, to-do lists, packing lists, gift lists, and invitation lists. A typical list saves time by condensing or summarizing all that is known on the topic into brief phrases. As Tristine Rainer notes,

> Lists are also particularly useful when you feel overwhelmed by the magnitude of something you wish to describe. . . . Even when nothing is resolved lists help focus problems and make them finite. When your head is swimming with unresolved issues, they seem infinite. On paper they become focused and concrete. You can do something about each item on a list. (1978, p. 73)

Thus, a list "objectifies" the task by taking it out of the brain where it is swirling around and setting it out on the page to be handled or checked off or prioritized and, for "to do" lists, ultimately and best of all, done.

When encouraging students to create lists, it is best just to brainstorm all items that could possibly be on the list. Creating a list through brainstorming can identify many and sometimes surprising things related to the topic.

Gayle's list in Figure 5.3 is her response to the instructor's question, "What are all the influences on a child's learning?" It is a long list and foreshadows many of the topics covered in the class, Theories of Instruction. Gayle, a high school art teacher, not only made the list but also doodled along the edge of the page as the class was brainstorming topics to be included.

Here are some ways to use lists for classroom learning.

Make a List of Brainstorming Ideas to Consider for a Term Paper or Project
Ask students to list the many possible topics that they have considered, and then read the list and select one or two that seem more appealing. Then students might do a focused freewrite on one of the topics.

Make a List of Responses to an Incomplete Sentence String
Creating a list from an incomplete sentence such as "Revolution is . . . " or "Biology is . . . " can generate a number of different ideas that tap student background knowledge. As an instructor, it is important to know what students already know before they begin studying a topic. That information can inform you as well and help you decide how much emphasis you put on any aspect of a new topic.

Figure 5.3
List: Gayle's Student Journal

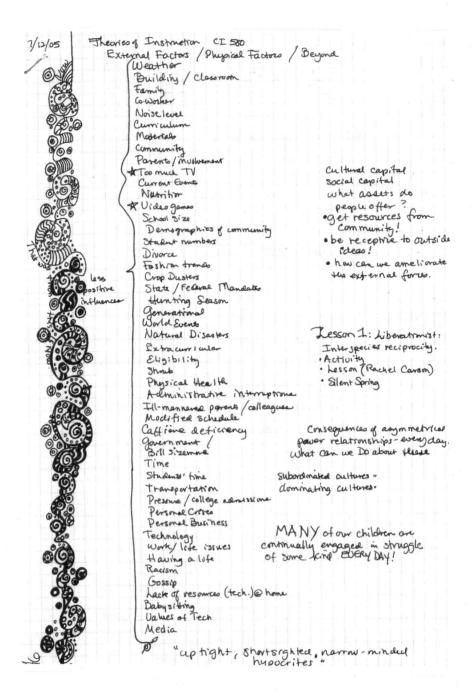

7/12/05

Theories of Instruction   CI 580
External Factors / Physical Factors / Beyond
Weather
Building / Classroom
Family
Co-Worker
Noise level
Curriculum
Materials
Community
Parents / involvement
★ Too much TV
Current Events
Nutrition
★ Video games
School Size
Demographics of community
Student numbers
Divorce
Fashion trends
Crop Dusters
State / Federal Mandates
Hunting Season
Generational
World Events
Natural Disasters
Extracurricular
Eligibility
Shrub
Physical Health
Administrative interruptions
Ill-mannered parents / colleagues
Modified Schedule
Caffiene deficiency
government /
Bill Sizemore
Time
Students' time
Transportation
Pressure / college admissions
Personal Crises
Personal Business
Technology
Work / life issues
Having a life
Racism
Gossip
Lack of resources (tech.) @ home
Babysitting
Values of Tech
Media

less positive influences

Cultural capital
social capital
what assets do
   people offer ?
• get resources from
   Community!
• be receptive to outside
   ideas!
• how can we ameliorate
   the external forces.

Lesson 1: Liberationist:
   Interspecies reciprocity.
• Activity
• Lesson (Rachel Carson)
• Silent Spring

Consequences of asymmetrical
power relationships - everyday.
What can we Do about these

Subordinated cultures =
dominating cultures.

MANY of our children are
continually engaged in struggle
of some kind EVERY DAY!

"uptight, shortsighted, narrow-minded
   hypocrites"

Make an Unprioritized List of Things to Do to Complete a Project

By making a list that is in no particular order, the students can see all the pieces of a project, both large and small. By reviewing the list, they can begin to practice how to cluster and prioritize the tasks needed to complete the project.

Make a List of Things Learned From the Lecture Today

Listing things learned in the lecture is a wonderful review activity. Although it appears simple, it encourages students to pay attention and to review what stood out in the lecture.

Make a List of Prior Knowledge and Underlying Assumptions

Constructivist learning theory acknowledges that prior knowledge is the best predictor of what students will learn about the topic. For example, what students already know about Picasso will help them more easily learn new things about Picasso.

Make a List of Concerns When Entering a Field Setting

Similar to the previous list, a list of concerns focuses on embedded assumptions that a student has about field work. Making a list of these concerns often opens up the door and allows students to look at what might be blocking their ability to observe as objectively as possible.

Make a List of Goals or Directions for the Future

Again, a list of future goals appears simple. Creating a list of goals should be done rapidly so that the internal judge, critic, or nay-sayer does not have a chance to interfere with spontaneous thoughts. When students review their lists, they can examine the various paths they might seek to travel in their lives. Writing a reflection on the list helps them think more deeply about the choices they have.

Log

A log is characterized by dated entries, brief phrases, and visually organized information. A log looks like a list, but is not a list. A log might have several categories listed in separate columns. The rows of a column (horizontals) can be the date of the activity being logged. Putting related information in columns facilitates understanding, quick review, faster access, and maybe even reflection when comparing columns. By looking across a log, we learn what happened that day. By looking down a log we can compare and contrast different aspects of the items in that column. For example, library research logs, field-site–visit entries, or books read during the year all lend themselves to a log format rather than as text in sentence and paragraph form. When students need to document dates, times, names, and a brief description of a class assignment or project, a log works well. A log not only promotes student accountability but also models how to organize a complex project into manageable bits. By reviewing a student log, you can quickly and easily assess what students are doing. When introducing a log, it is very helpful to show students an example of the log you want them to keep. A log of student group work on a community research project might look like Table 5.3.

Keeping a log can be a useful illustration for students of how a journal can be used. Students can easily and quickly learn how to keep the log. They will also see how logs can be a source of reflection on experience. When students review their log and look across and down the columns they can write reflections on the experience. A log invites students to identify patterns in their activities and abstract additional learning from the experience. From the log in Table 5.3, students can list the group and individual activities and keep a record of how the work is distributed and completed.

Some ways to use a log for classroom learning include the following.

Log Interactions in the Field

The date, names, time, and phrase or sentence descriptions of the nature of the field or clinical interactions can be logged. When students bring these to class, they can be used as a stimulus for written reflections and in-class discussions.

Table 5.3
Example of a Log for a Group Project

Date	Task	Work to Be Done	By Whom	Date Completed
4.11.07	Gather resources for group presentation in May.	Go to library.	Denis, Maura	4.15.07
		Talk to community partner.	Genaro, Molly, Denis	4.13.07
4.18.07	Share resources; write summary.	Bring notes to group meeting.	All	4.18.07
4.18.07	Proofread summary.	Submit to instructor.	Maura, Genaro, Denis	4.20.07

Log Dates, Times, and Activities of Small-Group Work
Whether during class time or out of class, students can be held responsible for recording date, time, and activities of their small-group work. One instructor had students write out discussion questions in small groups in class and then write the date, participants, and key ideas considered in their journal after the discussion. For accountability, students can photocopy these pages for instructor review.

Log Subtasks Completed and Record Final Task Accomplished
For long-term projects, students can list and then log their completion of subtasks. Instructors can quickly check students' logs to determine whether they are progressing in their assignment and also if they are able to divide a task into subtasks to facilitate completion.

Dialogue

Dialogue in journal writing is a "conversation" between people, parts, ideas, or things (Rainer, 1978). Dialogue enables students to distance themselves from other people, thoughts, feelings, and ideas; make them the "other"; and then write out an imagined conversation with the other. The dialogue allows the writer to objectify the other. When we objectify an experience, a relationship, our feelings, our worries, and our obligations, we gain some control and we can look at them from a different perspective to understand them anew (Kegan, 1982).

Progoff asserts, "Underlying these written dialogues, however, is the more fundamental sense of dialogue not as a technique but as a way of relationship. The dialogue relationship is a mutual meeting of persons each accepting, speaking out and most important, listening to the other" (1992, p. 125). Just switching to another voice allows the writer to explore a different perspective. Dialogue often uncovers hidden biases and misconceptions that can block understanding and openness to new ideas. More often than not students find that dialogue frees them to say things that they might not otherwise say. Depending on the dialogue, it can acquaint students with their well-hidden fears and anxieties. Description of other "voices" or perspectives in thinking is often a source of surprise and motivates students to write more, just to see what the other part is saying. Journal writers can dialogue with other people, works, feelings, inanimate objects, pets, their cars, or parts of the body. It is often helpful for students to dialogue with major projects like a thesis or dissertation. The first dialogue example in Appendix A from Alyssa illustrates how writing a master's thesis can be fraught with insecurities. To encourage students to make a dialogue seem more like a conversation, we suggest that students move to the next line when each "part" takes its conversational turn.

Here is a brief example from a student who was asked to have a dialogue with an inanimate object. This brief excerpt illustrates her initial skepticism and yet through dialogue she quickly reached an issue that she faced in her own life:

> **Emily (E):** I am talking to an inanimate object. . . . I must be crazy.
> **Inanimate Object (IO):** Hey! I have feelings you know.
> **E:** No you don't, you are not alive.
> **IO:** Oh yeah, well . . . blah, blah, blah. . . .
> **E:** You are a thing!
> **IO:** You have been a thing before too—people treat you like a thing with no feelings and you get mad. (Stevens & Cooper, 2007, p. 2)

Dialogue is natural for journal writing because much of journal writing can be a conversation with the self, parts of the self, significant others in one's life, or others we encounter in field or clinical settings.

Some ways dialogue can be used in college courses include the following.

Dialogue With Significant People in Course Material

Some faculty have had students write dialogues with figures in history, characters in stories they are reading, or leading experts in the field.

Dialogue With a Term-Paper Topic

Others have been successful having students dialogue with their term-paper topic. Students can start by asking what they need to learn and do to write a good paper on a particular topic. Writing a dialogue often enlivens the topic and can generate student enthusiasm.

Dialogue With Issues or Persons in One's Life

Having a dialogue with key issues in a student's life often stimulates deeper reflection. We have found that students have had interesting and insightful dialogues with time, procrastination, success, failure, roommates, and—well, the list is endless. The second dialogue example in Appendix A is a graduate student's dialogue with time.

Dialogue With Contradictions
and Conflicts in Thinking

Elbow (1973) encourages writers to pursue conflicts or contradictions in thinking as they write their journal entries. These foster deeper thinking and richer writing and help the writers to avoid ruts. Writing a dialogue, for example, between an environmentalist and a businessperson can illuminate both points of view.

Dialogue With Objects or Feelings

Ask students to list some inanimate objects that have meaning in their lives. They might list a car, an mp3 player, a special item of clothing, or a favorite food. For feelings, students could explore anger, frustration, exhaustion, and so on. Then have them greet the object or feeling in a dialogue and proceed to have a conversation with it. Often this results in a lively, playful, and interesting dialogue from which students gain some insight.

Dialogue With an Inner Mentor

To help students learn how to tap their own inner personal resources, we introduce them to having a dialogue with their "Inner Mentor," a wiser self whom many find has very good advice for them.

Concept Mapping

A concept map is a diagram with a set of "bubbles" or boxes that contain one idea, word, or phrase with arrows or lines connecting to other ideas. In addition to showing how these ideas link to one another through the arrows, the lines and arrows illustrate the hierarchical relationship between the ideas, moving from the general to the specific. Key ideas are arranged in clusters and the relationships between the clusters are identified by relationship lines; often the arrows indicate directionality. Concept maps enhance problem solving because students have to decide on the relationships between the ideas (Fox & Morrison, 2005). In addition, Novak and Gowan (1984) established that concept mapping fosters the development of deep and meaningful learning along with critical thinking.

Why would a journal be a particularly useful place to create a concept map? The map can be referred to repeatedly and ideas can easily be added. The ideas on the map can be used to organize and mobilize the writing of an essay or manuscript. The map is a visual display of ideas and the relationships between those ideas.

Figure 5.4 is an example of a concept map. In this case, the map is an illustration of how a graduate student, Serap, organized her core paper for her dissertation.

Sometimes students find that the concept map is all they needed to jump-start their ideas and see the relationships between these ideas. Paula wrote the following reflection on creating a concept map for a class reading assignment.

> . . . one of the first "ah-ha"-type moments in regard to this pattern of having time to reflect came when I used the cognitive mapping technique to outline one of our reading assignments. As I used this strategy, I found it a very comfortable and effective way of looking at the material and summarizing it. I loved being able to jot down main points, see relationships, and create an "at-a-glance" overview of the information. (personal communication, July 3, 2008)

Here are some ways to use concept maps for classroom learning.

Create a Concept Map of the Reading

You may have to teach students how to look for text structure elements, such as titles and subheads, in their course readings to put on the concept map. Paula's reflection was about an assignment to make a concept map of the class reading prior to class discussion.

Create a Concept Map of Students' Knowledge at the Beginning and End of Term

First have students list what they already know about the topic (e.g., architecture), and then place the items in a concept map noting the relationships between the ideas. If students do not know what a concept map is, show an example. At the end of the term have the students create another concept map of what they have learned. Having them write a reflection on how the two maps are different and how their notions have changed will deepen their own understanding of themselves as learners.

Create a Concept Map During the Lecture

Put a blank concept map on the board. As you lecture, fill in the parts of the concept map. Suggest that students create this map in their journal and fill it in as you lecture as well.

Figure 5.4
Concept Map: Serap's Student Journal

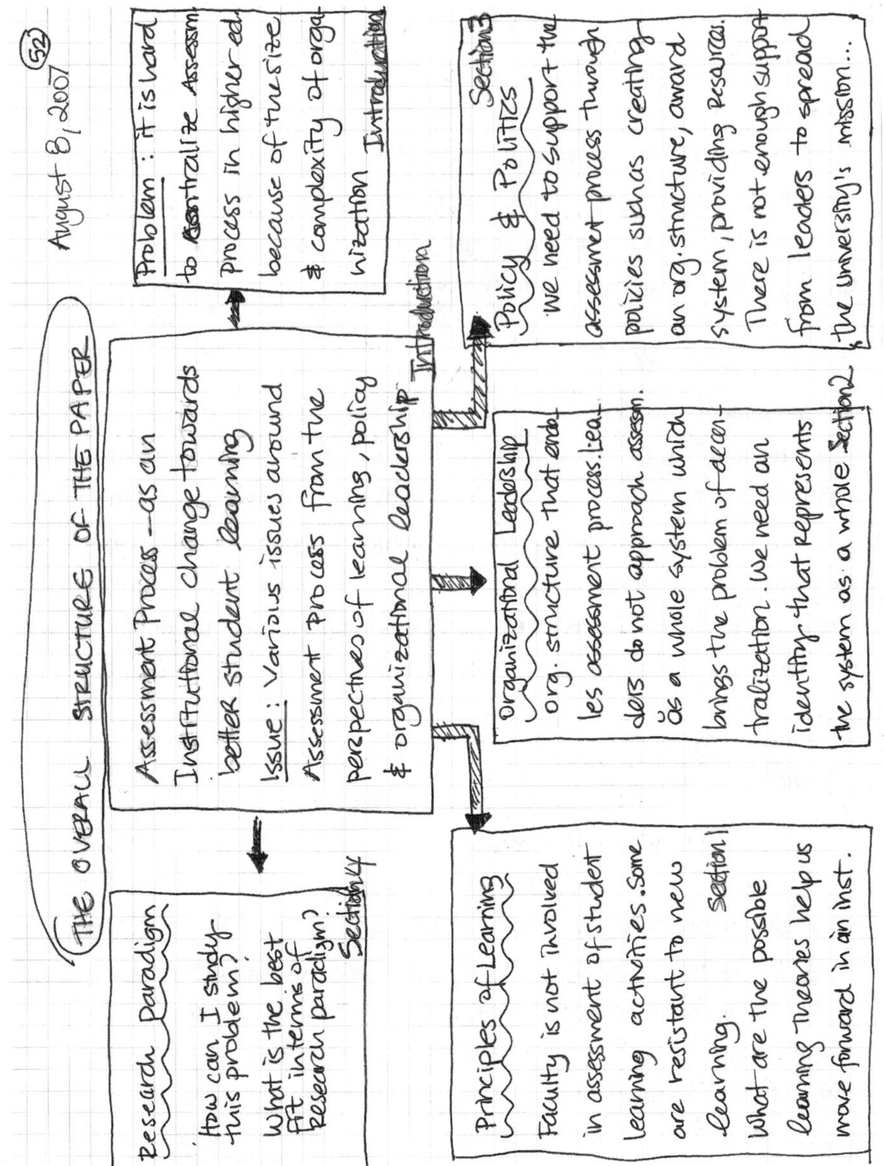

THE OVERALL STRUCTURE OF THE PAPER

August 8, 2007 (52)

Research Paradigm

How can I study this problem?
What is the best fit in terms of Research paradigm?
Section 4

Assessment Process —as an Institutional change towards better student learning
Issue: Various issues around Assessment Process from the perspectives of learning, policy & organizational leadership. Introduction

Problem: It is hard to decentralize Assessment Process in higher ed because of the size & complexity of organization. Introduction

Policy & Politics   Section 3
We need to support the assessment process through policies such as creating an org. structure, award system, providing resources. There is not enough support from leaders to spread the university's mission...

Organizational Leadership
org. structure that models the assessment process. Leaders do not approach assessment as a whole system which brings the problem of decentralization. We need an identity that represents the system as a whole. Section 2

Principles of Learning
Faculty is not involved in assessment of student learning activities. Some are resistant to new learning.   Section 1
What are the possible learning theories help us move forward in an inst.

Create Concept Maps of Chapter Content

Have students create concept maps of chapter content in their journals. Have the students form small groups to discuss with others what is important to remember in the chapter or readings.

Create Concept Maps of Key Ideas From the
Readings and Lectures for the Week

Creating maps of key ideas can be done individually or in small groups. When students create maps as small-group work in class, it is very active and engaging. As students discuss what is important and identify the hierarchical relationships between the ideas, they understand and remember them better.

Create a Concept Map of Ideas for a Term Paper

We have taught students how to use a concept map in the development of a term-paper topic. First, they brainstorm a list of all the ideas and questions that they have accumulated about the topic on one side of their journal pages. On the adjacent page, they can then create a concept map in which they cluster the ideas and see how they are related to one another. This can also be done with sticky notes; each note has only one idea and then is moved into clusters of ideas on the journal page. Then a sentence is written below each cluster to indicate what all the ideas in that cluster are about.

Metaphor

Metaphor describes one thing by comparing it to something else (Lakoff & Johnson, 1980). The two things may or may not be intuitively related; yet the metaphor helps highlight characteristics of each. For instance, we recently asked students to identify a metaphor for their action research projects. One student saw her project as a rock, something solid and impenetrable that she could not crack. Then, she saw how she was avoiding the rock and how she was fighting the ideas that were so impenetrable and difficult to understand. Another saw her project as a slinky, a continuous spiral of planning, action, monitoring, and evaluation that has been around for years. By using a metaphor to describe action research, both students saw their projects in a new and different light and were surprised about the value of using metaphor to understand their thinking.

Creating metaphors allows students to envision the objects or persons from a different viewpoint. For our journal-writing class, we take the students to the city art museum and have them find an object that attracts or even repulses them. We ask them to make a sketch of the object in their journal and give the object a voice and write down what the object says to them. Then they reflect on whether how the object speaks and what the object says has metaphoric meaning for their lives now. For example, Dom selected a transformation mask from one of the Northwest American Indian tribes for his object. He started with, "I am a mask. . . ." Figure 5.5 is a page from Dom's journal in which he drew and wrote about the object he selected at the museum and found that the object did indeed have something to teach him about himself.

Faculty in the sciences could easily adapt this metaphor activity to their field. In Anna's women's biology class she asked her students to create "body journals," and then at the end of the course to select one or two observations to be written onto a white dress. Each student posted an observation of the body, filling the white dress with journal entries. In Figure 5.6 the students are posting their observations onto a white dress. In this women's college the white dress has particular symbolism, because wearing white dresses and white gloves is part of an annual school ritual. (See chapter 9 for her full teaching case.)

Here are some other ways that metaphor can be used. Dannelle was the academic program coordinator for a group of 21 teachers from China who were visiting her university for 6 months. As part of their academic program, she introduced them to journal keeping. Besides using many of the techniques described in this book, she encouraged them to use their journals in a variety of other ways—to collect ticket stubs, take class notes, and work on English vocabulary.

One of the most interesting activities was a metaphor project that prompted the students to draw a tree at different points during the program. After giving the students colored pencils, she asked them to imagine a tree and then draw that tree in their journals. Then they were to describe the tree and its life. Over 6 months the students drew five trees. Trees seemed to be an appropriate and apt metaphor for spending a significant amount of time in a new culture, leaving their families, and living in student dormitories. Certainly all these activities challenged their abilities to adapt in foreign soil. The students were so engaged in the task that many students started their trees in the class but finished them later. Figure 5.7 illustrates a tree that Larissa drew in September about halfway through the visit. She wrote about a moon

Figure 5.5
Metaphor: Dom's Mask From Visit to Art Museum

Figure 5.6
Metaphor: The White Dress Journal From Biology of Women Class

festival that the Chinese have in September; yet for this festival she includes her American friends and families.

The tree metaphor helped these visitors summarize their experience over time, as well as observe how their trees and reflections changed as they progressed through the program.

Metaphor is the back door into deeper understanding of concepts taught in class and a way to understand the self through the extension of ideas in new directions. Ways to use metaphors for classroom journal writing include the following.

Create a Metaphor for Course Theme
A metaphor for a course theme might be, for example, "Biological diversity is a patchwork quilt. . . ."

Figure 5.7
Metaphor: Chinese Student Draws a Tree Representing Her
Experience in the United States

I miss . . . .
I need . . . .
she/he miss . . . . too.
she/he need . . . .
We are together.

September 25 is a tradinal festival — the Mid-Autumn Festival in China. This is a special time that everybody want to stay with family. But this year we is are in the USA. we can't accompany with family and friends. I think everybody miss hometown very much whe they saw the moon on the sky.

We had a celebration on Sep 24 night. Every roon made one or more delicious. Mooncake is the traditional food for the Mid-Autumn Festival, but we can eat them in the U.S.A. I feel very warm with all classmates. When someone leave home go to another place, she/he need friends and take care of each other. So I hope all of us have a happy day until we leave the U.S.A. Love each other. (103)

Create a Metaphor for Field Experiences

A metaphor for a field experience might be something like, "Going to the homeless shelter is walking along a path that I have never traveled before."

Create a Metaphor for One Aspect of Your Belief System

A metaphor for a belief system about how research is conducted might be "Research digs deeply into the soil of a garden looking for roots, bugs, and seeds." Here the belief system involves thinking of research as an activity in which the researcher digs below the surface for hidden elements that are not readily seen.

Revisit the Same Metaphor at Different Times

Just as Dannelle did with the Chinese teachers, select a powerful metaphor that can describe an experience and write about it several times to see how the writers' perceptions of it change over time, and how the writers themselves change over time.

Create a Metaphor for an Aspect of Your Life

To create a metaphor for an aspect of students' lives, for example, have students select and elaborate on a metaphor for their work lives, family, marriage, or relationships with others. There are endless ways to use metaphor for deep reflection.

Metareflection

Metareflection requires students to reread their journal entries generated over the term and write a reflection on what they notice about these reflections. Simply stated, *metareflection* means reflecting about reflecting. The word is derived from the term *metacognition,* which means thinking about thinking. People who have developed their metacognitive skills have a set of tested strategies for completing tasks and for learning. They are able to take the "balcony view" of themselves as learners and design and assess strategies for success. Research has shown that those who apply metacognitive skills to their learning are more successful in school. By having students reread, review, and reflect on their journal-writing entries, they can see what they have learned, highlight successful strategies, and practice reflecting on their prior reflections. Thus, we call this process metareflection. This builds the ever-so-important ability to monitor their learning and assess the effectiveness of strategies they employ.

What do students have to do to create a metareflection? First, students have to read their journal entries from across the term or semester; that in itself is a good way to review course material, and hopefully to note any changes in their perspectives from the beginning to the end of the course. When they compare what they thought at the beginning of the course with what they think now, students often find that their thinking has changed over time. As one student from our research noted, "The metacognitive journal entries helped me make more connections and really look back at my prior observations."

Recently we had a student who said he hated to reread his journal because he seemed so stupid. We asked him to consider that fact that once you write that page you can never write that same page again. In that way, the journal can really be an object that you examine to learn about your own learning and thinking style. In fact, as the days go by, you learn, change, and develop, and the self you were when you wrote that entry is now subject to review by your new self (Grumet, 1990). Liam, one of our students, wrote the following freewrite.

> I don't feel like I've ever committed to thinking about a particular problem, or even having a particular viewpoint. Each time, I've felt conflicted, because I tend to see these changes through multiple eyes: the eyes of an educator; the eyes of an administrator; and the eyes of a policy maker." (personal communication, November 11, 2006)

Later in a metareflection on this journal entry, Liam wrote,

> I meditated on the idea that I'm stuck in a neutral zone. While considering this question, I was blithely unconscious of the purple elephant in the corner. My life is currently a study in transition, with law school, a mandated 3-year neutral zone. Repeatedly over the last few years I've tried to explain to people that I'm in an "overexcited Alpha state," meaning that I'm learning more and encountering more new activities and expectations than in a normal life period. I've also told people, concerned for my well-being, that "Yes, my life is out of balance. But balance implies equilibrium or stasis. During a period of intense transition, balance consists of a series of constant adjustments, like a tightrope-walker or a surfer." For all my self-awareness in conversations at coffee shops or over dinner, I didn't really make the connection between my own transitional state and my difficulties defining my stance toward material in this class. (personal communication, November, 22, 2006)

When we ask students to write a metareflection on a significant journal entry, sometimes they choose to write on what they learned about keeping a journal over the term. Tobi, one of our students, wrote the following metareflection on the new role that journal writing will now play in her life.

> I have stuck my foot in the door of the wonderful world of journaling as a reflective practice. I now feel equipped to go beyond logging and recording the events of my life but to look deeper and learn from experiences. I plan to take more risks and leave any concerns of an imagined audience behind. My journal is a safe place for me to explore my thoughts, feelings, and concerns. It is a place to practice being me without criticism. It is no longer a place to chronicle events that happen to me but a place for me to happen, for me to grow into a complex, thinking adult who can make decisions for myself, by myself. (personal communication, July 16, 2008)

Metareflections also tell you how well students integrate course material into their lives. Sometimes our students select one of our lectures for their metareflection, noting how they continually turned back to this page to see the direction of the course. This is very valuable feedback for the next time we teach the class. Ways to use metareflection for classroom learning include the following.

Metareflection Over the Journal Entries Made During the Term
To make sure students use metareflection to think about previous journal entries, we have them select and photocopy significant pages and write a metareflection on those particularly significant entries.

Metareflection Over Particular Journal Entries
Have students select a certain kind of journal entry—for example, freewrites—and read those entries to look for common themes. Ask students to write a metareflection on the patterns they identify.

Metareflection on a Certain Activity in the Course
Have students select one particular aspect of the course, review their notes in their journal, and write a metareflection on what that particular aspect of the course meant to them.

This concludes our section on eight specific techniques that are useful when using journals for classroom learning. In the following three sections of this chapter we share some ideas about how journals can accomplish specific objectives. During workshops and conference presentations, faculty often ask us about how to use journal writing to:

- Encourage students to complete and reflect on course readings.
- Help students become better writers.
- Strengthen students' ability to reflect on their learning in field settings.

Although the ideas in the following sections are certainly not exhaustive, we hope they may help you get started.

Techniques to Encourage Students to Read the Course Material

In this first section, we offer suggestions on how to use the journal to address a perennial teaching problem: Students come to class unprepared to participate in class discussion largely because they have not done the readings. Research has shown that typically as few as 30% of the students have done the course readings for any lecture. Structuring the way that students respond to their readings is the key to getting students to read the course material. "Structuring" means giving students specific assignments to complete in their journals either at home or in class that are directly related to the course readings. We highly recommend that you use their reading responses or "learning logs" in class in some way as well. This requires students to bring their journals to class. Table 5.4 contains assignments that communicate that you expect the students to do the course readings. One residual benefit of these assignments is that the student not only has to read the material for the information but also has to think about it and create a response. Thus students have to be active learners. All of these activities originate in the journal. Students can then use them for review for exams as well.

Techniques to Improve Student Writing

The second specific way that journals can be used is to help students improve their writing skills. Journals are a classic way to help students develop their thinking and writing skills (Fenwick, 2001). Students need a place to write freely and begin to experiment with connections among fledgling ideas without having a judge sitting over their

Table 5.4

Journal-Writing Techniques That Encourage Students to Complete Course Readings

Interactive journal: Engagement	Students use two journal pages. On one page they take notes on the reading. On the other side, they "personalize" the content of the reading into a story, concept map, drawing, list, diagram, cartoon, or whatever comes to mind. This personalization facilitates recall.
Dialogue entries: Engagement	Students write out a dialogue with the author or with a key concept for that week. For example, in psychology class, the student might dialogue with motivation; in a biology class, with protoplasm. These dialogues facilitate comprehension and foster student engagement.
Letter: Perspective taking	Students write a letter in their journal to the author, character, or event that they are reading about. Tell them ahead of time if you expect them to read the letter in class. To write this letter, students must imagine the "audience" for the letter; this strengthens their ability to take the perspective of the other.
Concept maps: Ability to overview reading topics	Students develop a concept map of the key ideas in the reading. You can quickly assess assignment completion by walking around the room to see if they understand the relationships between the topics and have found the key ideas. In small groups they can share and compare their maps with one another, noting differences and similarities in interpretation.
Key questions or prompts: Focus on big ideas	Students can answer an overarching question for each class topic. Their answer must include citations from the readings. Students write answers to the question in their journals.
Pair-share: Talk about ideas from readings	Students discuss their written response to the reading with another student. If you warn them ahead of time to be sensitive to privacy issues, any of these activities—dialogue, concept map, letter, etc.—could be used as a pair-share.

(continues)

Table 5.4 (continued)

Sticky notes: Organize concepts from readings	Students use sticky notes to identify key, interesting, or surprising parts of the text that they discovered while doing the reading. They can share their notes in class in a small group or during a whole-class discussion. Sticky notes with notes from the discussion can be put into the journal as a reminder of what they learned.
Generate questions: Engagement with ideas	Students can formulate two class discussion questions from the readings. Or students can write a hypothetical midterm question in their journal. They could answer each others' questions in small groups. (Walden, 1988, p. 17)
Potpourri of responses	Over the weeks of the term, have students first write out key ideas from the readings in their journals on one page. On the opposite page have them respond to the reading a different way each week, such as with the four-column method, concept map, advertisement, comic strip, class discussion questions, letter to the author, focused freewrite, brochure, and newsletter. The variety of responses taps different learning styles for students and invites students to try different ways to engage with their readings.

shoulders scrutinizing their work (Elbow, 1973). Journals can contain the seeds of thought and flashes of insight that students can use when composing a paper and developing their own voices and perspectives.

In addition, journals help students learn about how writing works. Writing, of course, is not about coming up with a final product the first time the fingers hit the keyboard or grasp the pen. It is about working through, grappling, pulling apart, analyzing, summarizing, and finally finding an idea that authentically communicates something to another human being. Using some specific classroom journal-writing activities can open students to risk-taking and exploration with their writing, foster the ability to produce text, and build confidence in writing. Table 5.5 describes a variety of journal-writing techniques that improve student writing.

Table 5.5
Journal-Writing Techniques That Improve Student Writing

Freewriting	Students learn how to use freewriting to help get words, any words down on the page. This improves writing fluency (Elbow, 1973).
Lists: Topic selection	Students generate lists of as many ideas as possible before settling on one for a topic.
Focused freewrite: Paper topic development	Students write the assignment topic on the top of the page. Then they write out all questions, ideas, resources, directions, themes, people, steps to take, concerns, passions, interests, fears, anxieties, background knowledge—anything related to the topic—on one page.
Concept maps: Writing organization	After students have a list of ideas for their papers on one page, they cluster their ideas on an adjoining page. They can then draw lines between the ideas or put labels under the clusters and begin to show visually with lines and arrows the relationships between the ideas.
Log: Writing productivity	Students keep a log of their activities related to writing. The log could contain a variety of things related to writing: date, number of words written, references used, goals for writing sessions, or whether the goal was met or not met. (See a model in Silvia, 2007.)
Sticky notes: Writing organization	This is another way to develop a concept map to facilitate the organization of a paper. Have students write one idea for their papers on one sticky note. Put the next idea on another note and keep on going. When they have exhausted their ideas, they can begin to arrange the ideas in clusters on a journal page. Write labels or sentences under each idea. This begins to lay the groundwork for the organization of a paper.

Techniques That Foster Engagement
in Service Learning Projects

The third specific area that we address is how to use the journal to further student learning in settings outside of the classroom. Service learning; experiential learning; community-based learning; and even internships in professional practice programs like business, education, or nursing—all fall under the umbrella of learning outside the classroom walls. Often these involve learning in a setting that "belongs" to a community partner. Students have many wonderful opportunities to learn about not only the course content, but how to work with community partners. Faculty often assign reflective journals to help students garner much more from these experiences. As Hatcher and Bringle note, "Unlike the predictability of a textbook, a service experience can be unpredictable and confusing" (1997, p. 156). Reflective journal-writing activities can help students process their experiences and then share them with others.

When students go out into the field, the clinic, or the public school classroom as interns, they carry their excitement and their anxieties. They also carry their preconceived notions about how the world works. Students' prior notions can act as a set of blinders, limiting their observations, blocking their awareness, and crippling their learning. As a field supervisor or instructor using service learning or community-based learning activities, your job is to help students think more deeply about their observations and inferences. In addition, you can help students expose what they are bringing to their experience so that they can be open to new learning. Much of the literature points to reflective journal writing as a key to helping students get the most out of their field experiences (Ash, Clayton, & Atkinson, 2005; Jacoby, 1996). When designing reflective activities that include a component of reflective journal writing, Hatcher and Bringle (1997) offer these guidelines:

Link experience to learning outcomes.
Give guidance for reflective activities.
Schedule reflective activities regularly.
Allow for feedback and assessment of reflective activities.

Like all journal-keeping activities, these guidelines illustrate the need to integrate the journal into ongoing course activities and the assessment system. Table 5.6 catalogs

Table 5.6
Journal-Writing Techniques for Service Learning

Dialogue: Perspective taking of community partner	Have the students write an imaginary dialogue with one of their service learning partners. Write a dialogue with the service or project they are working on, for example, with the watershed they want to improve, with the hunger project, with the community they want to develop.
Concept maps: Organize and prioritize field work	Have students list key elements needed to complete a service project. From the list, create a concept map of the items, clustering things that are alike, and then establishing the relationships between the things.
Guiding questions: Critical thinking	Provide students with a list of thought-provoking questions to answer in their journals about the service project and relationship.
Log: Organize complex field work	Have students set aside about three pages in the front of their journals to create a log that includes the following: date of contact with the field, with whom the student met, result of contact, and date when they will meet again. Keep this in the front of the journal and fill it in each time they go out into the field.
List: Organize complex field work	Have students list all the things they need to do before they start meetings with field partners.
Three-column journal	Divide the journal page into three columns: 1. Service activity 2. Course material 3. Application to student's life
Service-learning vocabulary	Students receive a list of key vocabulary related to service learning that you want to see them use in their journal (Hatcher & Bringle, 1997).
Self-assess learning	Students ask these questions about themselves as a learner in a service project: Who am I in this project? What have I learned? How did I learn it?
Combine several journal activities	Students create a "swamplog" that uses four types of journal entries: daily log entries, summary log entries, reflections and explorations, and stepping-stones (proposed actions and noble intentions following service learning course) (Nicassio, 1992).
Values clarification activity	Students at the service site: 1. List words/phrases that describe their senses/feelings. 2. List word/phrases that describe their actions. 3. List word/phrases that describe their thoughts. 4. Describe what contradictions they sensed (derived from Hatcher & Bringle, 1997, p. 156).

ideas for journal-writing activities that help students achieve learning outcomes in service-learning settings.

Conclusion

This chapter offers a plethora of techniques for classroom journal writing. The success of assigned classroom journal writing depends on finding activities that engage students in their own learning. Instructor-guided journal-writing activities can increase student motivation to read course materials and engage in course experiences. The ideas and experiences in your course are then not a set of disconnected and inert facts. Journal-writing techniques encourage students to respond, relate, reflect, and encounter the subject matter at their own unique levels from their own unique perspectives. When students compare what they know with what the course offers, journal entries can reveal thoughtful reflection and critical thinking that can lead to transformational, not just informational, learning. Journaling helps students embrace the content knowledge of a course, making that knowledge their own. Maybe, it can even become a healthy habit for a lifetime.

Chapter 6 discusses how to assess journals while at the same time addressing the issues of privacy and the development of writing voice.

GRADING CLASSROOM JOURNAL WRITING

"All that hard work I put into my journal reflections ought to count," Julio noted.
"How can anyone actually grade my own personal reflections, anyway?" Sarah added.
Adapted from Crème (2005)

THESE TWO TYPICAL STUDENT COMMENTS APTLY ILLUSTRATE contrasting perspectives on grading classroom journal writing. On one hand, like all of the other required course assignments, some students would argue that the hard work on journal reflections should count. Shouldn't someone read the journal, provide feedback, and assign a grade? On the other hand, given the informal and potentially personal nature of journal entries, as Sarah implies, students may doubt that journal writing can be graded at all. Students are not the only ones concerned about grading journal writing. At our workshops and presentations on classroom journaling, faculty frequently ask, "How do I grade journal writing?" or even, "Should I grade journal writing?"

Grading or providing other forms of feedback on classroom journal writing presents challenges. Faculty members want journal entries that show how students are engaged with course content and how the course relates to their own life experiences. Some faculty members know that journals are also a particularly appropriate place for authentic observations and reflections on readings, clinical-setting observations, laboratory observations, and service-learning activities (English & Gillen, 2001; Fulwiler, 1987; Hatcher & Bringle, 1997). In other instances, journal-writing assignments may be designed to encourage students to probe deeply into their fundamental assumptions about the way the world works, in order to identify and think critically about their closely held beliefs in relation to course objectives (Brookfield, 1995). Yet as Orem writes,

> For a journal to be truly an instrument of transforming personal learning, the learner may need to be convinced of the safety of expressing what could be critical comments to someone who has the power to award a grade to [his or her] overall performance. (2001, p. 69)

One sure way to create a safe environment is to not read the journal at all, perhaps just checking it for completion, not content. Students might then have no fear of expressing critical comments and feel the freedom to explore any place their thoughts may take them. Yet if students are not given feedback and journal writing is not assessed and graded, students may not take journal writing seriously. Furthermore, not providing feedback may communicate that the task is unimportant, not worthy of the instructor's time. Therefore, a critical issue in classroom journal writing is whether to give feedback at all. If instructors decide to give feedback, the next issue is how to make sure that feedback creates a "safe" environment so that students take risks and garner the full benefits of reflective writing.

There is little agreement in the literature about grading student journals. In the sciences, Stork and Sisson assert that faculty should "respond to everything students write" (2005, p. 177) to send the message that informal writing is time well spent for science students. Boud (2001), on the other hand, insists that journal writing should be essentially private to avoid inhibiting deep or critical reflection on taken-for-granted assumptions. He assures journal keepers in his classroom that he will not read their journal entries. The content and quality of journal writing raises other important considerations. A journal (written, dated, informal, flexible, private) contrasts sharply with typical academic work. Even if you commit to reading student journals, the fact that journal entries are often informal, are written in colloquial language, can be variable in length and in quality, and may be seen as "private" makes the work very difficult to grade. Although you can grade whether students produce regular, dated entries, you may not be accustomed to grading informal student writing. In fact, the "sketchbook" quality of some student journal entries may not be suitable for grading against strict, preset criteria. Consider the fact that the journal entry may have incomplete sentences, misspelled words, unorganized sections, incomprehensible phrases, and even poor handwriting. How do you read, much less assess, those entries?

From another perspective, given the increasing emphasis on the importance of assessment in higher education (Banta, 2002), the question of how to assess student journal keeping becomes increasingly imperative. Coupled with the importance of using valid measures of student learning is the knowledge that active, engaged learning and enhanced critical thinking are important goals and can accrue from reflective writing (Weimer, 2002). Yet faculty are often left with many more questions than answers about assessing this powerful educational practice. O'Connell and Dyment's summary of the literature describes the many challenges of evaluating journals. They believe that ". . . evaluating journals can be a complicated, repetitive, daunting, time consuming and ethically challenging task" (2006, p. 681).

There are a variety of ways to think about and act on the issues that swirl around the larger question, "How do I provide feedback and grade student journals?" In this chapter we address these issues through the following questions:

- What role does feedback play in fostering classroom journal writing?
- What are the different ways to give feedback on journal writing?
- How can faculty handle the volume of student journals?
- What about privacy and the ethics of reading student journal writing?

The purpose of this chapter is to describe the key issues related to giving feedback and assessing classroom journals, and then to share a variety of ways to provide feedback and grade classroom journal writing.

The Role of Feedback in Fostering Classroom Journal Writing

Students want feedback. First they want to know *what* they are supposed to do, and then, over time, *how* they are doing in the course. When we hand out a syllabus, students look first at the assignments. Surely most of them are asking, "What am I supposed to do in this class to get a good grade?" Often it is not course content but the course requirements that catch their initial attention. The first class meeting is about expectations and requirements to complete the course. Therefore, if you want to get students' attention about journal writing, grade their work.

Questions about classroom journal writing coalesce around feedback: What is it? Why give it? How, when, and where should it be given? Grading student work is a form of feedback; yet grading is not the only way we provide feedback. We give students feedback in many other ways. Intentionally or unintentionally, instructors make feedback decisions as they design the course, talk about the requirements, and interact with students during the semester or term.

Feedback

Hattie and Timperley define *feedback* as "information provided by an agent (e.g., teacher, peer, book, parent, self, experience) regarding aspects of one's performance or understanding" (2007, p. 81). Feedback comes as the consequence of some type of performance and often can be seen as another form of instruction.

Why Give Feedback

The instructor is shaping the student's response to course content through feedback, calling attention to ideas, responses, and interactions that meet course expectations. In their review of the literature on feedback and its effect on learning and achievement, Hattie and Timperley (2007) write that feedback cannot be ignored; it is a major influence on learning. Feedback works to reduce the discrepancy between what students are doing and the expectations of the course. Feedback helps students monitor and adjust their work to meet course objectives.

Feedback is divided into two types: summative and formative feedback. Instructors may give feedback in a summative form, a formative form, or both throughout a given course. Grades are usually considered *summative* feedback because they serve as a rating of a total product such as a term paper, presentation, the final paper, final exam, or a summary of products for a course. Even though students may use the summative feedback on the next assignment, they may not go back and change their grade on the product. Summative feedback is set in concrete. Yet Crème asks, "If journal writing is valued as a 'process' ('making the process of learning visible. . .') then assessment that inevitably looks at a final product may distort that process" (2005, p. 290). In other words, summative feedback on journal writing without intervening formative feedback may undermine our basic objectives in assigning reflective writing in the first place.

Formative feedback gives students information about their work, usually without assigning a grade. Oral or written formative feedback is designed to help students develop their work and contributes to the "formation" of the work. Formative feedback happens when instructors provide students feedback on drafts of a paper before the final grade. Giving written or oral feedback without a grade on journal entries is also formative feedback. The assumption is that the work is not ready for a final grade; formative, nongraded feedback will periodically guide students about how to meet course objectives and learn more through their journal entries.

Journal writing is typically an ongoing activity over a semester or term. Instructors need to help students develop, refine, and reflect on their journal entries. Even though assessment of classroom journals can include a "grade," it does not always have to. Some faculty make it part of the participation grade. Most faculty allocate 10% to 30% (usually 20%) of the total student grade to journal writing (Cooper & Stevens, 2006; O'Connell & Dyment, 2006). Of course, you may want to allocate less than 10% or more than 30% to student journal writing; it just depends on what role journal writing plays in helping you accomplish your course objectives. For some students formative feedback without any grade may provide enough guidance for them to write enthusiastically and understand the value of reflection in their lives. They are happy to have an active audience that reads the journal and creates a conversation with them on paper. Others may need a grade to motivate them.

Ways to Give Feedback

This section addresses the question of what kind of feedback to provide on classroom journal writing. We present a variety of ways to give both formative and summative feedback. We have divided this section into three parts:

- Provide feedback using preset criteria.
- Write an individual response to each journal.
- Grade only for completion, not quality.

These parts address the questions: What are some ways to communicate your criteria for journal writing to your students? What kinds of criteria can be used to grade journal writing?

Provide Feedback Using Preset Criteria

Whether in the form of criteria check-off lists, holistic criteria, rubrics, or types of reflection, many faculty provide students with written criteria that explain the different aspects of the journal entries assessed. Both faculty and students benefit from preset criteria. When you use these criteria, there are fewer student queries (and office visits) to answer the question, "How is this going to be graded?" In addition, explicit criteria make it possible to grade more consistently in less time. Here are some examples of preset criteria: check-off lists, holistic criteria, rubrics, types of reflection.

Criteria Check-Off Lists

An architecture professor, Rudy, wants his students to develop the habit of keeping a journal in their professional lives. His many years of experience have taught him that beginning students need explicit criteria and feedback to guide their journal keeping. Table 6.1 lists the criteria he uses for "A," "C," and "F" grades. To arrive at a "B" or "D," he extrapolates the check marks in the adjacent sections. All of his 150 students turn in a journal three times during the term. Yet the first time he grades the journal, he does not record the grade. He makes comments on the journal pages and uses the criteria in Table 6.1 to determine the grade. He reduces his grading burden by training his teaching assistants to use the criteria sheets. The next two times that the students turn in the journal, he records the grade. Of course, to encourage self-assessment the students receive the criteria at the beginning of the term.

Rudy also requires his senior architecture students to keep a journal. Table 6.2 demonstrates that, unlike the criteria for first-year students, Rudy's criteria for upper-division student journals are less prescriptive, allowing more experienced students to express their individuality and to demonstrate their learning in a variety of ways. This is a journal that the students are required to complete when they are in Barcelona for a summer class.

Holistic Criteria

Another type of preset criteria is *holistic criteria* (Crème, 2005). When faculty use holistic criteria, they do not necessarily specify the different levels of performance, but indicate the qualities that a "good" journal will have. Table 6.3 shows how the faculty in a British university communicate the grading criteria for a "good record of study" in a second-year political anthropology class. A record of study can also be called a "learning journal" in which students summarize key points in course readings and reflect on these in the light of their own experience.

The criteria here indicate the importance of students documenting their thinking as well as their ability to weave course concepts and themes into their own lives.

Table 6.1
Journal-Grading Criteria

Architecture 100: Introduction to Architecture (Lower-Division Class)

Grading Criteria
Evaluation of the architectural journal is based on the categories of activities as described in the assignment handout.

"A" Journal (excellent level of performance)
___ Contains extensive entries demonstrating personal reflections about subjects and materials covered in classes.
___ Contains extensive entries demonstrating an engaged and consistent observation of works of architecture—how people use buildings and public spaces.
___ Contains critical judgments about works of architecture and the processes of making buildings and public spaces.
___ Clear demonstration of analytical and critical thinking about architecture.

"C" Journal (satisfactory/average level of performance)
___ Contains multiple entries demonstrating personal reflections about subjects and materials covered in class.
___ Demonstrates a casual and inconsistent observation of works of architecture.
___ Includes critical judgments about works of architecture and the process of making buildings and public spaces, but lacks consistency and/or only includes minimal examples.
___ Average demonstration of analytical and critical thinking about architecture.

"F" Journal (failing/inferior level of performance)
___ Near absence of personal reflections about subjects and materials covered in class.
___ Demonstrates minimal observation of works of architecture—buildings or spaces.
___ Absence of critical judgments about works of architecture and the processes of making buildings and public spaces.
___ Journal consists primarily, or exclusively, of class lecture notes.
___ Fails to demonstrate analytical and/or critical thinking about architecture.

Additional Comments:

_____

_____

_____

_____

Another example of holistic criteria in the literature comes from teacher education at the graduate level (Table 6.4; Fenwick, 2001). Here the instructor decided to grade the journal "holistically," meaning that the whole journal or student-selected entries were read in their entirety and a global assessment was made. The students were given these descriptions ahead of time.

Table 6.2
Journal-Grading Criteria

Architecture: Barcelona Field Experience (Upper-Division Class)

The primary requirement for this course consists of developing and maintaining a working journal that can demonstrate individual participation and personal engagement with class activities and with Barcelona. Above all, this journal will encourage you to experience and reflect on your days in Barcelona, from the day-to-day activities like morning coffee to the once-in-a-lifetime experiences like crawling up the towers of Gaudi's Sagrada Familia.

There are no easy answers as to length or quantity of pages; however, a minimum of two pages a day or session would seem to be satisfactory. Journal entries will likely include a variety of impressions, from sketches to written notes or longer narratives to collages.

Format: The journal itself should be spiral bound or hard bound; anything larger that 9 × 12 inches is typically unwieldy and difficult to carry around. The journal will be checked on an irregular basis and will typically be returned on the same day.

Table 6.3
Assessment Criteria for a "Record of Study" in Political Anthropology

---

A good record of study:

- **is comprehensive**—meets requirements such as an introduction and conclusion, and demonstrates syllabus coverage
- **shows understanding** of the material
- **shows ability to select, summarize, analyze, and show relationships** between concepts, both within the course and outside it (e.g., other courses and ideas, life situations)
- **shows self-awareness** of the writer as learner, both in relation to the ideas and ethnographies in the course, and to course activities, processes, and colleagues
- **demonstrates risk-taking**—shows that writers are prepared to "take risks with the material and in relation to their own political and intellectual position"

(adapted from Crème, 2005, p. 290)

One of the reasons Fenwick grades holistically is that students should not be expected to cover all criteria in every entry. For example, she emphasizes that not all individual entries have to include feelings. However, the whole journal needs to show some attention to feelings.

Rubrics

A third way to communicate your expectations and assess journals with preset criteria is through a rubric. A *rubric* is a scoring guide that communicates criteria over a number of different dimensions like organization, analysis, content, and conventions.

Table 6.4
Holistic Assessment Criteria

Teacher Education at the Graduate Level

Holistic evaluation of five student-selected entries. Photocopy selections.
   Five entries due at midterm and in final week of class. Scoring description:

5 Thoughts and feelings are purposeful and insightful. The content is either detailed or approached philosophically. The unique voice of the learner is present and sustained. Significant risks in thought may be evident. Readers can follow the entry easily.

4 The thoughts and feelings expressed are purposeful—either insightful and general, or detailed and conventional. The expression is clear, easy to follow, and appropriate for the context.

3 Thoughts and feelings are present but not always clearly connected to the purpose for language use. Language and thinking may be very conventional and lack development. Readers can follow the writer, but may need to work a bit to do so. The language is generally appropriate for the context.

2 Thoughts and feelings are not consistent or connected but are related to the purpose and context. The content and expressions do not anticipate the audience. The writer knows what is meant but does not lead the reader through the intended meaning.

1 The content is very confusing or even conflicting. It may be only tangentially related to the intended purpose.

INS Sample is too brief to score.

(derived from Fenwick, 2001, p. 44)

Rubrics may describe only the highest level of performance, known as a scoring-guide rubric, or it can describe several levels of performance, such as a three- to five-level rubric (Stevens & Levi, 2005). Because the rubric is divided into dimensions, rubrics help students separate and attend to different aspects of a complex assignment. In our experience, students, especially nontraditional students, like rubrics because they communicate the often unclear and sometimes hidden expectations that instructors use to score student work. Table 6.5 is the scoring-guide rubric for journals in our graduate research methods class.

Table 6.5 is a complicated rubric. It contains the task description, cut and pasted from the syllabus. Having the task description printed on the top of the rubric helps students keep track of the task expectations in relation to the grading criteria. Because this is a scoring-guide rubric, and not a three- to five-level rubric, it only describes the highest level, the exemplary level of task performance. A scoring-guide rubric is more suitable at the graduate level and requires more feedback from the instructor because the middle and lower levels of performance are not included in the rubric.

Besides using the rubric for scoring, we also make written comments on the student metareflections themselves. Because in a scoring-guide rubric the other levels of

Table 6.5
Rubric

Journal Keeping in a Research Proposal Class

Journal-Keeping Rubric: 20 points

Task: You are expected to keep a journal during this course to record your insights, log your research, take lecture notes, and brainstorm your ideas for your final research proposal. You can use the journal to record other events in your life as well, such as taking notes at meetings, recording lecture notes for other classes, keeping a phone log, recording a handy list of Websites, keeping a list of books read, etc.

At the end of the term you will turn in photocopies of the table of contents and three significant journal entries. For each of these three selected journal entries, you will write a one-page *metareflection*. Your metareflection results from your re-reading, reviewing, and reflecting on what you have written in your journal over the term. Select the entries that catch your attention. There can be any number of reasons why these entries capture your attention—they might be unusual, insightful, surprising, meaningful, helpful, etc. Questions that you can **consider** when writing the metareflection are:

- Since this entry caught my attention, what does that tell me about myself now?
- How does this journal entry help me to understand and integrate the course themes into my professional life?
- What are some of the underlying and essential assumptions and beliefs about research and my research topic reflected in this entry? Do I still agree with them?
- Looking back on this entry, in what ways has my thinking changed since I wrote it?
- What next steps or future ideas might come out of reflecting on this entry and its implications?
- In what ways has keeping a journal for this class changed my thinking and beliefs about writing and/or the value of keeping a journal in my professional life? How does this journal entry reflect those changes in my beliefs?

Dimension	Description of an Exemplary Journal	Points
1. Format	Bound book Table of contents includes date, title of entry, and page number Pages are numbered throughout	3
2. Freewrites	Table of contents indicates that three freewrites were done each week outside of class.	3

3. Metareflection	___ Photocopies of at least three significant and meaningful journal entries. These entries can be from your lecture notes, field observations, freewrites, research, brainstorming, or other entries.
	___ Write a metareflection about EACH of the selected entries. Some criteria for the metareflection are below (not all of these criteria have to appear in a single metareflection):
	    ___ Refers to specific parts of the journal entry.
	    ___ Describes clearly how thinking or beliefs have changed.
	    ___ Integrates at least three course themes into the analysis of the journal entry.
	    ___ Clearly defines course themes and relates entry to relevant course themes.
	    ___ Provides evidence of willingness to revise ideas and beliefs.
	    ___ Shares how basic values and assumptions have changed.
	    ___ Provides evidence of creativity, playfulness, or unique approaches.
		14

PLEASE TURN IN THIS RUBRIC WITH THE ASSIGNMENT.

performance are not shown, it is important to make more written comments on the rubric and on the students' work itself. However, by placing the basic criteria on the rubric, it saves time so that we do not have to repeat the same comment over a series of student papers. We also include information on the rubric about our expectations for the formatting of the journal: In this case we require that the journal be a bound book, have a table of contents, and that the pages be numbered. This rubric is for a graduate-level class. Undergraduate classes will more than likely need more specific criteria that can be found on a three- to five-level rubric (Stevens & Levi, 2005; see www.introductiontorubrics.com).

For many years, nursing educators in particular have relied on reflective journal writing to help their students begin to "think like a nurse." Reflection on experience is an essential part of any kind of medical education (Durgahee, 1998; Shapiro, Kasman, & Shafer, 2006; Winningham & Preusser, 2001). Guided writing activities push student nurses to think more deeply about what background experience they bring, what they already know, and how they can respond appropriately (and quickly, if necessary) to challenging incidents in clinical settings (Glaze, 2001; Krmpotic, 2003).

Because they were dissatisfied with the low levels of reflection that their students were demonstrating, nursing program professors Butell and May developed the rubric shown in Table 6.6 for scoring student journal reflections on their psychiatric nursing practicum (personal communication, June 18, 2008).

Table 6.6 indicates that there are different dimensions to the student nurses' reflections and there are levels of acceptable performance within those dimensions. The instructors sought to include some seemingly difficult-to-grade categories like "spirit of inquiry" to alert students to their expectations. The professors showed students examples at each of the levels to anchor the dimensions and descriptions of those levels. After the introduction of the rubric, Professor Butell noted, "I definitely feel the journal writing has improved!" (personal communication, June 18, 2008).

Criteria for Types of Reflection
This section on preset grading criteria would not be complete without some attention to the literature on assessing the types or levels of reflection in student journals. Based on their work in adult development (Mezirow, 1981), several researchers have explored ways to provide feedback to students using the different types of reflection (Crotty & Allen, 2001; Jensen & Joy, 2005; Spalding & Wilson, 2002; Valli, 1993, 1997; Wallace & Oliver, 2003). Valli (1997) developed four types of reflection by

Table 6.6
Rubric

Reflective Journal Keeping in a Clinical Psychiatric Nursing Class

Task: You are expected to write weekly reflections on your experiences in the clinical psychiatric setting. You should consider what your goals were for the week, how your prior knowledge and beliefs affected the quality of your interactions, and your ability to do the work. In addition, it is important to develop a "spirit of inquiry" about your nursing practice. In other words, describe what questions your interactions generated and where you might seek answers for these questions in the future.

Levels of Performance

Dimensions	EXEMPLARY	SATISFACTORY	NEEDS WORK
Analysis of Therapeutic Interaction	Students use range of verbal and nonverbal therapeutic communication with in-depth analysis of interaction.	Students use basic verbal and nonverbal therapeutic communication with minimal analysis of interaction.	Students demonstrate nontherapeutic social interaction with minimal or no analysis.
Therapeutic Use of Self	Students share how they think and feel about themselves and clients in-depth and use this knowledge and insight to meet client-student outcomes.	Students share basic thoughts and feelings about themselves and clients.	Students do not share thoughts and feelings.
Awareness of Beliefs/Values	Students show awareness of client's values and beliefs, and awareness of students' own values and beliefs in relation to client. Take appropriate action.	Students show awareness of client's values and beliefs (families, individuals, and populations).	Students show no awareness of beliefs or values.
Spirit of Inquiry	Students effectively propose ways to seek answers to two to three substantive questions.	Students raise two to three substantive questions related to client care.	Students raise superficial questions or no questions.

which to assess student journals: reflection in/on action, deliberative, personalistic, and critical. Table 6.7 defines these levels.

Spalding and Wilson (2002) studied the use of these types of reflection in student journal entries. All instructors in the study gave students examples of what these types of reflection might look like. One instructor handled feedback this way: Next to the student entries, she wrote "R" for reflection in or on action, "P" for personalistic, "D" for deliberative, and "C" for critical. Sometimes she had the students label

Table 6.7
Typology and Definitions of Reflection for Student Teachers

Type of Reflection	Definition of Reflection
Reflection in/on action	Reflecting on one's own teaching performance
Deliberative	Reflection on a whole range of teaching concerns, including students, the curriculum, instructional strategies, the rules, and classroom organization
Personalistic	Reflection on one's own personal growth and relationships with students
Critical	Reflection on the social, moral, and political dimensions of schooling

(adapted from Valli, 1997)

their own entries with these letters before they turned them in. This indicated whether her perception of student entries was the same as the students'. The study concluded that the "preservice teachers benefited from spending class time on defining, discussing and viewing models of reflection" (Spalding & Wilson, 2002, p. 1393).

Write an Individual Response to Each Journal

Another way to respond is to write an individual response to each journal. Rebecca requires students to keep a "learning journal" on the course readings (personal communication, May 15, 2008). Rather than a long list of preset criteria for the journal entries, she provides feedback to students by writing her own reflections on the readings and reading her reflections to the class each time they begin the discussion of the readings. This is one way the students begin to see how to "respond" to the course readings in their journal. She does this "to model how to reflect on the readings and connect them to personal experiences. The students are often not sure how to use the journal for recording responses to the readings and, therefore, they appreciate a model. I fear that long lists of criteria might discourage students from experimenting with journaling" (personal communication, May 15, 2008). She collects the journals at midterm and at the end of the term and writes comments in the journals. She selectively reads and responds to different entries and puts a check mark above each entry that she reads. Her responses are more like a conversation than an evaluation. She might ask a question or make a personal comment like, "What other things can you remember about how teachers treated you in elementary school?" or "Wow! I felt that way about my first grade teacher, too."

In some courses Joanne reads the entire journal and, while reading, writes a narrative response to the student on her computer. It is much like a personal letter to each student. In her response she may write about the whole journal, or about specific entries, and the type of reflection that students have engaged in. This narrative response may include questions and may seek to "converse" or create a dialogue with students about their work. Students are encouraged to fold over those pages that they do not want her to read. There are no checklists or explicitly stated criteria; however, her comments seek to guide the quality of student journal entries. Students seem to set aside privacy issues and often really appreciate her full, personal response to their work. Students receive full participation points (20%) for a complete journal.

There are a variety of ways to communicate individualized comments to students. Some instructors prefer to make their comments on student work in pencil rather than pen, and, if they use pen, certainly not red pen (Fenwick, 2001). Other faculty make comments with sticky notes in journals so that their own handwriting is not on the original student journal page. The student journal at the end of the term then reflects only the work of the student, not the comments of an outside reader, the instructor.

Students benefit from this type of written dialogue with the faculty member (Spalding & Wilson, 2002). Some faculty benefit, too. Reading all entries in student journals is one way to learn more about how students think and what interests them. Kofi, an instructor in one of our cases in chapter 9, takes his students to Africa during their senior capstone course. He states, "Reading the entire journal helps me assess the group dynamics in the field and helps me figure out what to do next time" (personal communication, June 18, 2007). Rebecca notes that reading the journal is a better way than class discussion to find out about her students. If the journal is assessed several times during a term, journal entries also show faculty where the students are confused or concerned about the way the course is proceeding, and the faculty member can adjust course activities accordingly.

Grade for Completion, Not Quality

The final way to give students evaluative feedback on their journals is to grade the journal only for completion. For some instructors, if the student fills in the journal pages, it means that the student has participated in the course. Occasionally, Dannelle does what she calls a "power-grading" method. Students turn in their journal at midterm and the end of the term. She quickly flips through all the pages of the journal, not reading any total page at all, but looking for key words used in the course. She returns all the journals in the next class. If the journal is complete, students receive full credit for participation in the class to that point. Dannelle wants "to convey the message that students are indeed accountable for completing the journal entries. However, I also want to convey the message that the journal writing is for them, not for me; for them to explore their ideas and responses, not to prove to me that they have thought a certain way. I also want to know that they have kept up with the assignments in the journal."

Handling the Volume of Student Journals

As faculty walk out the office door with a giant stack of journals to grade, they may sigh and wonder what kind of monster they have created. Obviously, the time-consuming nature of giving feedback to students on the many pages of their journals is an issue. Crème notes that several of her colleagues eventually discontinued using learning journals or what she calls "records of study" (2005, p. 288) because they just took too much time. Some have dealt with this challenge by telling students that the journal is completely private, but requiring that quotations from the journal be used in the final reflective essay for the course (Boud, 2001).

Here are some tips for handling the volume of student writing in journals:

1. Read only half the journals at a time over a weekend or stagger the dates that they turn in their journals over the entire course.
2. Have students use a highlighter to mark key phrases or sentences that have meaning for them and read only those entries. A further extension of this activity is to have the students then use those highlighted quotations in an end-of-term reflective essay.
3. Have the students select a set number of entries to photocopy to turn in as a sample of their journal work. Having the students write a reflection on these selections allows them to create a metareflection; that process is fully described in chapter 5. Having students photocopy selected entries and possibly write a metareflection also addresses student reluctance to give up their journals. Some students may have integrated the journal so much into their lives, using it for several classes and keeping personal notes in it, that they are quite reluctant to hand it in.

4. Train teaching assistants to read student journals. Rudy, whose architecture classes have 150 students, states, "Students need and deserve feedback but it takes a lot of time" (personal communication, June 12, 2007). This situation makes preset criteria helpful. He has detailed descriptions of scoring criteria for the journals (see Tables 6.1 and 6.2), and he has trained his teaching assistants to do some of the midterm feedback.

We have learned from these experienced instructors that successful use and assessment requires that journal writing be an integral part of the classroom feedback and assessment system. Whatever method of evaluation faculty choose, journal-writing assignments should not be ignored.

Privacy and the Ethics of Reading Student Journal Writing

The journal is generally considered a place for private musings; for exploration; and for honest, authentic responses to the world outside and within. It is a place to be oneself and not be "on stage," nor be concerned about the opinions of others. It can be a place to explore knowledge, assumptions, beliefs, values, attitudes, dreams, and hopes, as well as a host of feelings such as anger, fears and worries, frustrations, and joy—all without fear of censure. Hence, the dilemma for instructors who assign journal writing is determining the audience. Certainly, faculty can assure students that the journal will not be graded for grammar or punctuation. However, the classroom journal is not totally private and can have a powerful reader, the instructor.

Moon (2006) suggests that students need to learn how to regulate the level of disclosure that is appropriate for a particular learning task. The world itself is contentious and there are many ways to write about any issue, with some versions being more appropriate than others for a particular assignment. Students need to be alerted to different ways to approach these different versions or interpretations. She points out that levels of disclosure of thoughts, feelings, and responses may also depend on what is appropriate within the students' cultural backgrounds and experiences. Learners may also reveal material of a sensitive nature, such as criminal activity or, in the case of journals in clinical practice, the unethical behavior of colleagues. All these issues can be addressed at the beginning of the course, when the journal assignments are being set up.

Another consideration is how "public" student journal writing should be. Ghaye and Lillyman (1997) point out that students have certain rights and should not be coerced into making public what is written in their journal. Swartzlander, Pace, and Stamler (1993) go further, discussing the fact that students may have been asked to make inappropriate self-revelations in their writing assignments. The result can be students who believe they will receive a better grade if their writing is emotionally charged or displays the most drama. Most importantly, Swartzlander, Pace, and Stamler (1993) underscore that for students who have been victims of abuse, it is difficult for them to set appropriate boundaries. These students need clear guidelines about appropriate disclosures.

First of all, instructors should be careful not to give the impression that students are expected to deal with their emotional problems in their writing, or that they will succeed in the course if they write about dramatic personal experiences. In a course entitled "Writing to Heal," Susan, the instructor, clearly states her limits in writing in her syllabus:

> I am not trained medically; I am a writing teacher, so I offer this as a tool anyone can use to more deeply engage and understand his or her life. What is uncovered may be something that needs to be discussed with a professional outside of class; I am not a therapist. (personal communication, June 23, 2008)

Beyond this, instructors should find ways to help students learn what is appropriate and inappropriate to share in their journals. Some of our suggestions follow.

1. Make sure students know well ahead of time (at the beginning of the course and before they start writing in their journals) how you are handling the entries and their responses. Are you reading every word? Or are you having the students select what they want you to read?

2. Never insist that students read from their journals in class unless you warn them of this requirement before they write. They have the right to know that, if their entries are shared in class, they will remain confidential. Talk to the entire class about the issue of confidentiality at the beginning of the course.

3. Tell students that if they do disclose something that indicates abuse or harm, instructors are obligated to report that information to others, such as counselors or administrators.

4. If there are entries that students do not want you to read, ask them to turn down and staple the pages they want to keep private.

5. Do not have students turn in their whole journal. Have them reread and select significant entries, then make photocopies and write metareflections on these

entries. This way they can keep highly risky and personal things to themselves, and they do not have to share them with you.

6. Tell students that the journal is where they are free to explore their ideas, feelings, and viewpoints, and that this may look messy, illogical, embarrassing, or uncomfortable, but that this exploration is part of their own development. This helps students who find their own writing to be depressing, whiny, or excessively negative.

In general, faculty should consider the rights of students to privacy, self-respect, dignity, confidentiality, and informed consent, as well as the ways in which students might be assured of these rights in the classroom. These rights must be balanced with the benefits of journal writing so that students learn the power of reflection in their learning and their lives.

Conclusion

In this chapter we detail the variety of ways to provide feedback to students about their journal writing. Feedback is important because students respond to feedback and it helps them to develop reflective thinking and writing practices. Feedback, whether formative or summative, is a form of assessment. By thinking about your expectations and communicating them clearly to students, you will enhance the journal-writing experience for your students.

To summarize this chapter, we have created a chart in Table 6.8 of the various types of criteria that might be scored in a journal. What you select to score, of course, depends on your objectives for using a journal in the first place.

Table 6.8
List of Possible Assessment Criteria for Journals

Journal Dimension	Criteria That Can Be Assessed
Formatting	Date—date is easily found Length Presentation: 2-column method, or margins Legibility Type of book used for journal—bound, notebook Organization: Table of contents, numbered pages Headers—Clear link to course readings using bibliographic formatting Log: date, brief description
Completeness	Number of entries Regularity of entries Included quotations from readings
Type of entries	Used a variety of types of journal entries: dialogue, freewrites, focused freewrites, concept maps, unsent letters
Observations	Clarity of description of observation Inferences derived from the observations Separation of inferences from observations
Openness	Evidence of speculation Evidence of willingness to revise ideas Evidence of examination of closely held beliefs Honesty and self-assessment
Depth of reflection	Thoroughness of reflection and self-awareness Depth and detail of reflective accounts Thoughtful, comprehensive Levels of reflection: descriptive, critical, transformative Sought out, described, and challenged personally held assumptions related to field observations or course content
Type of thinking	Evidence of creative thinking Evidence of critical thinking Representation of different types of cognitive skills (comprehension, synthesis, analysis, evaluation)
Entries related to course objectives	Entries clearly related to any relevant course work, theories, work in field settings Match of the content and outcomes of the journal work to course objectives, learning outcomes, or purposes that the journal is intended to fulfill
Number and quality of questions	Inclusion of questions that derive from course readings and lecture Quality of the questions that arise from reflecting on field observations or on the journal itself

7

JOURNAL WRITING IN PROFESSIONAL LIFE

I don't naturally come to the orderly management of paper. I'm sort of like
Pig Pen when it comes to how to manage the various parts of my life.
My journal has given me a wonderful sense of always knowing where things are.

Jean, university dean

JEAN HAS BEEN KEEPING A PROFESSIONAL JOURNAL since she became a dean in 1995. Her journal contains dated notes on meetings as well as lists, outlines for things she's working on, doodling, drafts of letters, and other reflections. She says, "The act of writing things down makes them accessible to me even if I don't look at it again" (personal communication, June 16, 2006). It is in many ways a memory device for her.

Richard, a doctoral student in education, began keeping a journal when he entered his doctoral program a year and a half ago. He writes almost daily on his lunch break about his life as a graduate student and his work as a teaching assistant. He states that keeping a journal has taught him a lot about himself and that his professional decisions are now based on "good evidence" from his own writings and thoughts. He feels he now understands himself much better and states that he is able to "give himself time" through his journal (personal communication, October, 17, 2006).

Like these two journal keepers, faculty and administrators use journals for a variety of purposes. How might you enhance or even jump-start your own journal writing and reflecting? This chapter is filled with suggestions from our research as well as the experiences of a number of academics about how to use a journal in your professional life to get organized and to stimulate your own reflections. We present these techniques not as a comprehensive list, but simply as ideas to get you started.

Journal keepers in higher education may employ many of the eight techniques listed for classroom journal-writing activities, including freewrites, focused freewrites, lists, logs, dialogues, concept maps, metaphors, and metareflections. This chapter suggests different ways to use these eight techniques, plus three others, in the context of professional life. We will also discuss the ways that academics format their journals, including spiral-bound notebooks and conventionally bound blank books, as well as electronic venues such as word processing files or blogs. Finally, we include three sections that highlight how to use the journal for improving your writing, developing your research, and reflecting on your teaching.

The key questions for this chapter are:

- What are the uses of journal writing in professional life?
- What techniques are used when keeping a journal in professional life?
- What formats work well for those who keep a journal in professional life?
- How can the journal be used to improve writing skills and productivity?
- How can the journal be used to develop research focus and topics?
- How can the journal be used to reflect on and improve teaching?

This chapter focuses on why and how to use a journal successfully in academic life. We will share numerous examples, techniques, and insights from faculty as well as administrators and graduate students who have found ways to sustain journal keeping precisely because it enhances both their professional and personal lives.

Uses of Journal Writing in Professional Life

Although there is more published research on the use of journals in the classroom than there is on the use of journals in professional life, our research (Cooper & Stevens, 2006) indicates that higher education professionals use their journals for two central objectives:

- To manage day-to-day and long-term work expectations
- To develop skills and insights

In chapter 1 we provided references pertaining to these two broad goals.

Professional Objective I:
Manage Day-to-Day and Long-Term Work Expectations

Professionals use their journals to manage their day-to-day activities as well as to tackle long-term work expectations. The dated, archival characteristics of the journal make it particularly suited to this purpose. One of the major benefits that both administrators and faculty report is that keeping a journal at work helps them to have everything in one place. Because most journals are arranged chronologically, the record of the on-going series of events in professional life proves invaluable. This avoids frustrating searches for files, and provides a way to track not only ongoing events but also research ideas and expectations.

In the left column of Table 7.1, we list various specific professional objectives, and on the right we suggest some useful journal-writing techniques to accomplish each objective. An extensive description of each technique can be found later in this chapter.

Faculty and administrators use their journals to record committee activities and decisions (Cooper & Stevens, 2006), to take notes on advising sessions with students, to make to-do lists from the meetings they attend, list phone calls, and generally think on paper about their work responsibilities. Entries are often dated and major decisions or agreements noted. Often there is a list of who attended the meeting, and commitments made for particular tasks. For example, Skip, the director of a research unit, says his journal provides him with a quick reference to past meetings and leads to a more organized life. In addition, as a place for self-analysis and constant self-evaluation, his journal is his conscience, creating a set of checks and balances that help him to maintain a sense of teamwork and camaraderie in his organization. It is a vital part

Table 7.1
Journal Writing for the Professional

Objective I: Manage Day-to-Day and Long-Term Work Expectations

Professional Objective	Suggested Journal-Writing Technique
Record committee activities and decisions.	Log, listing
Keep a dated log of professional activities for promotion and peer review.	Log, listing
Track and organize research activities.	Focused freewriting, listing, concept mapping, log
Reflect on and address problems and issues in the work setting.	Freewriting, focused freewriting, dialogue, unsent letters

of his work life, a valuable tool, and something that he believes he could not do without.

One question that arises is that of time. We often hear academics say, "I don't have the time to sit and write! I'm too busy!" When asked about this issue, Gerry, a department chair in engineering who keeps four separate journals, smiled and said, "Managing your life takes time" (personal communication, June 13, 2007). Many professionals find that being disorganized ("Where are the notes from our last meeting . . . somewhere in this office!") takes more time. They see the journal as a time-saving device because everything is in one place.

Another way to save time through journal use is to keep a dated log of professional activities for promotion and peer review (Stevens & Cooper, 2002). Busy as we are, gathering evidence over a 3- to 5-year span for promotion and tenure can be a daunting task. Yet a dated log kept in one place allows for a level of organization faculty might not otherwise have and one they will be grateful for when the time to submit tenure or promotion papers arrives. As Gerry commented further, his journal is a place to "unload his mind" so he doesn't have to remember everything and can work "without anxiety" (personal communication, June 13, 2007).

Faculty members also use journals to develop and organize research activities to manage the day-to-day and long-term expectations of their research lives. They often use their journals to plan their research agenda and jot down ideas for future research as they come to mind. In addition, they may use their journal to create an audit trail, conduct imaginary dialogues with research participants or research partners, as well as clarify their roles as researchers (Kleinman & Copp, 1993). Vasti Torres, an associate professor of higher education, for example, reflected on how to analyze her qualitative data in her research journal:

> Going in-depth into the second year interviews and I'm back to the question of how to treat the data? Last year I decided to look at the interviews as a whole. When I do that with this set—I keep going back to the individual first year interviews. Perhaps I will try to focus on the emerging categories instead of figuring out if there is fit with previous data. . . . (Jones, Torres, & Arminio, 2006, p. 85)

Faculty and administrators can use their journals to reflect on and address problems and issues in the work setting (Penney & Warelow, 1999; Shepherd, 2004). These unresolved issues may be confidential, such as a university president who has conflicts with the governing board. Here the journal can be a private place to work out questions as well as to vent frustrations. One administrator wrote, "I have learned that keeping a journal helps me articulate my feelings and emotions more fully. This has been important when dealing with some of the more frustrating aspects of work . . ." (Shepherd, 2004, p. 221). Writing in a journal can be a place for professional renewal as well as a place to vent. Rick and Marcy Jackson, leaders of the National Center for Courage and Renewal, name journaling as a way to sustain themselves, stating, "We found ways to give voice to unlived parts of ourselves through journaling and creative expression, to let the used-up parts take a rest while discovering that we are more than what we do" (Jackson & Jackson, 2005, p. 185).

Professional Objective II: Develop Skills and Insight

Professionals also use their journals to develop their writing skills and to think about the meaning of their work, as well as to reflect more deeply about their professional plans and purposes. Richard, our graduate student quoted previously, falls into this category, using his journal to reflect on his place in the academy and his purpose in pursuing a doctoral degree. Journal-keeping practices that fall into this second set of objectives can engender surprising new insights about work. In addition, research indicates that regular journal writing about highly stressful challenges improves health and reduces stress (DeSalvo, 1999). Table 7.2 lists specific professional objectives related to developing skills and insights in the left column. On the right are techniques

Table 7.2
Journal Writing for the Professional

Objective II: Develop Skills and Insight

Professional Objective	Suggested Journal-Writing Technique
Converse with the self.	Dialogue, focused freewriting, freewriting, unsent letters, time travel
Improve writing and increase clarity of thought.	Freewriting, focused freewriting, concept mapping
Reflect critically on teaching expertise.	Listing, freewriting, focused freewriting, dialogue
Develop professional identity.	Freewriting, metaphor, focused freewriting, dialogue, time travel
Examine deeply held assumptions.	Focused freewriting, metaphor, unsent letters, dialogue, time travel

that are useful for each objective. Each of these techniques is discussed in more detail later in this chapter.

The development of skills and insights includes conversations with the self (Durgahee, 2002; Glaze, 2002; Grumet, 1990). Dialogue is one journal-writing conversational technique for uncovering issues and clarifying professional problems and solutions. Progoff advocates the use of dialogue to "activate," "stimulate," "draw forth," and "give direction" to growth (1992, p. 141). In the following extract Kristen is working on questions of professional writing. Her "other" self gives some quite valuable and concrete advice:

> **Me:** I don't have enough time to write this dissertation. I want the proposal pretty much done by the end of the semester and fine tune it during the summer, but I feel as if I haven't even started it yet. I have all these areas I want to look at but I don't know how it is all going to fit together into this proposal. Which direction do I head in and how am I going to write this proposal when I know I always veer off on other topics?
> **Myself:** Stop looking at the entire picture. Break it down into small pieces. What do you have to work on first, or right now?
> **Me:** I have several areas that I want to look into the literature about.
> **Myself:** What are they?
> **Me:** Benefits of living on campus, benefits of living in a themed community on campus, millennial students, current sophomore experience programs, student experiences of first-year experience programs.
> **Myself:** What intimidates you the most?
> **Me:** Looking at current sophomore experience programs.
> **Myself:** Why?
> **Me:** Because most of it is web-based and I don't think they will give me what I want.
> **Myself:** What do you want?
> **Me:** I want to know why and how they developed the programs.
> **Myself:** What will the web give you?
> **Me:** What the program entails and what it offers.
> **Myself:** Will that be beneficial?
> **Me:** Yes.
> **Myself:** Then just use the web for that. What resources could you use to gather the information about why and how they were developed? (personal communication, January 23, 2007)

Here we see how a dialogue can help the writer move through insecurities and questions about how to proceed with a large writing project. Her "wiser" self helps her find a way through her dilemmas.

Keeping a journal also improves writing ability and increases clarity of thought (Boice, 1990, 2000; Elbow, 1973, 1981; Klein & Boals, 2001). Ostermann and Kottkamp, for example, found in their study of school leaders that "the act of writing one's thoughts seems to have a substantially different and greater impact" (1993, p. 73) than oral statements. Freewriting, dialogues, and the use of metaphor all contribute to boosting the effects of journal writing. Boice's research indicates that writing every day produces more material and moves faculty toward publication versus waiting for inspiration, or waiting until there is a large chunk of time to write. He advises that faculty write for at least 20 minutes a day. A journal is a perfect place to collect these daily writings, to jot down connections among ideas, or to plan future writing projects. Likewise, Elbow (1973) extols the virtues of freewriting as a way to find your voice and to produce material that can later be edited and used in the creation of publications. For those with serious writer's block, a journal can free up creative juices and allow professionals to make progress toward producing more and better writing.

Educational professionals also use their journals to reflect critically on teaching and professional expertise. The journal can be used to evaluate roles and responsibilities. Faculty, for example, can use their journals to examine who they are as teachers and to work to become more engaged in the classroom. Teaching journals are useful for recording responses to classroom lessons, reflecting on their significance in relation to past events, and pulling out implications for future planning. Gee (2004), for example, feels that keeping a teaching journal has helped him to become a more insightful and relentless evaluator of his teaching abilities and to acquire an academic conscience. The journal can also be used to simply sustain faculty as they teach. One journal keeper wrote,

> I need to recognize that [journal keeping] nourishes my inner self. . . . I need to remember that just as I need to nourish my body to invest myself in my teaching, I need to nourish my inner self as well. I will look for activities and causes in which I can truly invest myself. Lastly, I will work to remember that I need to bring my whole self to my teaching and to whatever else I may do. (Doris, personal communication, July 16, 2007)

Administrators also find journal keeping helpful. For example, CJ (see her case in chapter 10) uses her journal to sort through issues she faces in her role as a community-college board member. She deals with many issues that require confidentiality during her executive sessions with the Board of Education. Because she describes herself as "pathologically open," it is helpful for her to review and reflect on these issues in her journal because she cannot discuss them with anyone. She says she can tell if she is not writing enough because she gets upset about trifles. In general, CJ states that journaling "keeps her sane" (personal communication, March 17, 2005).

An important task for both faculty and administrators is to develop their professional identity. University administrators, faculty, and graduate students all use their journals to reflect on their career paths and professional identity (Cooper & Stevens, 2006; Cooper, Stevens, & Chock, 2006). John V., one of our students, put it this way:

> My journal has become a way to stay in contact with myself. With all the challenges I face at work, I had lost close contact with my most trusted advisor: my inner voice and that relationship with myself. Being on sabbatical, I now have some time to reflect and think. My journal writing has become a place where I can think without being interrupted, review my past actions, think of new courses of action, and keep a record of those thoughts. (personal communication, December 3, 2007)

Questions of leadership are also a part of the professional identity issue. Warren Bennis, one of the most creative thinkers and prolific writers about leadership of our time, states, "The point is not to become a leader. The point is to become yourself, and to use yourself completely—all your gifts, skills, and energies—to make your vision manifest. You must withhold nothing. You must, in sum, become the person you started out to be, and to enjoy the process of becoming" (Moxley, 2005, p. 256). The process of "becoming" is greatly enhanced by keeping a professional journal, a place to deposit thoughts, doubts, and to be honest with oneself. Many leadership development programs use reflective journaling to help leaders look within. For example, researchers in the field of women's leadership development state that keeping a journal is especially useful for achieving wholeness and gaining self-clarity (Ruderman & Ohlott, 2002).

Keeping a journal also aids professionals in examining their deeply held assumptions about their research and their work. The journal can be a safe place to examine ethical dilemmas, clarify values and biases, or reflect on one's role as researcher (Janesick, 2004). Lincoln and Guba (1985) recommend the use of a reflective journal to clarify the researcher's role and make decisions regarding methodology. Here the journal not only serves as a record of what decisions were made, but it "can provide a venue for reflection about the research decisions and prompt further questioning of subsequent issues that can emerge" (Jones, Torres, & Arminio, 2006, p. 99). Journals are also a useful way to clarify one's assumptions and personal biases as a researcher. Davis, who studied the effect of gender on male development, wrote,

> For me, this meant being aware that I might try to make the interview data fit my preconceptions (Self) rather than allowing the participants (Other) to speak for

themselves. . . . I . . . clearly have biases associated with my own development as a White, heterosexual, Italian American male. (2002, p. 512)

Davis was able to use his journal to explore these biases and then avoid using them to make premature interpretations of his findings.

Finally, research indicates that regular writing about both problems professionals encounter and their feelings about traumatic events helps to reduce stress and improve health (DeSalvo, 1999; Kalb, 1999; Lepore, 1997; Pennebaker, 2004). Louise DeSalvo (1999) has documented the ways in which journal keeping has improved the health of asthmatics and others with chronic diseases, such as arthritis. She reports that in her own experience, journal keeping dramatically improved her asthma, making her life and her illness much more manageable. Journals can also be used to reflect on the meaning of illness in personal and professional life (Krmpotic, 2003). Thus, journals facilitate powerful insights that can affect one's health and understanding of life experience.

Techniques for Keeping a Journal in Professional Life

The eight techniques listed initially in chapter 5 are all useful in keeping a journal in professional life. These techniques are freewriting, focused freewriting, listing, logs, dialogue, concept mapping, metaphor, and metareflection. Three additional techniques, writing unsent letters, using time travel writing to envision future career or organizational moves, and intuitive writing, are also discussed. Please note that ours is not the only way to frame journal-writing techniques. From her analysis of a large number of professional journals, O'Hanlon (1997) describes four spontaneous modes of keeping a journal: report writing, interpretive writing, deliberative writing, and integrated writing. Although we prefer to be more explicit about these techniques, these categories include most of the techniques described in this section. Appendix A contains summary charts for each writing technique with a definition, objectives, procedures, and examples. These will enable you to quickly reference the technique should you wish to use it in a class or your professional life. Let us now turn to a discussion of how to use these techniques in your professional life.

Freewriting

Freewriting is the foundation of the professional journal. It allows journal keepers to explore what is on their minds or check in on daily thoughts and concerns, to jettison these daily concerns, or even just to "clear the deck" to make way for more formal writing. Peter Elbow (1973), a champion of freewriting, recommends that it be used to build writing fluency, playfulness, confidence, and creativity. One faculty member we know uses freewriting for 10 minutes to warm up before proceeding to more academic writing. Here is an example of a freewrite from Joanne's journal:

> We are all being here, to the best of our ability, struggling with what that means in our lives as academics, in our lives as partners, parents, children of aging parents, grandparents, and just plain old human beings! People on the planet. I try to remember to ask myself, when I am 80 or more, what will have mattered? What matters now? The problem is that what matters seems to shift and bend and change with the wind, the time, the day, the context. And yet some things are timeless. Some things always matter: integrity, love, making a living, being or becoming the person you want to be. It's like a kaleidoscope—flashing before your eyes, putting you in some kind of a trance where you can easily get bamboozled into wandering down the wrong road and end up asking, "How the heck did I get here?" Such an important question!

Ways to use a freewrite in professional life include the following:

- To check in: Freewriting can be a way to check in with yourself to find out what is on the surface of your thinking and feeling for the day or week. Letting the words tumble out onto the page during a freewrite can be quite interesting and even surprising to the writer. Setting aside dictums about grammar, punctuation, and all the constraints of formal writing often allows unconscious ideas, unanticipated observations, surprises, and creative connections to flow from your pen. As one of our doctoral students wrote in an anonymous survey on journal writing, "Freewriting allows information to spill out (that) you didn't know was there" (personal communication, March 22, 2007). Another nonnative English speaker found value in freewriting, stating, "The freewriting was helpful, especially in my own language. I wrote without thinking in English grammar. I love the idea to write in my first language. Gracias" (anonymous survey, March 18, 2007).
- To "clear the deck": Before beginning more formal academic writing, some academics allow themselves 5 to 10 minutes of freewriting. Even though their freewriting is not directly related to an academic topic, this activity gets the "writing juices" flowing, and allows emotions and other distractions to be vented. After having warmed up with a freewrite, it is then easier to approach academic work. As one faculty member wrote, "Freewriting is a good way to clear out the clutter

in my brain so that I can think and see more clearly" (anonymous survey, March 18, 2007).

Focused Freewrite

Focused freewrites are similar to regular freewrites except that they are focused on a particular topic, rather than being totally open-ended. Like freewrites, they are generative and are especially useful when exploring a teaching or research topic or, for an administrator, an organizational concern. Focused freewrites are most commonly used to generate ideas; raise questions or concerns; explore interests; or to summarize ideas around one theme, topic, or question. A focused freewrite is like a brainstorm that can list questions, concerns, insights, resources, interests, roadblocks, strengths, weaknesses, opportunities, threats, and ideas. Here is an example of a focused freewrite that highlights the questions that arose when Dannelle was doing the initial organization for the chapter on assessment in this book:

> Focused Freewrite: Chapter on Assessment of Journal Entries
>
> If I am reading a chapter on how to assess student journals, what would I want to know? I would want to know about: grading student journals—how? Why grade student journals? Because I want students to take journal writing seriously and I know they pay attention to what they are graded on. I don't really want to dampen their enthusiasm for journal keeping. Yet, what criteria should I use? Depends on my objectives; depends on my time; depends on the message I want to give students about what is important in this class. Hmmm, I am really not satisfied with anything I have read about assessment of journals. There isn't much and it is all over the place. I need to look for more references. The research I have doesn't really help me answer these questions. We want to give the reader a potpourri of choices for assessing student journals and we want to be specific. And journal writing is different from assessing other kinds of academic work. . . . Ah, there is a key idea, I definitely want that idea in the chapter. . . . (June 25, 2007)

Ways to use a focused freewrite in professional life include the following:

- To generate ideas: A focused freewrite is one of the best ways to generate ideas about a research project, a paper, or an administrative project. Faculty who are going up for promotion often use this device to help them get all the ideas down about what they have been doing over the last few years—a daunting task—and find the central theme in their work. You can also use focused free-writes to explore a topic, discover what you know, or what your questions are before you begin a piece of academic writing or a project you are launching as an administrator.

- To summarize ideas: Before a project is completed but after much of the work is done, it is revealing to do a focused freewrite on what has been learned. It often brings up ideas that had not been considered before. The loose structure allows the introduction of ideas that might not have been considered impor-tant thus far in the life of the project.

Lists

Making lists is a very common writing technique. Lists help faculty and administrators keep track of and prioritize their responsibilities, generate ideas for research projects or new programs, plot steps needed to complete a manuscript or a project, or summarize major stepping-stones or significant events in one's career. Making a list of feelings about a person or problem at work can often help objectify and even clarify challenges. One advantage of lists is that they are usually short phrases and can be easily viewed on one page. This allows the writer to quickly review the list to compare, contrast, or gain insight from the ideas on the list. Ranking and prioritizing the items on the list can lead to the identification of hidden patterns that might not have been obvious before.

Here is an example of a list, in this case a list of jobs the graduate-student jour-nal writer, Joe, has held. He used this list to acknowledge the breadth of his experi-ence as well as decide what he really wanted to do in the future.

Jobs I Have Had

Mortuary Assistant	Retail Store Clerk	Window Washer
NursingHome Assistant/CNA	Retail Music/Video Rental Guy	Live-In Caregiver
Paperboy	Canoe-Rental Clerk	Baby Sitter
Carpenter's Go-Fer	Rock Show Security Guy	Dog Sitter
Housepainter	Cook/Caterer	Flower Delivery Guy
Illustrator	Waiter	Artist
Webmaster	Gas-Station Attendant	Teacher (school) (personal communication, July 22, 2005)
Landscaper	Janitor	
Production Assembler		
Bartender		

Ways to use lists in professional life include:

- To use as to-do lists
- To gather ideas for a research project
- To identify steps needed to complete a paper or project
- To gather what you already know about a project
- To place stepping-stones or identify significant events in your life
- To elicit feelings about a person or problem at work

Log

Although logs are similar to lists, they are usually more detailed and extensive. Placing the date at the beginning of each entry is one of the central features of a log. Logs often chronicle events or steps taken during a project with others. They are often organized in columns. An example is a ship's log on a long voyage or a log of steps taken in a research project. Progoff (1992) describes a log as a place for the factual data of our lives. Although the entries may involve a great deal of emotion, they are to be made as briefly, directly, and as objectively as possible. The log sections of his journal process are "the collections of the raw empirical data of our lives" (Progoff, 1992, p. 26). The accompanying feelings and thoughts about these events are later recorded in other sections of the journal. In this way, Progoff asserts, "We place ourselves between the experiences of our past and the possibilities of the future. . . ." (1992, p. 16).

In a log of events, the thoughts and feelings about those events can be recorded along with the event, but often they are not. Whatever the purpose, one of the strengths of a log is the cumulative and neutral, fact-like record that is created. Over time, patterns appear. Even the discontinuities in a pattern are informative. As Progoff states, "Events that seem to contradict one another are all part of the unity of process by which life unfolds" (1992, p. 19). Through a log, an entire journey can be viewed from a distance and therefore be better understood.

Ways to use a log in professional life include:

- To document research in the library: Here is a set of column titles that might be useful when creating a research log: date, task, research descriptors used, database, result.
- To document steps taken in a research project or personnel issue: Here is another set of column descriptors that might be useful for working on a larger

project such as a collaborative research project or a personnel issue: date, persons involved, topic, decisions, action.

- To log interactions with community partners: Sometimes it is difficult to keep track of community-partner interactions and expectations. Some faculty devote a single section of their journals to this highly variable, demanding, and complex outreach work. Here are some column headings you might fine useful: date, names/contact information, type of activity, tasks to be done, who is responsible, actions taken.

- To log phone messages: Keeping track of phone calls is often difficult. We have found that a phone log in our journals makes it easier to be sure that we respond to calls. The columns we typically use are date, time, phone number, person, request, check box for completion of request.

- To log advising appointments: Another challenge is to make sure that student-advising requests are attended to in a timely manner. Again, a log seems to help us organize student advising appointments. Useful column headings are date, student, contact information, request, action.

- To log interactions around a personal issue: Logs, like lists, often provide perspective and opportunities to reflect on a particularly stressful interaction in your life. Keeping a log with these column descriptors may help you identify patterns that are destructive as well as those that are fruitful: date, time, who was involved, what happened, my feelings, actions taken.

Dialogue

A written dialogue is a "conversation carried on with yourself to help you gain insight into a person, event, or subject you wish to understand better" (Rainer, 1978, p. 103). Dialogues help the writer to deal with a situation or person, and to clarify the relationship or a particular issue. In a dialogue you address the person or subject directly and simply allow the person or the subject to speak to you in response.

Dialogues with people are most useful for working out relationships with colleagues or students. Dialogues may evolve out of previous journal writings in which a particular person or issue arises repeatedly. Dialogues with inanimate objects, such as a program or project, are also useful in dealing with frustrations or planning issues. They often allow the writer to obtain some distance from the issue or person they are struggling with as well as to give voice to an issue and allow hidden understandings to surface. Dialogues often take on a playful or poignant quality and can offer surprising insights that come from unexpected directions in the dialogue. Here, for example, is a dialogue that Dannelle wrote after she noticed that in the last year she was fond of using the word "eek" in her freewriting. She wrote the following dialogue with "eek" to see if "eek" had something to say to her.

DDS: Hi, eek, how are you?

E: Eeek, eek, eeeek

D: How many Es do you have?

E: At least two, sometimes three, and other times, particularly the most frustrating times 4—eeeek!

D: Ok, ok, ok. Now. . . . Answer me. What are you doing in my writing?

E: OK, I am trying to get your attention. . . . You have done a lot of me lately. You have found only one way to express your feelings. You like me. Do I get your attention?

D: Kinda'.

E: Yes, I do! Yes, I do! EEEEK!

D: All right, OK, you are the red flag seeking my attention! You are the exclamation point at the end of the sentence! You are a spout on a tea kettle. You are an important part of me. And you say nothing.

E: Oh, yes, I do.

D: I don't let you out—you are just in my journal. Say, . . . maybe you allow me to express my stress and tension. And you are not a real word. You are a sound. You're a substitute for a more detailed and descriptive set of words. Yes, that is what I don't like about you. You don't push me to clarify my emotions. I depend on you and you fill a void.

E: Yep, you got it! Why should I be anything else? You only use me occasionally.

D: Too much lately! Anyway, I like you because you remind me that I am really stressed about something and you point to or "eek" at these important things.

Like most good conversations, this dialogue was not planned ahead of time. Dannelle just wanted to explore her use of the word "eek" in her journal reflections. She learned that it is related to very strong, often unspecified, emotions and can also hide some deeper emotions that could be worthy of exploration and reflection.

Ways to use dialogue in professional life include:

- To explore alternative perspectives on a project or program: Here you can examine how you are feeling about a particular project as you begin, or you can determine what is going on if you get stuck in the middle of implementation.
- To understand a colleague or supervisor's point of view: Here the object is to clarify the relationship or to plan how to approach someone about a particular

topic. One leader we know uses dialogue to plan how to approach parents of students in her school. Others use this technique to understand the actions of their bosses or supervisors. Still others use the technique to clarify troublesome relationships with colleagues.

- To describe another's point of view in a conflicted situation.

- To help uncover these deeper issues that writers may not be aware of when they first start the dialogue: It is sometimes helpful to write a summary of the dialogue and what insights you may have gained from it. See the chart on dialogue in Appendix A for an example of a dialogue with time, an issue we all struggle with, as well as a metareflection on the dialogue.

- To explore patterns in your life: You can use the dialogue format to explore a recurring pattern in your life that you might want to change, for example, being late for meetings or always saying "yes" when asked to do something.

Concept Mapping

A concept map is a cluster of ideas in boxes or circles that are connected to each other. It is a schematic or drawing that helps the writer to gain a visual image of a set of ideas or themes and their relationships to one another. Figure 7.1 is a copy of the first page of one of Dannelle's journals for the year 2005 in which she created a concept map. At that time, she was working on several projects and wanted to see how they might be related to a larger idea. Drawing the concept map and adding to it over several weeks helped her identify the central role that reflection—teaching it, studying it and writing about it—plays in her professional life. As she looked across her activities in teaching action research, keeping a journal herself, writing a book on rubrics, and coordinating a master's program, she realized that her interest was in how reflection fosters her own and others' professional development.

Ways to use *concept mapping* in professional life include:

- To brainstorm, generate, and organize ideas for research papers, grants, or large projects: In creating a concept map, you can list and then organize ideas in clusters to see how they relate to one another. Labeling the clusters or writing a sentence under the clusters helps you to see the underlying relationship between the ideas and relate similar ideas together.

- To compare and contrast several ideas: Venn diagrams in particular facilitate the comparison of several ideas.

Figure 7.1
Concept Map: Themes in Work and Research From Dannelle's Journal

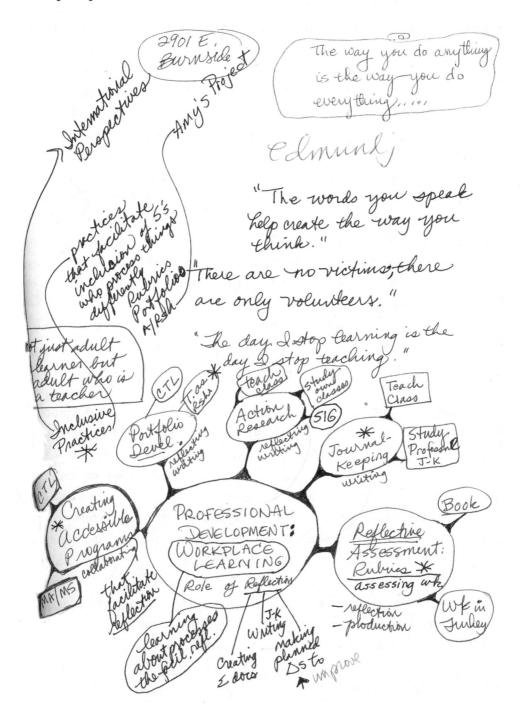

Metaphor

Lakoff and Johnson (1980) assert that we live by metaphor. Our lives are filled with metaphors that influence how we think and how we see the world. "[M]etaphor is pervasive in everyday life, not just in language but in thought and action" (Lakoff & Johnson, 1980, p. 3). Metaphor influences the way we speak and think, and can be a powerful vehicle for understanding ourselves and our organizations. Morgan (2006), for example, has used metaphor to guide our understanding of the organizations we spend our lives working in. He suggests that we view our organizations as machines, organisms, and psychic prisons in order to understand them better. Basically, metaphor is an implied comparison and thus helps the writer to explore comparisons or contrasts between two things. Metaphors inform our thinking and help us to see ourselves, our organizations, or our programs in new ways. In addition, metaphor helps us to approach a topic indirectly and perhaps come closer to truths that may be painful to face. As Palmer states, ". . . truth through metaphor can emerge from and return to our awareness at whatever pace and depth we are able to handle. . ." (2004, p. 93).

Metaphors can be used in journal keeping to understand ourselves as professionals, as well as to understand the schools and colleges we work in. They can also be used to help us envision programs we are designing, running, or working in. Metaphors can be visual as well as written.

Joanne's watercolor (see the back cover of this text) was painted at the beginning of program planning. She envisioned the blossoming program as "pink with possibility" even though it grew out of an old and gnarled tree. These images helped influence how she thought about a budding program, as well as how she spoke to others about it. Likewise, how you think of your professional self, whether as a flattened tire or a garden in full summer bloom, has a definite influence on how you approach your work. Exploring those metaphors in your journal can uncover some deep perceptions that guide your behavior, limit or enhance your full engagement, and color your interactions with others.

One way to explore a metaphor of your professional life is through a series of questions. First, bring forth as many characteristics as you can about the object, person, or experience to which you are comparing an aspect of your experience. For example, when we teach a class together we feel like we are gardening in the same plot of earth. You can ask questions like: What are the characteristics of this object (person, experience)? Where was it created? How is it used? Where does it live? Who uses it? What is its history? Why is it the shape, color, or texture that it is? What is its future? If it could talk, what would it say? Second, ask: How do all these aspects of the metaphor compare with my life? How is my professional life like any or all of these characteristics? Finally, write a reflection on what you learned about yourself from comparing and contrasting the characteristics of the object with your life.

The use of metaphor is definitely a powerful instrument in the journal keeper's repertoire of techniques. Some scholars suggest that you can readily use metaphor to undergo transformational learning about your work (Deshler, 1990). For example, Deshler suggests that you first generate metaphors for yourself or your organization as it is now, and then explore metaphors that represent how you would like it to be. Seeing the difference can help you understand how you view your work and suggest paths in new directions.

Dannelle's use of metaphor as a way of understanding her work started when the dean asked her about how school–university partnerships were progressing; she responded, "It is like being in a surreal painting. The reality of the university is so different from the realities of schools. It is just plain surreal." Then she proceeded to write an article comparing the work to what it must be like to be in the middle of a Magritte painting (Stevens, 1996). Since then, Dannelle has used several different metaphors as themes for research articles examining her work as a school–university partnership coordinator (Stevens & Everhart, 2000).

Ways to use *metaphor* in professional life include:

- To better understand your organization or yourself as a professional
- To understand different perspectives about a project
- To develop creative responses to challenging problems at work
- To look at something from a different point of view

Metareflection

Metareflection involves writing a review of previously written journal entries. The process requires rereading, rethinking, comparing, contrasting, and identifying patterns in prior journal entries. After this review, the journal keeper writes a reflection on what she has noticed, on what stands out, or on what has stimulated her thinking and insight. This is a wonderful way to affirm progress over time, to identify recurring destructive patterns, or to objectify experiences, and then be able to analyze them more deeply to foster positive change. As one graduate student noted in an anonymous research survey, "metareflections showed me how to step back from a situation and disengage some emotions in order to allow clarity of thought" (March 13, 2007).

Rather than just using their journals for reflecting on teaching and their work, sometimes faculty find that the journal is useful for personal reflection. Mary Jane chose one of her personal journal entries to reflect on her life as a public school teacher, mother, and graduate student. Figure 7.2 is her word collage, and her metareflection on it follows.

> This reflection is rather personal. It deals with things I found out about myself as I was putting my self-reflective word collage together. I had to write those "things" out in order to gain meaning and understanding of my thoughts. This is the first time in a long time I've actually allowed myself to think about me. Over the last couple of years my life has gone through some major changes. As I was choosing the words that seemed to have meaning to me and my life now, in general they seemed pretty positive. That is pretty much how I feel these days. Then, looking back, I noticed how a few of those positive traits ended up having some negative real-life scenarios associated with them. Spontaneous and impulsive, they are my main trouble makers! (Mary Jane, personal communication, March 18, 2008)

Ways to use metareflection in professional life include:

- To review work over time and check direction of work with goals and objectives for academic life.
- To reflect on previous writing, looking for patterns, surprises, hidden meanings, underlying assumptions, or general direction.
- To obtain an overview of an experience over time, such as an end-of-semester reflection on previous journal entries about one's teaching, or an end-of-year entry about progress toward tenure: Metareflections can provide an overview of a term or a year's work.
- To develop strategies to address ongoing challenges: By photocopying pages from the journal that are relevant to a challenging committee or a personnel issue, you can take a "balcony" view and write about what patterns you see and how you might address the problem from a fresh perspective.

Figure 7.2
Metareflection and Word Collage: Mary Jane's Journal

Unsent Letter

Even if never sent, letters written to others can clarify relationships, provide insights into the motives of others, unburden you by saying the things you want to say but never would or could, and even allow closure. Unsent letters can be "an exploration of whatever a particular person evokes when you think *to* them. The letter you actually send may differ substantially from the first draft written in the diary, or you may never send the diary letter in any form" (Rainer, 1978, p. 78). In addition, an unsent letter can express thoughts to a certain person when actually doing so would be rude or inappropriate. The fact that the letter is unsent gives journal writers the freedom to express their thoughts and feelings honestly. Here is an example of an unsent letter from a woman who "decided to write a letter to my house in order to say goodbye." Jolina wrote:

> Dear 944 SE Lexington,
>
> With a heavy heart I say goodbye to you. It has been a wonderful experience living within your walls, being protected by your embrace, and growing alongside you. You are a simple soul, not many luxuries, not many remodels or updates and that's what I loved about you. You were charming, old fashioned, traditional, and historical. You looked so great with the American flag on your porch and a manicured green lawn that Josh planted himself. You were so close to the park, the shops on 13th, nestled near the river, in a community of caring people and loving neighbors. I remember when we found you. It was like destiny. We weren't really even looking, but there you were needing someone to rent you. It was so easy to get to know you, to move in, and start our life. Remember, the first day we brought Hooligan home? How he explored every room and wanted to know who you were? Hooligan loves you too. He misses you, I can tell. At our new house his nose gets confused. The smells are not what he is used to. (personal communication, May 15, 2007)

Ways to use unsent letters in professional life include:

- To explore unresolved issues with a colleague or supervisor: These letters are often a place to express feelings that might be damaging or inappropriate if they were sent or said out loud to the person. They are a way to speak the unspeakable and thus reduce tension in a relationship.
- To practice an important upcoming conversation: The letter can provide a dress rehearsal for a conversation that will take place in the future.
- To bring closure to a relationship: Unsent letters are also a way to say goodbye and let go of relationships that have ended. The person may be physically unavailable or simply unwilling to hear what you have to say.

Time Travel

Using the journal as a time machine can involve writing from the past or from the future to your present self. This can take the form of recalling the past, exploring a road not taken, or charting your future. As Rainer states, "Just as memories of the past exist in the present, so do seeds of the future" (1978, p. 241). Traveling into the future is similar to writing an unsent letter except that the letter is sent by the writer from an imagined future back to the present self or from an imagined past to the present self. When used as a letter from the future, it is a form of goal setting or a way to clarify what you are really working toward. By imagining yourself in the future (1 year, 5 years, or at age 80), you are able to imagine possible futures and to give yourself advice about how to proceed with a career, job search, or other current endeavors to make that future real.

Here is an example of a letter from the future. In this case the journal writer chose to write from 10 years into the future.

> August 10, 2013
>
> Things are weird, as usual. I have been spending a huge amount of time working on The Novel again and it's becoming something of a joke among my friends and perhaps a metaphor for my life in general. I keep going back and making it incrementally more perfect—someday it will be published, and I can lie down and die! In the meantime, however, it's a week until the 5th Annual MEAT, WIRES, AND COFFEE festival, the art event in the desert we put together when it became obvious that Burning Man had blown out its circuits and strayed from its artistic beginnings. How I found such strange and kindred spirits is beyond me and a happy mystery. Paint and Motion and Music and blazing fiery electricity . . . who would have imagined a place like this for me a decade ago. (Joe, personal communication, July 14, 2003)

This letter illustrates the power of writing from the future. The writer can begin to imagine possible futures that were fuzzy or nonexistent before sitting down to write. The advantage is that you can be more alert to these possibilities in your life once you have written about them.

Ways to use time travel in professional life include:

- To explore possible future career moves or job opportunities: A letter can be sent from a future date describing the kind of job you have obtained. It can thus be used as a template for the kind of job you really want while you are job searching.

- To explore the consequences of your career choices if you have to choose from two different paths: The journal writer would write two letters, each reflecting a different choice. It can thus be a valuable tool in the decision-making process.
- To gain the long view as a program or grant begins or ends.

Intuitive Writing

According to Rainer intuitive writing (also known as *free association, stream of consciousness, free-intuitive writing, automatic writing,* or *active imagination*) was a primary tool of Surrealist writers and painters. It is similar to free writing. However, it "comes from a deeper place in the psyche. It is primarily an intuitive language, a message from the inner consciousness. Free-intuitive writing releases the voice of the subconscious by removing or putting aside the control of the conscious mind" (1978, p. 61).

The power of intuitive writing is in evoking the subconscious mind through writing. Sometimes it releases emotions that are hidden so far into the subconscious that they cannot be tapped any other way. Artists use this method to generate genuine, creative responses, whereas psychologists have used this method to find the deeper motives and feelings that affect client behavior. According to Rainer,

> No matter what you call it, the technique is simple. You relax and try to empty your mind. You don't think about anything. You simply wait for whatever comes into your mind, and you write it just as it comes, without worrying about whether it makes sense. You let your hand do the writing. You record what you hear from the back of your mind. Nothing is irrelevant. You try to capture every word and image that occurs to you. It may all seem silly, just nonsense, but you write it anyway. It may seem embarrassing, but you write it anyway. You write fast, so fast that you don't have time to think about what you are doing. You don't take time to censor or make sense. (1978, p. 62)

One way to tap this part of your brain is by writing with your nondominant hand. When Dannelle used one of Rainer's suggestions for intuitive writing, not looking at the page as she wrote, she found the following intuitive writing bubbling up into her consciousness:

> Letting looking up the trees are there moving grey clouds days come along trees & bees & bugs & bother bearing bubbles words flow from my pen to the pretty page

Tracking words shower dedicate the book to Anita Pearl Friedrich Smith Fitzsimmons 1919–2007 my mother & my best teacher, was she?—yes she was—the best teacher I know her girls she always was so proud of her girls, her girls who were they? Little, bright, smart, 4-H, swimming took us swimming every day in the summer in San Rafael—for her to go shopping For us to make sure we did not drown—drown down in life—drown & go & feel free to go in water. (June 26, 2008)

When Dannelle started the intuitive writing, she did not know that it would end up at a very significant and recent event in her life, the death of her mother. Yet this writing released many deep emotions and insights about the role that her mother played (and plays) in her life.

Ways to use intuitive writing in professional life include:

• To learn to listen to your inner consciousness
• To "play" with words
• To engage in a totally unrestricted way of getting words down on the page

In this section, we have shown you a variety of techniques to use while journal writing. The joy of journal keeping is its inherent flexibility and suitability for a wide range of activities in academic life. In the next section we address how to format the journal. Finally, in the last three sections we discuss ways to use the journal for three purposes: to improve your writing, to facilitate and reflect on research, and to reflect on and improve teaching.

Formats That Work Well for Journals in Professional Life

Faculty and administrators in higher education use various journal formats depending on their needs. There is quite a wide array of choices available today. The books can be conventionally bound, spiral bound, or loose leaf. Journal entries can also be kept on a computer, depending on the preferences and learning styles of the journal writer (see chapter 8 for more information). Whatever format you choose will be superior to Gee's (2004) original method, which was to write frantically after class on grocery-store receipts or whatever he found in his pockets, or to jot his thoughts down on a stray folder when he got back to his office. Having everything in one place is a huge time-saver.

Some journal writers prefer dividing the journal page into two columns—for example, one smaller column for noting the date, participants, the to-do list generated from the event, and questions about the activity; and the second column for notes, meeting minutes, concept maps, and other larger pieces of text. Dannelle uses this method and likens the larger column to a river in which external information flows past her consciousness (e.g., meeting minutes, notes, phone log, and project to-do list); she likens the smaller column to the river's bank, in which she observes, reacts to, and reflects on the river (e.g., date, participants, key ideas, immediate to-do list, reflections, questions). Having two columns makes it easier to find things later. A description of this method is shown in Figure 7.3.

The entire journal can also be formatted into two sections: The front section is where the journal keeper writes entries every day while going through her day, whereas the back section is for deeper reflections and freewrites that are more personal and private. One way to make the sections is to make the first section from the front of the journal as usual. To create the second section, turn the journal upside down and start writing from the back. When the two sections meet in the middle, it is time to purchase a new journal. When you fill a journal, it can also be helpful to write a table of contents that contains the date, the title of the entry, and the page number. This helps remind you of what is inside and where to find a particular piece of information you may be searching for.

Inside the front cover of this book is an example of one of Dannelle's tables of contents from one of her journals from 2007. She does not write the table of contents until the journal is full. Then, usually on a long plane flight, she will number her pages and make this table with the date, the activity, and the page number. When done, she will use one highlighter color to mark particular activities in the table of contents. For example, topics related to journal keeping (notes from interviews, conference presentations made, conference sessions attended on journal keeping, reflections from teaching students about journal keeping, conversations with Joanne, and so on) will get one color. Other key activities like rubrics will get another color. This way she can quickly find the entries. When she is ready to write an article, teach a class, or even write a book like this one, she peruses her tables of contents and her journals over the previous few years; photocopies all the pages related to the topic, say, developing the ideas around the assessment of student journals; and then uses the ideas as fuel for her writing, committee work, research, and teaching.

Figure 7.3
Two-Column Journal Method: "River" and "Bank"

How to Keep a Journal in Your Professional Life: The Bank and River of Experience

Dannelle D. Stevens, Ph.D.   Joanne E. Cooper, Ph.D.

A journal for your professional life has several key components =======➔ to log and record professional activities
=======➔ to collect notes from meetings, conferences, reflections

	JOURNAL FORMAT SMALL COLUMN (1–2 inches) "Bank of the River"	JOURNAL FORMAT LARGE COLUMN (3 to 6 inches) "River of Experience"

CONTENTS	Narrower than large column
	Put in date of entry
	Meetings: List names of those present
	Note ideas that are
	    Interesting
	    Link to other activities
	    Spark your imagination
	    Require more work
	Write out comments, reflections & responses
	"To do" list
	Grocery list
	(to get it off your mind)
		Wider than small column
		Notes on the activity (minutes, agenda, key topics covered, etc.)
		Diagrams, concept maps that summarize thinking
		Narratives from freewriting (or turn journal upside down and write from the back for the more personal reflections)
		Quotations from participants at the meetings
		Agendas glued-in, Power Point miniature slides from handouts, business cards
		Notes from conference sessions, speeches that can be used for ideas for future research
		Rough drafts of writing and research ideas
		Phone log with "to do" list
		Stickies organized in concept maps
		Notes from research collaborations with colleagues
		Resources found: Web sites, books read, references
		**Often useful to photocopy key pages and use for discussion & reflection

BENEFITS	Written reflections over time: trail of dates & ideas "To do" list to follow up on commitments Confusions to track later Easy to find when pages numbered and table of contents used	Actual record of what happened, what was said and by whom Quotations from participants allow you to reflect on other perspectives Track dates and activities as evidence for promotion Opportunity to reflect on activity after the event No fumbling for folders and notes from previous meetings Way to pull together ideas for future projects (photocopy relevant pages)

© D. D. Stevens, 2008

Rudy, a professor of architecture, uses another formatting method. He prefers to use large, spiral-bound books that can be taken apart in order to reorganize the pages. He does not like to write in chronological order and may later want to organize the entries according to when they were written or to compile the entries according to topic. Size is also a consideration. Most academics like a small notebook that can be easily carried from meeting to meeting. The classic Moleskine journals offer variety and quality. Whatever format is chosen, it should be carefully selected for the particular purposes and tastes of the journal writer. One of the beauties of journal keeping is its flexibility, allowing for a wide array of possibilities. Of course, it may take a few iterations of organizational systems to find the formatting system that works well for you in your complex professional life. Our cases in chapter 10 illustrate the variety of formats that academic professionals use.

There are three central areas of professional life that can be enhanced through the regular use of a journal: improvement of writing, research, and teaching.

Using a Journal to Improve Writing Skills and Productivity

As noted previously, there are a variety of journal-writing techniques that develop writing skills and increase writing production: freewriting, focused freewriting, dialogue, and so on.

In this section we apply these specifically to writing improvement. Any skill, such as playing tennis, that is practiced on a regular basis will improve that ability. This is also true of the skill of writing. In Table 7.3 we list specific techniques that improve writing skill and productivity.

Your journal can also be a powerful tool in helping you to plan and conduct research.

Using a Journal to Develop Research Focus and Topics

Many of the journal-writing activities that you can use for the development of your writing can be applied to the development of your research. Research strongly depends

Table 7.3
Using the Journal to Improve Writing Skill and Productivity

Freewriting	Build writing fluency through freewriting frequently.
Focused freewriting	Generate ideas about a paper you want to write. If you use freewriting or focused freewriting in class, write in your journal when the students write in theirs. It provides a powerful role model and sometimes it precipitates that flash of insight needed to further your writing project.
Dialogue	Write a dialogue with your manuscript, with your perception of yourself as a writer, with your writing block, with time, with paper topics, with students.
Concept map	List all the ideas you have for a paper. Then, on the same page, put them into a concept map, clustering like ideas and beginning to establish relationships between ideas. Sticky-note alternative: Write one idea per small sized sticky note. Generate as many ideas, questions, concerns, and insights as possible. When you are done, you will have a stack of ideas. Read them, and then cluster them in groups on two pages of your journal. Write sentences below the clusters that summarize the ideas in the cluster. Number the sentences in some logical order and begin writing your paper.
Metareflection through photocopying	Reread the sections of your journals that contain notes from conferences, ideas from readings, reflections, notes made during reflections, or that are related to a particular topic. Having a table of contents and numbered pages readily facilitates finding these old journal entries. Flag these pages with sticky notes, and then photocopy all these pages. Now you have in your hands photocopies of the seeds you have already planted for writing and developing your topic. Read them. Summarize them and write from them. See Figure 7.4 for a typical journal page that could contain seeds for further reflection and writing.
Read articles and books about writing	Become a student of academic writing. Read books and articles on writing in academe. Here are a few (full citations in reference list):
	Boice, R. (1990). *Professors as writers: A self-help guide to productive writing.* Cooper, J. E., & Stevens, D. D. (Eds.). (2002). *Tenure in the sacred grove: Issues and strategies for women and minorities.* Elbow, P. (1981). *Writing with power: Techniques for mastering the writing process.* Hiatt, G. (2008). *Reducing over-complexity in your scholarly writing.* Rankin, E. (2001). *The work of writing: Insights and strategies for academics and professionals.* Silvia, P. J. (2007). *How to write a lot: A practical guide to productive academic writing.*

on the craft of writing—for example, recording observations, documenting interactions, and capturing insights. Consequently, a journal can be a repository for data, reflecting on it, and writing about it (Janesick, 1998, 2004). Figure 7.4 not only illustrates the two-column method but also shows how the ideas gleaned from a research conference can be summarized. The balloons were ideas that interested Dannelle from the Professional and Organizational Development (POD) Conference regarding the "scholarship of teaching and learning" (SOTL). She said to a friend, "I floated some of my own ideas and collected some ideas from others about SOTL at the conference." In the plane on the way home, she decided to summarize these in her journal in the form of balloons.

Research also often involves many participants, as well as outside contacts. It can be difficult to keep track of the many details involved in a research project—participants, contact information, resources used, instruments used, references needed and used, and so on. A journal can be a perfect single location to gather and track this vital, research-related information. Some faculty devote a single journal to a research project (Jones, Torres, & Arminio, 2006). Others integrate their research activities into the rest of their professional journal and can easily find their research activities through numbered pages and the table of contents. Table 7.4 is a list of several different ways to use the journal to facilitate your research.

In addition, many times new academics have a difficult time identifying a research agenda. The writing techniques in this chapter, such as focused freewriting, dialogue, listing, and concept mapping, can help the researcher examine and explore her or his research focus.

Using a Journal to Reflect On and Improve Teaching

Keeping a journal while you are teaching can be extremely useful. A journal can be a helpful planning document or a place to brainstorm teaching ideas. After each class, you can reflect on what went on for you and for your students in the class. If you try something new, you can take some time to reflect on how it went and what you might do differently next time. As Gee, an English teacher in a 2-year college, states, "It could very well be that the unexpected minor occurrences in a classroom are the most precious educational pearls for a teacher to record and preserve" (2004,

Figure 7.4
Using a Journal for Research: Balloon Collection of Ideas From a Conference

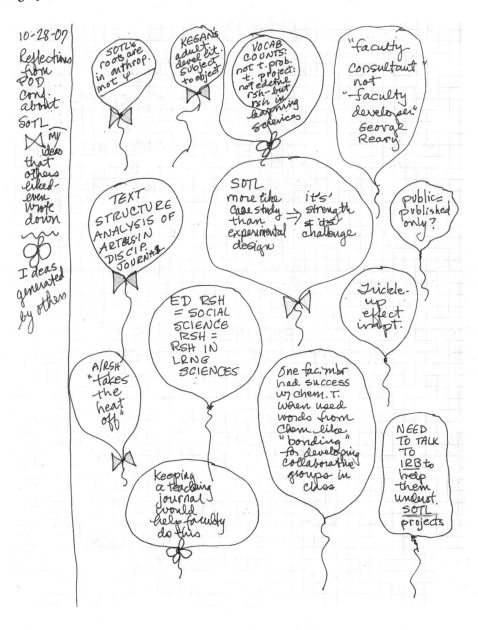

Table 7.4
Using the Journal for Research

Lists and logs	Keep to-do lists, phone logs, and reference lists.
	Keep lists of key words used in doing literature searches.
	Keep a list of research participants and contact information in one place in your journal.
Meeting notes	Keep notes during meetings with fellow researchers. These are invaluable.
	If you use the two-column method, put the to-do list in the smaller column so you don't lose the task that needs to be done.
Research focus	In the front of the journal, keep a list or concept map of key questions, topics, and themes in your research.
Conference notes	At a conference take notes in your journal during sessions related to your work and review these for ideas and contributions to your own thinking and research.

p. 26). Gee "tries to write a brief evaluation of my instructional odyssey every day" (2004, p. 26). He asks about what worked, what didn't, and why. He also uses his journal to record the stories he relates to help make an assignment memorable or il-lustrative examples he uses to bring home a particular point. He asks, "Are all these notes a waste of time? Certainly not for me. I prepare for my classes each semester by both evaluating my texts and carefully reading my journal" (2004, p. 30).

When we give in-class writing assignments, we also use our own journals and write along with our students. It is always powerful to model the behaviors you desire in the classroom, and we have had more than one student thank us for writing along with them. Your journal is also a handy place to keep references, Websites, and to remind yourself of books or articles you want to read in preparation for teaching. Colleagues often suggest resources at professional conferences. If you have your journal with you, both the source and any teaching ideas you pick up can quickly be jotted down.

Finally, it is sometimes helpful to generate metaphors for yourself as a teacher in order to get a grasp of what is going on with you in the classroom. Here is a meta-phor Joanne wrote at a time when things were particularly frustrating:

When I am teaching I feel like a snorting horse.
I glisten sometimes in class, but mostly I worry that my students think I'm all wet.
I am struggling under the weight of all this work. It weighs on me like a heavy saddle and sometimes I just want to buck it off.

Someone is always reining me in, jerking on the bit in my mouth, trying to get me to say "hegemonic" and "epistemologically."

How can I learn to love this saddle? To see it as a way to help people get from here to there?

When will someone bring me a carrot? Take me for a long ride in the country?

When will I take myself out for a long ride in the beautiful countryside?

This exercise helped Joanne to see that perhaps she needed a break from all the struggles. It was a surprise to realize that she had been waiting for someone else to come along and relieve her load, when in reality, she needed to rescue herself. Whatever your insights, a journal can be a valuable tool in your teaching life, one we highly recommend. Table 7.5 summarizes some of the ways that you can use your journal to reflect on and improve your teaching.

Conclusion

Keeping a journal in your professional life furthers two major goals: to increase your organization and to enhance your ability to reflect on the meaning of your work and

Table 7.5
Using the Journal to Reflect On and Improve Teaching

Lists and logs	Create to-do lists, lists of teaching resources.
	Brainstorm teaching ideas.
	Keep lists of what worked and what didn't when you taught a lesson.
	Keep a log of what is going on with a particular student or group of students.
	Keep lists of teaching ideas or references from a conference.
	Keep a list of valuable Websites and other resources inside the cover of your journal.
Notes of teaching or advising efforts	Keep notes of what you planned and what you actually did in the classroom.
	Keep notes on how well your efforts worked.
	Keep notes on student conferences
	Keep notes of observations of teaching interns.
Focused freewriting	Generate ideas, questions, reflections, and concerns after each class or after a term.
Metaphor	Use metaphors to help you get a metacognitive grasp of what is going on in your classroom or who you are as a teacher.

work-life events. Although keeping a journal can offer professionals in higher education a chance to reflect on their work and to grow, this understanding does not come easily. As Whyte states, "Maturity and energy in our work is not granted freely to human beings, but must be adventured and discovered, cultivated and earned. It is the result of application, dedication, an indispensable sense of humor, and above all a never-ending, courageous conversation with ourselves, those with whom we work and those whom we serve" (2001, p. 4). Your journal can be the location for those courageous conversations.

8

JOURNAL WRITING
IN THE COMPUTER AGE

Rebecca A. Schulte

Learning without thought is labor lost.
Confucius

IN PREVIOUS CHAPTERS, journal writing in academe is defined as an activity that supports thinking and reflection. The journal is a place where the labor of writing can result in learning about the self and life through examination of ideas and experiences. We have emphasized journal writing in the blank pages of a bound book. However, for many the journal written on the computer is a preferred substitute for the handwritten journal as an all-in-one tool for the creation, retrieval, and organization of information. To ignore the computer as a tool for journal writing would likely disincline those more comfortable typing than handwriting, and could result in overlooking ways journal writing can be a similar yet distinct experience in a computer environment. We address the following questions in this chapter:

- In what ways is journal writing different when typed on the computer?
- How can you incorporate the computer in classroom journal-writing assignments?
- How can you use blogs and the Internet to facilitate classroom journal writing?

The computer presents a different journal-writing experience compared with a handwritten journal. These differences reside not just in the tool, but also in the approach to writing based on the computer environment. Word processing software has transformed the means and methods of writing and creating typed text. This chapter first compares and contrasts journal writing by hand versus journal writing on the computer using word processing software. The last half of the chapter focuses primarily on the use of the Internet and blogs for generating and sharing journal entries. The goals and benefits of journal writing are reinforced while showing how the process can be both enhanced and limited when using technology and the Internet.

Differences in Journal Writing When Typed on the Computer

Journal writing is generative. Like an improvising jazz musician, the writer cannot know in advance where the strokes will lead. Sometimes journal entries come from bursts of inspiration when least expected, and sometimes they emerge from a dot or a scribble. Journal writing can be arduous, or can flow freely and easily toward bigger ideas and better understandings. The important thing is to put pen to paper, or fingers on keyboard, and play with words and ideas. Claxton states that the creative edge is where focus and intuition reside and that "writing is itself a creative fumbling towards something" (2006, p. 352), rather than a linear stream of words and sentences. The challenge is not so much which tool to use, but to commit time, remain open, and trust that journal writing will foster learning and professional growth.

The handwritten journal is an object or artifact in itself, literally a book you can open to any page. It is inherently unstructured and allows many possibilities in how and where the author accesses, creates, constructs, and organizes entries. The computer is a viable option for journal writing but is a more structured environment in which technical skills are required to create and organize journal entries. Unlike a handwritten journal, word processing software contains writing tools to correct, support, and enhance the typed text, but can also make writing more formal. Comparing and contrasting the basic elements of typed versus handwritten journals will help you make an informed choice about how one or both meet your classroom and professional needs.

Characteristics of the Computer That Can Facilitate Journal Writing

Computers are a powerful and pervasive tool for writing and organizing information. The computer provides an unlimited space to write and save text, while sparing paper. Keeping a journal on the computer has the following advantages:

Multiple Interfaces

The computer environment is multifaceted, so many tasks can be accomplished by switching back and forth between calendar, e-mail, the Internet, and various documents. A journal-writing folder can easily fit into the multitasking environment, making journal writing a more convenient exercise for busy people who rely on their computers to organize the events of their day.

Transferability

Journal writing on the computer makes it easy to manipulate and transfer ideas and information within a word processing document by highlighting, cutting, and pasting text. This can be helpful when combining and organizing information into journal entries that share common topics or themes.

Storage in Folders

When preparing to write long papers or documents, a computer journal folder can be created for dumping, organizing, and categorizing text in preparation for putting together the longer document and creating more polished writing.

Compatibility With Online Resources

When reading research articles, weblogs (blogs), or Websites on the Internet, a blank word processing document can remain open on the desktop and serve as a place to capture key information and incorporate thoughts and ideas.

Sharing Content With Others

Sharing journal writing in the academic context, and responding to that writing, can be more simple and efficient with access to the Internet.

Emphasis on Typed Text

On a computer, of course, the emphasis is on words and the mode of writing is typing. When presented with blank pages in a bound book and a pencil, some people are more inclined to engage in freehand doodling and artwork than writing. On the other hand, some are adverse to handwriting or drawing altogether and are more inclined to produce writing if allowed to type. For those who find blank pages in a journal book too open-ended, or for those who prefer typing over writing because handwriting is difficult or less efficient, the use of the computer can result in more focused and productive journal entries. Individuals who have difficulty with both typing and handwriting might consider exploring digital voice recorders or voice activation software on the computer.

Although regular journal-writing practices can be accomplished using word processing software, the technical characteristics inherent in the computer can also present challenges. These challenges, discussed in the next section, can sometimes make the process of capturing and organizing thoughts more cumbersome and less appealing compared with the handwritten journal.

Characteristics of the Computer That Hinder Journal Writing

The computer can seem in many ways a logical place to keep a journal. After all, it is a sort of personal library in a digital environment, and is a repository for thoughts, ideas, and information. However, the computer environment involves a different set of skills and challenges that can hinder sustained journal-writing practices. The following is a list of points to consider when using the computer for journal writing:

Distractions in the Computer Environment
Because the computer has multiple interfaces, the writer can be tempted to abandon the journal to check e-mail or search for something on the Internet. The distractions on the computer are often difficult to ignore and can interfere with time alone to reflect and think.

Limited View of Text
Display of text in the average word processor at 100% view is limited to a block window of approximately half a page. To read or view the text that comes before and after those few paragraphs, you must scroll up and down. This restricts the writer's attention to that which can be seen, and can interfere with planning, translating, and reviewing the text as a whole (Fatton & Eklundh, 1997).

Propensity for Perfection and Conventions
The computer environment can make the writer preoccupied with conventions and edits, and may foster the perception that writing requires perfection and "readiness." The word processor automatically highlights mistakes in grammar, spelling,

and sentence structure (although this feature can be turned off). This could cause the user to be less likely to write freely, take risks, or play with words, and could disrupt the flow of ideas.

Time and Skills for Technology

The computer has functions that allow the writer to make lines or boxes and play with the format of the text, similar to what might be created in a handwritten journal. However, these functions take time to learn and time to incorporate. Without these skills, computer journals are not as likely to be playful or spontaneous in their construction. In addition, computers can be complicated and fickle, requiring the assistance of a technician. However, over time, more and more students are becoming computer savvy and are capable of using or learning how to apply word processing tools for journal writing with little difficulty.

Software products such as OneNote, Scrivener, www.livejournal.com, Life Journal, and others still being developed are designed to allow for more variability in the computer-writing environment by replicating some of the flexible features of handwritten journals with electronic sticky notes and multiple-page viewing. However, programs such as these share some of the same limitations as the word processor: There is a learning curve and confinement to the computer desktop. Using the computer for journal writing, regardless of the software, can affect when journal entries are made (their accessibility) and what journal entries look like (their aesthetics). These may be important characteristics to consider when deciding between typed and handwritten journal entries.

Efficiency and Portability of
Computer Journals and Handwritten Journals

Frequent journal writing is recommended to develop habits in reflective and critical thinking. Like any developing habit, the more often it occurs, the more it becomes a part of daily life. Therefore, the student and professional new to journal writing should be prepared to write at any time in any place. Maintaining an ongoing journal is more likely to occur if it is easily accessible and practical to use in everyday situations.

For many faculty and students, working and writing on the computer is a part of the daily routine, and journal writing will most likely occur if done in the computer environment. Using a laptop computer for journal writing can seem most efficient because it is a portable space for creating and storing a variety of information and for multitasking. Although using a computer can be a viable journal-writing option, computers are not the best method for some types of journal-writing activities. There are many situations in which using a computer could be intrusive, inconvenient, cumbersome, or not customary. In addition, when creating a computer journal entry, access requirements (e.g., opening it, having it securely placed, being plugged in or sufficiently charged) can impede its use for journal writing.

In many circumstances, the handwritten journal can be easier to access than a computer for making quick journal entries. Faculty in higher education may find that handwritten journals allow for more natural engagement with students while facilitating discussions on readings or presentations. Personal insights or thoughts and student comments can be recorded more randomly and spontaneously during class on the blank pages of a journal book. In addition, the journal book can be retrieved with ease from a handbag or briefcase to record quick thoughts in a variety of situations such as informal social events or family gatherings, on the bus, at the park, and in the garden.

Thoughts and ideas worthy of capturing often appear when we least expect them. Schön (1983, 1987) describes these as opportunities for "reflection-in-action." In these moments, unexpected connections between what is happening in the moment and past experiences have the potential for "effective surprise," which Jerome Bruner considers the "hallmark of creative enterprise" (1969, p. 18). When using the computer to journal, it may not be as easy or convenient to jot down surprise connections, fleeting thoughts, or ideas that are worth remembering, and explore them in more depth.

There are technologies available today that enable the tech-savvy individual to achieve flexibility similar to that found in a handwritten journal, making it possible to capture fleeting thoughts and ideas. Web-enabled cell phones can connect with the Internet; e-mail and services such as Twitter can be used to send messages, which then can be transferred to a word processing document.

However, efficient use of these tools involves technological skill and resources, and although there are some advantages to these tools, there are inherent limitations in the style and amount of content of such journal entries.

When determining which journal-writing tool is most efficient, it is important to consider the circumstance, your technical skills, and the possible outcome of the journal entry. A handwritten journal can be more versatile for quick journal entries or "reflections-in-action" because it can be used more inconspicuously and with more flexibility. The computer journal may be a better choice when journal writing can occur in the office, school, home, or a café.

The Aesthetics of Journal Writing

Journal writing can be accomplished with a handgrip on a pen to create strokes on paper, or by tapping keys on a keyboard. Either way, ideas and reflections can be recorded, but handwriting and sketches as attributes of journal writing are compromised when using the computer. The computer keyboard does not allow for spontaneous and playful construction of words on the page, sketches, asides, and doodles that can collectively contribute to a personal journal aesthetic. The journal pages of contemporary artist Guillermo Del Toro (2008), who directed films such as *Pans Labyrinth,* and journal writer Anne Frank (van der Rol & Verhoeven, 1993) aptly illustrate the unique characteristics of using a pen or pencil to create handwritten, stylized text and imagery. The pages of Anne Frank's journal are uniquely constructed, consisting of handwritten entries often surrounded by sketches and side notes, suggesting time devoted to thought and intimacy with the journal pages. Creative and artistic aspects of her personality that are embedded in her design would not have been so easily translated had she used a computer, where the personal style and character of the writer can only be interpreted through the typed text.

This comparison of handwritten and typed journal writing demonstrates the differences that extend beyond the mode of writing to the environment in which the writer is working. Certainly, journal writing can be accomplished on the computer or in the blank pages of a bound book, but understanding the differences inherent in each is important when selecting your journal-writing tool.

Incorporating the Computer Into Classroom Journal-Writing Assignments

Typewritten and handwritten journals allow for valuable but different journal-writing experiences for students. This section explores some specific ways journal-writing assignments can be incorporated in the classroom using a computer. We look at how journal entries typed on the computer can be an alternative to a handwritten journal. In the following section, we elaborate on using the Internet to extend the journal-writing assignments to a broader audience.

Even if you choose to have students keep handwritten journals, when planning to include journal writing as a class assignment, it is important to think about the option of typing journals on the computer. This is recommended because inevitably at least one student will be interested in using the computer. Thinking about these options ahead of time will help you decide whether to allow handwritten or typed journal entries or both. In addition, it will help you be aware of what students need to know when using the computer to create and maintain journal entries. The following are points to consider when incorporating journal-writing assignments in the classroom:

- What are your student learning objectives for using the computer for journal entries? (learning, review, reflection, observations, and so on)
- What journal-writing techniques (e.g., freewriting, reading responses, reflection, dialogue, field notes, log) and other classroom experiences (e.g., field trips, group work, and so on) help you accomplish your objectives?
- What is your classroom environment (face-to-face, small groups, large lecture hall, online)?
- What are your own experiences and preferences in using a computer?
- What are the computer skill levels of your students?
- How will the computer journal be graded or reviewed?
- In what ways can the attributes of journal writing be incorporated in the computer journal?

Objectives and Activities for Journal Writing

Journal-writing techniques and classroom activities can help you reach certain course objectives. Journal techniques such as reading reflections, dialogues, logs, or narratives can easily be accomplished on the computer or in the handwritten journal. The unstructured environment of the handwritten journal is most effective for classroom assignments that include drawings, diagrams, artifacts, or field and observation notes. On the computer it is possible to integrate text with photos, links to Websites, charts, and so on. Table 8.1 shows what types of journal-writing activities are best achieved with a handwritten journal and which are best achieved with the computer journal. Obviously these lists are not exhaustive, but are meant to suggest that some activities may be more suited to one or both mediums. As an instructor you will have to decide which medium fits your instructional objectives.

Table 8.1
Activities Suited to Handwritten and Typed Journals

Handwritten	Typed or Handwritten	Typed
Field notes	Narrative stories	Team e-mails
On-site or spontaneous	Freewriting	(see Laura's case in chapter 9)
observations	Dialogues	Blogs
Combining text reflections with	Lists and logs	Online course programs like
graphics, diagrams, and artifacts	Reading reflections	Blackboard or Web CT
Reflection during experience	Reflection-on-action	
	Metareflections	

Classroom Environment

Journal writing for students can take place during class or outside of the classroom. Journal-writing assignments specifically for the computer can be useful when the instructor has limited contact with students, such as in large lecture halls, for online classes, or during fieldwork. The Internet makes it possible to share journal entries easily and efficiently with the instructor, or with part or all of the class. Regular reflections can be submitted through e-mail or an online learning management system such as Blackboard, or through blogs. When allowing students to use their computers for in-class journal writing, be aware that typing journal entries during class might interfere with the concentration and thought processes of classmates. It is also tempting for students to multitask, tune out, and surf the Internet if their laptop is sitting in front of them in class and wireless service is available.

Experience and Preferences of the Instructor

In addition to the nature of the assignment and the classroom environment, the instructor's experiences with journal writing and personal biases regarding computers can have an influence on the assignment. If the instructor feels that some students will be more inclined to write their journal entries on the computer, allowing either mode as an option for students is a good place to start. Freedom of choice in classroom assignments is one of the important factors to consider in sustaining motivation and engagement in students (Flowerday & Schraw, 2003). If you give students a choice, students may choose to combine typed and handwritten journal entries. Joanne's students sometimes write handwritten entries in class and computer entries at home. Once you explore and understand the various aspects of journal writing and have clarified your goals, you may give students a choice to use their preferred method, or to limit the assignment to either handwritten or typed journal entries. Experience and experimentation with journal writing is key to developing your preferences for journal-writing methods and tools.

Assessing the Computer Skill Levels of Students

Some students will choose to use the word processor for journal writing because they are competent and literate with computers and it is their preferred writing tool. Other students may choose to use the word processor because they would rather not write in a journal, but they may lack the skills or knowledge to use the computer well enough to be successful in developing journal-writing habits. Others may be more physically comfortable with a keyboard rather than a pen or pencil. To effectively use a computer for long-term journal writing, it is important for students to understand:

- How to create, manipulate, and organize multiple file folders on the desktop with different titles such as personal reflection, Psych 101, cohort meetings, school observations, and so on.
- How to use various tools from the tool bar and formatting palette to manipulate and highlight the text; add boxes and diagrams; and make bubbles for concept maps or tables for logs, dates, and text. If students are not aware of how to access the different tools in word processing software, there may be limited variability in the typed journals, and a learning curve that could hamper their journal-writing experience. Learning these steps may require some extra time and instruction.

Many colleges and universities now have computer labs or require the purchase of a laptop when beginning college. It is more and more likely that students have computer skills that exceed that of the instructor, in which case, these students could provide creative examples of computer journal writing to the class and perhaps assist struggling students. Faculty should consider the classroom environment, personal readiness, student skills, and student access to computers when planning instruction.

Grading and Reviewing Typed Journals

Providing the option of typed or handwritten journals in class assignments results in different products for grading. You will get some that are typed and stapled together or e-mailed, and others will be written in a bound book. Handwritten journals may contain random and juxtaposed text with handwriting that is sometimes difficult to decipher. The typed journal may appear and read more like a traditional school assignment with formatted and typed text, but may also contain some random and incomplete thoughts and imperfect conventions.

The same grading strategies suggested in chapter 6 for handwritten journals can be applied to typed journals, such as the use of rubrics or a check-off system. Criteria could also include evidence of using word processing software tools such as tables to organize and log journal entries to support journal-writing practices. Be aware that in a typed journal it is more difficult to tell if students did the journal-writing assignment all at once or right before the due date. Of course, these quickly conceived and generally unreflective entries defeat some of the basic reasons for journal writing. If journal writing is done using blogs or systems like Web CT or Blackboard, the date and time of submissions is tracked, and students are accountable for making entries by certain due dates.

Incorporating Journal-Writing Attributes Into Typed Entries

The attributes of journal writing can be incorporated into basic word processing skills. Table 8.2 outlines the various attributes of journal writing, their function, and how they can be easily incorporated on the computer.

Finally, it is important to note that neither the typed nor handwritten journals guarantee critical examination of readings, deep reflection, or transformative learning, which are the potentially powerful outcomes of reflective writing in journals. Therefore, it is still important to follow the guidelines presented earlier for introducing and structuring the classroom journal, as well as clarifying expectations and providing feedback to ensure active engagement and student learning.

Using Blogs and the Internet to Facilitate Classroom Journal Writing

The handwritten journal and word processor are two environments in which the writer can openly and deeply examine their experiences and explore perspectives *in private*.

Whereas private journal entries from either process can be shared with classmates or colleagues, the computer environment can connect the user to larger audiences using the Internet. E-mail, blogs, and social networking Websites allow thoughts, experiences,

Table 8.2

Six Key Attributes of Journal Writing Adapted to Typed Journal Entries

Attributes of a Journal	Function of Attribute	Suggested Adaptations for Typed Journal Entries
Written	Journal writing consists of words on a page related to thoughts and reflections of past and future events.	Differentiate between journal writing and other types of writing related to school, work, and personal documents. Keep the computer journal separate from other written documents and in a location on the desktop that is readily accessible.
Dated Entries	Dated entries allow the journal writer to chart and compare perceptions and learning over time and help keep track of meetings, conversations, and professional contacts.	Date each entry at the top of the page or use tables such as this one to organize and label entries by date and topic. Create a separate table of contents page for particular journal folders to include dates and content.
Informal	Students are free from rules and conventions related to writing so as to not inhibit the flow of ideas.	Reassure students they will not be evaluated on conventions. In fact, encourage them to save documents without editing or deleting entries. Introduce "floating" ideas, in which sentences and words can exist separately from a body of text using drawing tool boxes or tables.
Flexibility of Expression	Allows for variations in style, use, and form.	Review with students systems for organizing and storing journal entries (e.g., integrate tool bar options, tables, combined archives, and text). Encourage variation in style (italics, bold, underline, colors). Explore a variety of computer software and online options (blogs, e-mail, outlines, lists, a mix of journal-writing techniques and tools).
Private	Journal writing is a reflection on experience and a process for exploring ideas and biases that is best done in private.	Reinforce that the journal is for personal growth and reflection and sharing is optional or negotiated. Demonstrate how journal writing can prepare for dialogue or expression in class or with a broader audience on the Internet.
Archival	The life of the journal keeper can be chronicled and saved.	Highlight or color key words so ideas and entries are easier to locate. Use columns to create a river of information and a bank as described in chapter 7. Create individual documents with titles and store in a titled folder. Create folders that are titled by classes taught, participation in committees, books and journals, faculty meetings, etc. Avoid editing and erasing past journal entries. Journal entries can be saved on a CD.

and ideas to be shared. They also allow students and professionals to retrieve and integrate information, and engage in dialogue around a subject or topic in new and different ways. We will explore how blogs and the Internet can contribute to thinking and learning for students and faculty, and enhance journal-writing practices.

Definition of a Blog

The term *blog* is shortened from the term *weblog*, which is derived from its function as a simplified Website and a log of information, text, and images created and maintained by an individual for personal or public use. A blog is a type of online diary of single entries in reverse chronological order. Since the advent of blogs in the late 1990s, many thousands of computer users have used blogs to write short reflective narratives and share news and personal stories. The surge in blogs is due in part to Websites such as Blogger (http://www.blogger.com), which allows anyone to create a blog for free and without the need for high-level technical skills or programming knowledge (Blood, 2002).

Many blogs are written and maintained by experts and many others to share experiences, thoughts, and feelings related to politics, travel, hobbies, or personal life (Martindale & Wiley, 2005). Blogs can be personalized through options that allow the blog author to choose different layouts; invite open comments from the public or a selected audience; and integrate pictures, video, and links to Internet web pages and articles for others to view. Blogs have been credited with contributing to the resurgence in journal writing (Kajder & Bull, 2004). Although blogs are often referred to as online journals, they are very different from private handwritten or typed journals.

Similarities and Differences Between Blogs and Journals

Blogs are considered a type of public journal because they share some of the same features as private handwritten or typed journals. Blogs contain the ideas, thoughts, expressions, and opinions of the author in a format that is dated and archived. In addition, a collection of blog posts has the potential to reveal changes in the learning, thinking, and perspective of the writer over time. A primary difference between a blog and a journal is that blog entries are written for a public audience. The function of a blog is to start or add to a conversation and communicate with others. As a result, blogs may not be as conducive to exploring random thoughts, ideas, biases, and assumptions as freely and uncritically as in a private journal.

Another feature of a blog that differentiates it from a private journal is the option of accessing and integrating information from the Internet. Blogs allow the author to extend a search outward to a broader network of information, people, and perspectives, and incorporate selected links into the construction of a blog post. Although exploring and integrating Internet searches can be informative and interesting, this activity can also lead the writer away from the blog journal entry and out of the moment. In contrast to the private journal, in which writers are typically alone with their thoughts and the page, bloggers are easily connected to alternate activities.

Using Blogs to Foster Reflection

The objective of journal writing is to create continuity between experience, reflection, and learning. In chapter 3, informational and transformational learning are introduced as two types of learning, linked by reflection. Experience without reflection is not sufficient to foster personal growth (Dewey, 1933). In blogs, the author has access to information and the potential for reflection, but as with a handwritten journal, learning to reflect requires some facilitation (Black, Sileo, & Prater, 2000).

Blogs have been effectively used in higher education to enhance the quality of reflection in students working toward their teaching licenses (Kaplan, Rupley, Sparks, & Holcomb, 2007; Kuzu, 2007), to support and enhance learning a foreign language and aspects of different cultures (Ducate & Lomicka, 2008; Wassell & Crouch, 2008), and to elicit discussions and guide research in doctoral leadership studies (Martindale & Wiley, 2005). Blogs allow time and space for dialogue among students and with a broader community, which has contributed to more class participation, opportunities for reflection, and enhanced group identity among classmates (Kuzu, 2007; Wang & Fang, 2005). However, two features of a blog considered essential for fostering quality reflections are (1) the facilitation of community among students and (2) feedback from students and the professor.

Stiler and Philleo (2003) introduced blogs instead of handwritten journals to graduate students in education to foster reflection. Their research showed that many of the blog posts shared among classmates contained more analytical entries than existed in handwritten journals from past classes. However, the research also found that students were less inclined to write blog posts about sensitive or controversial topics, and more than half the students in the study reported being unsatisfied using the blog as a journal because of technological hurdles and loss of anonymity. To remediate discomfort with sensitive content and technological issues, and to guide quality reflections, frequent and regular feedback from the instructor is recommended. Another study showed that feedback from a small group of peers rather than the entire class and the instructor can foster more thoughtful and open reflections because students don't feel they are being judged (Kaplan, Rupley, & Holcomb, 2007).

These studies illustrate the contribution that the combination of social interaction and journal writing can have on the development of quality reflection among students, and how a fear of writing, sensitive topics, and lack of confidence with technology can inhibit journal writing and reflection when using blogs. Offering the option of handwritten journals and sharing in small or large groups can ensure that all students have an opportunity to participate in journal-writing practices. Using a written journal for personal reflection and a class blog for synthesizing those reflections could combine the best elements of both media types.

Blog Communities

Higher-level critical thinking is stimulated by social interaction and interconnectedness (Vygotsky, 1978). Chapter 3 introduced Baxter Magolda's (2001) theory on peer partnering, in which shared writings can enhance the process of self-authorship and critical reflection. Students are often more motivated to engage in journal writing when they know it will be shared with peers because it creates reasons for participating other than for a grade (Kaplan et al., 2007). Sharing journal entries with peers can contribute to reflection and learning (Black et al., 2000), and can be done through open dialogue or online with e-mails or blogs. Blogs extend the conversation with and about the self through public discourse, and can be a place to present or perform what develops out of private journal writing. In addition, blogs might improve writing skills by giving students the opportunity to view the writing and reflections of other more skilled writers (MacLeod, 1999). Blog Websites such as Edublog (http://www.edublogs.org) can facilitate community, learning, and reflection among a select group of students. Other options for creating community and discussions among students include e-mail listservs or proprietary course management systems like Blackboard or Web CT, although many report them to be less accessible and more difficult to navigate than a standard blog (Martindale & Wiley, 2005).

Feedback on Blogs

Feedback on journal entries contributes to metaphoric reflections because unexpected connections and social interaction add new perspectives. One feature of blogs is the comment option, which is activated or deactivated by the author of the blog. The comment feature allows anyone to respond to blog posts. Instructors can use the comment option for questioning to elicit more reflective thinking.

After making field observations in schools, an education student might write about middle school children who talk to each other during instruction and don't seem interested in learning. You might reply with questions such as, "What do you remember about your schooling and how students behaved during a teacher's instruction? How is this different from what you are experiencing now? What do you look for in students to determine that they are interested and ready to learn?" These questions help the student think more deeply about how past experiences might influence expectations, and about how he or she can evaluate these interpretations and expectations of student behaviors.

Peer feedback might focus on problem solving and include questions that relate to what is learned in class about classroom management, or what they have seen or done that is effective. Despite the research that shows the benefits of peer feedback, research also shows that many students, unless required, are reluctant to give feedback to peers (Ellison & Wu, 2008; Lu & Bol, 2007; Yukawa, 2006). You can require that students post a minimum number of comments on peer blogs, or break students into smaller collaborative groups to help those who are shy about writing public comments feel more comfortable.

Using Blogs to Support Learning for Students and Faculty

As mentioned, much blog software makes it easy to include pictures and video, and incorporate links to Websites and research. Faculty can use these features to extend teaching and learning. Glass and Spiegelman (2008) found that incorporating blogs in the class syllabus or instruction can extend student learning, connect students with the content, and enhance community in the classroom, in addition to orienting students to the practical uses of technology.

Dr. Michael Flower, a biologist and professor of Interdisciplinary Science Studies at a state university, uses blogs as an organizational tool for his undergraduate university studies classes (personal communication, May 9, 2008). He posts the syllabus, assignment descriptions, and an overview of what will be discussed in class on his blog at least 2 days prior to class. During class he takes digital pictures of drawings, diagrams, and findings that have been captured on the white board and imports these as images to the blog. With access to the Internet, students can review what emerged in class discussions. These course content reviews can be helpful for students when studying, for clarifying lecture points, or for retrieving content when absent.

Dr. Flower has found that creating and maintaining blogs for students has contributed to his own professional growth because it connects him with research and discussions outside of the academy. Online learning and research using blogs can lead faculty to connections with other professionals engaged in particular areas of study, and can contribute to scholarship (Martindale & Wiley, 2005; McLeod, 2007). Educator blogs, those written by educators about education (Online Education Database, 2008), are on the rise. However, many professors in higher education reportedly don't blog because of time pressures and because they are not familiar with blogging (McLeod, 2007). Indeed, becoming familiar with blogs, exploring topics through blogs, and creating and maintaining blogs takes both time and consistent effort.

Assignment of Blogs

When incorporating the use of blogs in the classroom, sufficient time and guidance is needed for students to explore how to create a blog before actual posting and journal writing begins. The learning curve with blogs varies among students in a class, depending on their experience. Students should be comfortable with the technical aspects of blogs before they begin to engage in reflective thinking and journal-writing practices for public view. It is recommended that students read multiple blog posts and experiment with the links and comments features prior to writing a blog themselves as a class assignment (Ducate & Lomicka, 2008). Although an increasing number of students are entering colleges with computer skills, a digital divide still exists among students, and it cannot be assumed that all, or even most, students are computer literate or have regular access to the Internet (Trotter, 2007). Instructors considering blogs as a journal assignment will need to be prepared to provide varying degrees of technical support.

Before guidance and technical feedback can be provided, instructors should first explore blogs themselves: Read multiple blog posts, create a blog, learn what makes a good blog post, and learn how to make comments on a blog (Blood, 2002). To foster reflection and critical thinking, you can provide guiding questions and prompts related to course lectures, discussions, readings, and research, which can direct discussions and provide a framework or structure for students when blogging.

Assessment of Blogs

Student blogs should maintain a level of formality and academic rigor, but should also be a safe place to express thoughts and experiences. Blog entries can be graded on content, quality of reflection, or participation, but should not be graded on writing conventions. The number of blog posts required can vary based on the type of assignment. It is important to remember that too much emphasis or demand on class blogging can cause "blog burnout," resulting in hurried and mundane blog posts or comments by the students, as well as hours of monitoring blog posts and comments for the professor (Dawson, 2007; Kolar & Dickson, 2002). Dawson suggests that faculty provide options in addition to blogs for demonstrating knowledge and understanding, and find ways of accommodating those students with different learning styles. Not all students are comfortable with blogs or the Internet, and the focus should be on the learning objective of the class without too much dependence on technology. Dawson (2007) encourages professors to include students in the discussion of the expectations for the blog assignment. Negotiating outcomes with the students will help you maintain reasonable expectations as well as determine the level of interest, feasible workload, and needed support.

A Note on Privacy in Blogs

Although blogs are typically created for public view, many can be made relatively private by selecting a preference, which indicates the choice to not be indexed by Google; this makes it very unlikely that the public will stumble on the blog when on the Internet. Some blog software has the option of password protection. In this circumstance, the exact web address can be shared with a select group and the blog cannot be accessed without knowing the password or logging in. It is important to recognize that there is always a risk when putting content and opinions on the Internet. Authors can change what is written on their own blogs at any time; however, there is a permanence that exists because blog posts can be printed, copied, or cached. Students should not divulge personal issues in blogs used as part of a higher education curriculum. Self-censorship of personal views and perspectives in blogs is recommended, particularly among professionals in the field of education (Read, 2006).

In summary, blogs afford users certain flexible alternatives to traditional journal-writing methods. Individuals considering blogs or similar online journal-writing activities should take the time to review the goals of the journal-writing exercise to ensure that the technology is suited to the activities planned. In addition, information, perspectives, and connections can be gleaned from public blogs, then processed and reflected upon in private journals. In this way, blogs in conjunction with private journals have the potential to extend and enrich learning for students, faculty, and administrators in higher education.

Conclusion

The exercise of learning through self-examination, by exploring our private thoughts about life, is a fundamental element of journal writing. This chapter explores how journal writing can be effectively accomplished using word processing software and the Internet. Typed and handwritten journals are inherently different in their structure, organization, and use. Yet both can be used by students and professionals to engage in reflective thinking and self-expression.

Advances in Internet and computer technology allow for new and different experiences and social interactions, as well as alternative journal-writing tools and methods. As technology changes and evolves, it will continue to influence how we document, share, and reflect on experiences. However, what is most important is that writing supports thinking, and that private time be created without distraction to reflect both in the moment and on past experiences. Without the creation of this time and space, "we cease knowing how to be fully present, or how to give our wholly undivided attention to one matter" (Kabat-Zinn, 2005, p. 157).

So, what do professionals, administrators, or students in higher education keep with them to be prepared for different types of journal writing? The answer is to always be prepared with a journal book, a laptop, or both. Whatever the tool, it is the practice of ongoing reflection that is essential to personal and professional growth and learning.

Part Three

A COLLECTION OF CASE STUDIES
Teaching With Journals and Keeping Journals in Professional Life

9 Case Studies: Teaching With Journals

- Case 1: Dance—Reflection on Movement
- Case 2: Architecture—Ways of Seeing
- Case 3: Food Chemistry—Learning Logs
- Case 4: International Studies—Field Journal
- Case 5: English—Teaching Poetry
- Case 6: English—Team E-Mails
- Case 7: Nursing Education—Reflection on Clinical Settings
- Case 8: Community Health—Using Metaphors
- Case 9: Service Learning—Using Student Feedback
- Case 10: Biology—Observing the Natural World

10 Case Studies: Journal Keeping in Professional Life

- Case 1: A Department Chair in Engineering
- Case 2: A Professor of International Studies
- Case 3: A Professor of Teacher Education
- Case 4: A Doctoral Student
- Case 5: A Professor of Integrated Studies

- Case 6: A Director of a Research Unit
- Case 7: An Associate Dean
- Case 8: A Community-College Board Member
- Case 9: A Retiring Dean

9

CASE STUDIES:
TEACHING WITH JOURNALS

In this section of the book we present two chapters with cases. Chapter 9 contains cases of 10 faculty who use journals in their classrooms and chapter 10 contains cases of 9 higher education faculty, graduate students, and administrators who use journals in their professional lives. Because these cases are derived from interviews and depict the stories of journal use by individual faculty, they offer details that are missing from the standard research format. They use what Clandinin and Connelly describe as "personal practical knowledge" (1998, p. 150), knowledge that is embedded in practice, or what Brookfield (1990) would call *theory in use* rather than *espoused theory.*

The cases in this chapter are from faculty who have been using journals in teaching for many years. These are not novices who are just trying journals for the first time, but veterans who have worked out the bumps and scrapes of journal use in the classroom and fine-tuned their effectiveness to match their particular curricular needs. Each of these faculty members was asked a similar set of questions about their teaching practices in recorded interviews (Stevens, Cooper, & Lasater, 2006). They were asked about their learning goals, their assignments, and their grading procedures. In addition, they were asked about what the practice of assigning journals has taught them about teaching and learning, as well as what effect it has had on their students.

There is much to learn from these examples. First, they exemplify the flexibility of journal use. They show you how the journal can be shaped to fit the learning needs of dancers, administrators, chemists, architects, nurses, teachers, and international studies

185

students who travel to far off countries. Second, they help the ideas presented earlier in this book to come alive. With these concrete examples, you can find your way to the particulars of your own classroom needs. These cases present a rich array of possibilities for teaching, as well as a wide variety of methods for assessing students' writing. Finally, these cases contain the wisdom of seasoned teachers, faculty who know the pain of lessons gone awry and who have worked out some of the problems you may encounter, leaving you with creative solutions to ponder.

Consider these cases as gifts from the faculty who have so generously shared their experiences with us. We gladly pass their experience on to you, knowing that many of you may already be using journals in creative ways, but may welcome the ideas of fellow travelers in the pedagogical world. In *The Skillful Teacher* (2006) Stephen Brookfield compares teaching to white-water rafting. One minute you are up, exuberant, and triumphant; the next you are awash in the fear and disappointment of a lesson gone terribly wrong, wondering why you ever became a faculty member in the first place. These cases present the wisdom of others who have braved the rapids of the classroom and come through with some thoughts to share. It is our hope that they can lead you to new encounters in learning with your students, new ways to understand their learning journeys, and fresh insights into their confusions and frustrations as learners. Please send us your experiences with these techniques, your questions, and your successes. With your permission, we will gladly share them with others. We have a Website, www.journalkeeping.com, designed for faculty to upload the stories of their experiences using journals.

Table 9.1 is a quick reference list of the cases in this chapter.

Case 1: Dance—Reflection on Movement

Gregg is department chair for the dance program at a large public research university. He has used journals in many of his dance classes over the past 20 years, from the time he first started teaching.

He shares that journal writing helps his students learn how they observe movement, as well as different ways of looking at movement. In essence, the students are learning a different language. The journal and the regular use of dance language in the journal serve as additional entry points into the discipline. The physical effort of writing and expressing one's thoughts using a discipline's constructs appears to be

Table 9.1
Teaching With Journals by Discipline, Courses, and Unique Journal Uses

Case Number/Name	Discipline	Course Title	Unique Journal Uses
#1 Gregg	Dance	Bartenieff Movement Fundamentals & Laban Movement Analysis	Reflection on movement Learning and practicing the use of key dance vocabulary
#2 Rudy	Architecture	Introduction to Architecture, and Seminar: Architecture in Barcelona	Document ways of seeing Journal formatting Upper & lower division
#3 Miguel	Food Chemistry	Experimental Foods	Content learning log Values and vision for entering freshman students
#4 Kofi	Black Studies/ International Studies	Seminar: Field study in Ghana	Field journals in international settings
#5 Jane	English	Introduction to Poetry	Teaching poetry with journals
#6 Laura	English	Freshman English composition	Using team e-mails
#7 A. N.	Nursing	Senior seminar in hospital clinical setting	Reflection on complex clinical settings
#8 Isabelle	Community Health	Freshman seminar in community clinical office	Using metaphors Understanding the perspectives of others
#9 Vicki	University Studies/Service Learning	Senior Capstone class in University Studies	Using student feedback from journals to shape direction of course
#10 Anna	Biology	Developmental Biology Botany Biology of Women	Observing the natural world Keeping a body journal Writing from prompts Drawing from life

beneficial for students. As students become comfortable using new words and phrases to express their thoughts, the frequent use of this new vocabulary and phrases may produce a shift in how they see and understand dance. Students can also become immersed in the discipline through the use of this new vocabulary. Their journals can contain more than written narrative entries. They can contain poems, include pictures, photos, drawings, and other means of communication for students to express themselves. Students should have a sense of ownership, a sense that whatever is included in the journal "is mine." The dance journal is to be used only for Gregg's class. It is not to contain homework assignments from other classes or other information unrelated to the dance class or the dance journal.

Gregg uses journals as another lens by which to view and assess his students. The course requires students to write in their journal on a regular basis. Gregg collects about eight journals at a time, two to three times per semester. He states, "I try to look at each [journal] individually. It's not like I'm trying to hold them to one particular standard. But I try to see how they see the class and I try to augment this with my comments." Journals are a good way for Gregg to get to know the students and to have a sense of how to personalize his teaching to meet the individual student's learning needs. He reads everything in the journal and writes individual suggestions into the student's journal. As an educator, the journals allow him to see how his students may be approaching the material in an entirely different way than he had planned. This insight allows him to determine other ways to present the material.

Using journals in his classes seems to be successful. Gregg says, "You've got to inundate yourself with everything possible, if you want to really learn . . . and [journal keeping] is just another tool to use."

Case Two: Architecture—Ways of Seeing

Rudy is a professor in the Architecture department of a large public university, where he has been for 15 years. He is currently serving as chair of a five-person department. He uses journals in two of his courses: a 100-level course entitled Introduction to Architecture and a 300-level summer course that involves traveling to Barcelona to study.

The introductory course usually has about 140 students, both majors and non-majors, who are all required to keep a journal of their observations of architectural elements throughout the city. Their sketchbooks or journals (they make no distinction here) should contain drawings, as well as reflections and analysis of what they have drawn. Rudy encourages students to purchase a spiral-bound book of some sort and to start anywhere in their book. He tells them not to be chronological to reduce their anxiety and "the terror of the white page." His aim is to increase their observation skills, and the journal can include records of things such as a walk through their neighborhood. He wants students to combine sketching with narrative comments and to understand that these exercises are "not about making art." They should use their journals to help them think and to remember what they've seen. It is easier to remember if they draw it. He says many of today's students are "camera happy" and tend to snap digital photos when he wants them to draw and write about what they are seeing.

Rudy uses a rubric (see Table 6.1) to give beginning architecture students a general idea of how their notebooks will be evaluated. He describes an "A" journal, a "C" journal, and an "F" journal. The journal is about 20% of the grade. Rudy tries to indicate what he wants students to do and not do. He has a set of mandatory exercises and another list of recommended activities, and he tells the students that three to four pages a week is satisfactory. He doesn't grade artistic ability because he believes that is unfair. He also keeps a journal along with his students, because he believes that it is helpful for him to do the assignments with the students.

During the term he conducts two progress checks, in which he does not grade the journal but uses sticky notes to give feedback. He says students are conditioned to want a grade, but he tends to assess the pace of the journal keeping rather than the quality because he believes the assignment is more about a "journey, not a destination." The journal tells him about the level of engagement that the student has with the class. He has teaching assistants read the journals first and make comments, and then he reads them. On the issue of time, Rudy says, "Students need and deserve feedback but it takes a lot of time" to grade 140 journals. He hopes to limit the class to 80 students next year.

Students' responses to having to keep a journal are "all over the map," according to Rudy. Some respond with, "Oh no, it's another journal." The more engaged students find it helpful. He says, "I've gotten over the depression about lack of performance." He tries to deal with students' initial resistance in several ways. To overcome their "inertia and anxiety" he shows them unfinished work, sometimes sharing his 5-year-old son's journals. He has them do a sketch and then rip it out of their journal and throw it away in order to illustrate that the work is not something precious. It is a tool to further understanding. He tells students, "If you can't draw, start out by writing and making lists." He wants students to reflect on the mundane as well as the monumental.

Over the years he has learned to acknowledge the students who succeed with journal keeping. He talked about a student that he actively discouraged from taking the class because he was legally blind and the field of architecture is so visual. But the student persisted, was interested, and engaged. He "took the time to understand the material" and created one of the most "interesting and compelling" journals Rudy has seen. If students wander into personal issues, he asks them to turn the corner of the page down and he does not read that page.

When asked what he would change about the way he uses journals in his teaching, Rudy says he wishes he didn't have to grade them. He has the same problem in the studio, "having to calibrate different levels of performance." He believes that the journals are about learning and reflection and that assigning journals "puts students in an arena of constant reflection and helps them to be more critically aware of their world." Using journals has also helped him to become a better coach. He believes that the process "is not about just looking, but about seeing"; journals are a path, "a place where you talk to yourself" about what you are seeing.

Case 3: Food Chemistry—Learning Logs

Miguel is a professor of food science with a specialty in food chemistry. He has been teaching for 30 years, has served as an associate dean in his college, and has served as an interim vice chancellor for the university.

About 15 years ago he began to ask himself how he might make a difference in the classroom before he retired, ". . . and that's when I started to get involved in trying to develop students." Around that time the Secretary's Commission on Achieving Necessary Skills (SCANS) report was issued by the U.S. Department of Labor, which encouraged the infusion of skills such as critical thinking, working with others, resolving conflict, and values education into the college curriculum. He began to reformulate his classes to help students develop as whole individuals. Miguel focused on student development, using food chemistry to help develop specific skills identified by employers as important.

He used a book entitled *Be a Kid Again* (Sneath, 2001), which emphasized the development of values and vision through intensive writing. Students questioned his assignments, asking, "Why are we doing this? It doesn't have anything to do with food science," to which Miguel replied, "No, but it has everything to do with your life!"

As part of his class requirements he has students write two journal entries a week; one entry is on values and vision and another on the technical content of the course. He uses a rubric to grade the journals. He doesn't grade on grammar or spelling, but is much more interested in having his students think and write. By the end of the semester his students have examined their values and report that they have learned so much in the course about foods as well as their own values, and about themselves. The journals written at the end of the semester often reflect the growth and development of students' thinking, as they sort through "where they were off-base and why." He reports that most of the students also "felt very comfortable about writing by the end of the semester and could do it in half the time it took them at the beginning of the semester."

Miguel requires that students' journals be typed and turned in every Monday morning. Students must follow a rubric that requires them to give examples and reasons for the statements that they make. The journals they write total about four typed pages per week. In the last few years he has enlisted undergraduate teaching assistants (TAs) to read the journals and make comments before he makes additional comments. The TAs are always students who have previously taken the course and so are very familiar with the journal process and the kinds of comments to make. The TAs receive "Directed Reading and Research" credits for their efforts and they enjoy seeing teaching, learning, curriculum development, and grading from an instructor's perspective. The TAs write their comments on the typed pages. Typical comments include "What is your main point?" "You don't have any examples," or "Are there any counter examples?" and so on. Previous to that, Miguel read all the journal entries himself. He states, "The most important thing to me about requiring journals is if you put a lot of time into reading and commenting on their writing, the students feel that what they say is important and subsequently put considerable time and effort into writing about their perspectives."

"The students report that writing journals reflecting on human values and on the technical content of the class really helps them to clarify their thinking on these topics. Sometimes the students write back to me the next week and say, 'I disagree with you,' and then I think OK, this is great, we have a dialogue going on here." Miguel believes it is important for the students to have immediate feedback. "I think if you have students write and you collect their entries every 2 or 3 weeks, it's not as effective. They receive a grade for their journals every week, although the first 2 weeks are grade-free until they get a sense of what is expected of them."

Miguel strongly feels that having students write about different human values is worthwhile. For example, he says that, after reading the chapter in their textbook entitled "Keep Trying," students sometimes write about how they gave up on something. They write in their journal, "You know, I really should try harder," and Miguel says, "Sometimes I do notice a major change in their work ethic, the quality of their written work, or their attitude. . . . They start thinking about issues in a different way and even make major changes to the way they do things when they realize that their usual ways of doing things are not that effective."

At the end of the semester he asks students to compile all their journal entries and write an evaluation of the worth of the journals to them. He says, "That's when it all comes out." "Students become very honest and tell you how they hated journaling at the beginning of the semester and that they just went through the motion of writing something because it was a requirement." However, for many of the students there is a change in attitude toward the middle of the semester as they realize how writing seriously about "passion," "time management," or not getting along with members of their group can be very helpful in understanding the "why" of their positions on various issues. Miguel states, "It's what we all become teachers for . . . to know that you made a difference. And that's what I was trying to do when I changed my philosophical approach to teaching." He has published an article describing his approach in the *Journal of Food Science Education* (Iwaoka & Crosetti, 2008).

His colleagues feel that he makes the students do too much work. "You know," he states, "you find out you can get students to work really hard and not complain endlessly if they find the work to be meaningful and beneficial to them. They say they spend 50% of their time on my course during the fall semester and yet because of what they get from it, most of the time I get good teaching evaluations." In fact, Miguel has won several teaching awards. His students who go on to medical school report that his classroom processes are very similar to problem-based learning, so they feel comfortable with that format when they encounter it in medical school.

The students' journals have become a valuable resource to Miguel when he is asked to write a recommendation for a student. He asks to see their journals and will often quote from their journals in his reference letters, restating what the student said they learned, what they felt about integrity or honesty, and so on. "So," he says to his students, "if you want any recommendations from me, you need to keep your journal."

Miguel feels that using journals in his classes has taught him the value of letting the students do the work. "Whenever we 'teach' or 'lecture,'" he states, "we do all the work. We condense the material; we summarize it; we present it to them. If we do all that for them, we learn the most. They should be doing that. We take away a lot from the students when we do the work for them. We need to let them compile, condense, and summarize the material, ask questions about the material and let them get muddled, confused, and . . . hopefully develop the skills of solving problems." He believes that through this process we will be developing better critical thinkers, problem solvers, and hopefully better employees and citizens.

Case 4: International Studies—Field Journal

Kofi has been teaching in higher education for 31 years in the United States, Ghana, and Jamaica. He currently holds a joint appointment in Black Studies and International Studies at a public university. Kofi uses journals in his capstone course in International Studies, which involves a 4-week field project in Africa. The students begin their journal before they leave the country. The journal includes logistical information, lecture notes, immunization records, and passport information, as well as library materials, contact information for people they interview in the field, and photos related to the students' projects. These journals are checked while they are in the field, turned in 2 weeks after students return, and are graded on completeness, on their initiative (the inclusion of supplemental library information), and on presentation (the way the journal is written—in outline form or complete sentences). The journal constitutes 20% of the student's grade.

Kofi reads each student's entire journal and writes comments on a separate sheet of paper. He gives students a lot of freedom to create a journal style that works for them. He says, "They show their true selves if you give them freedom." In addition, he reads to assess the group dynamics in the field and to figure out what to do next time. "The journal often reveals how effectively students have used their time and how they are progressing on their research projects." He says to his students, "You are paying to learn something; you don't want to just sit on the beach." The journal also gives Kofi a sense of how students are experiencing and conducting their field study. He tells his students, "When you do an interview in the field, don't come back and ask me for phone numbers or directions. How can you interview somebody and not get the information you need?"

Kofi asks the students to number the pages of their journals ahead of time. This way, he ensures that they won't remove any pages they don't want him to see. He sometimes checks the journal after 2 weeks in the field, just to look at their numbered pages. He wants to learn about how they are thinking about their entire experience. He encourages students to keep their journals and reread them a year later. Some continue to keep a journal during the following year or years. His overall goal is that their journal be a record of their experience and their learning. "Sometimes," he says, "they think I'm a slave driver, but I tell them 'You won't enjoy the trip unless you are prepared and think about what you are experiencing.'"

Case 5: English—Teaching Poetry

Jane holds a Ph.D. in medieval literature. She has been teaching English composition at a community college for 20 years. During that time, she has honed her use of journals in the classroom and says that this technique, which she uses to teach poetry, is the culmination of all her years of using journals in writing and literature classes.

At the beginning of the term she has each student draw a number from a paper sack. Each number corresponds to a poem that they are then assigned for the rest of the term. She selects 30 poems that are not in any of their texts. Students are to write their final term paper analyzing this poem. Then, as the term progresses, Jane covers various topics such as metaphor, images, symbol, stanzas, and so on. Students are asked to write in their journals about these topics and how they pertain to their individual poems. They are required to produce several journal entries on each topic. What are the images in the poem? How does the poet use metaphor in the poem?

The journals are collected three times during the term, so that Jane can evaluate students' progress in applying the ideas in the course. She writes back to them in their journals, making suggestions if students are too superficial in their analyses, or guiding them to what they should look for in the poem. She holds individual conferences with each student twice during the term. They are to bring their journals to this meeting. She discusses whether the student is going in the right direction and encourages them with suggestions about what might lie ahead in the course. For example, she might say, "When we get to metaphor, you will find more ideas that apply to your poem."

At the end of the eighth week of the course, students are to turn in all journal entries and a final paper analyzing their assigned poem. In this paper they are to find one theme (the most important theme in the poem) and discuss how the poet developed it. This paper is 25% of their grade.

Jane states that the students often learn a great deal not only about poetry but about the poet's perspective on a particular topic. For example, she had a student who believed deeply in cutting forests for their lumber. He drew a poem by Gary Snyder about saving forests. He came to the professor in complaint and she reminded him that the drawing of the poem was perfectly random. By the end of the term, this student had learned to understand what Snyder was seeing, through his poetry. This provided the student with a new perspective on the long-standing battle between loggers and conservationists.

Jane believes one of the reasons this method works is that entries are tied directly to course content. Without a direct focus on course material, students tended to produce random chatter, writing in large script on small pieces of paper. Jane says, "Journals without direct focus on class material are a waste, except in women's literature in which the focus on women's lived experience allows for the effective use of more personal and autobiographical entries." Jane states that this is "the most successful use of journals I've ever had." She says this technique works so well that she would "do it again in a heartbeat."

Case 6: English—Team E-Mails

Laura is an associate professor of English and has used journals in her undergraduate and graduate English courses for the past 11 years. She often uses what she calls a "team e-mail" approach that she learned from a colleague. Earlier in her career, her students wrote individual journals for her classes. However, Laura found students often wrote too many entries the night before the journal was due; she wanted more interaction from the journals. There are two unique aspects to team e-mail journals. First is the use of e-mail technology or courseware like Web CT for students to stay in touch and communicate with each other. The second is the creation of small groups of students who are formed into teams. Team members interact with each other through the collaborative development of a team journal. Laura has turned away from using individual journals to the use of team journals because of their interactive value.

Laura groups five students together to form a team. Team members agree to trade e-mail addresses. The journal assignment requires the students to write something that is related to the class. At the first class meeting one student in the team must agree to start the e-mail journal by writing the first entry. The student sends his or her entry to all team members, and the next person's e-mail is sent to everyone in the group by selecting "Reply All." The entry is copied to Laura. Any one of the team members can respond to the first entry. It is very important that the students react to one another's comments in some way. She gives students a weekly deadline, such as getting their entries into the journal by noon each Friday.

Laura includes a statement in her syllabus saying that interactions online are governed by the university's Student Code of Conduct. She wants the students to know that it is inappropriate to forward things that someone has written within the context of the class without asking permission first. She believes team e-mail journals allow her to create and maintain manageable teacher–student boundaries. If Laura finds team e-mail journal entries inadequate, she tells the student. Typically team e-mail journals are 10% to 15% of the final course grade.

Laura writes out the first journal assignment. She reads everything the students write. She likes the reflective nature of journal writing and that journal writing allows students to develop a "writer's voice." This gives Laura the opportunity to share with students the different voices that each individual can present through writing. She does not routinely provide written feedback to the journals unless there is a point she wants to make or clarify. She tracks who is participating in the e-mail journal in her grade book. Sometimes she notices that a student "is missing" and will take the student aside to try to find out what is happening. She also schedules times during the semester when students don't have to post, unless they have missed entries and need the time to make up the work.

Laura believes the more you can get students to write, the better their writing will be. Journals provide more points of connection with students and broadens the audience for their reflective writing on class topics. Some teams continue their journaling beyond the end of the semester, a sure sign of their success in fostering more reflective students.

Case 7: Nursing Education—Reflection on Clinical Settings

A. N. teaches nursing students at a large public university. Her students are in their fourth and senior year of the nursing program, seeking the Registered Nurse license along with their bachelor of science degree. During the semester they write four reflective journal entries about their clinical study with an experienced registered nurse. A. N. does not see them face-to-face every day and depends on the electronic submission of journal entries to tell her what they are learning from the clinical setting.

At first A. N. gave students a lot of latitude for their journal entries. However, there was much variance in their response, from articulate and insightful to distant and technical. She was not persuaded that the latter entries demonstrated that the students were reflecting and learning. To "push them a bit, I decided I needed to structure the reflections and chose the Clinical Judgment Model [Tanner, 2006] that seeks to give us a common language in nursing to describe what we do and know in our clinical settings." She allows students to handwrite their reflections; however, most send them via e-mail. First they identify a specific incident from the previous week in the clinical setting, and then apply the Clinical Judgment Model to their interpretation and description of what happened, how they responded to the situation, and what they learned from it.

A. N. assigns journals "because they allow me to assess student thinking and I seek to heighten their awareness of clinical judgment in nursing care: noticing, interpreting, responding and reflecting. The Clinical Judgment Model is a rich way to explain what we do as nurses. I believe that this assignment helps them internalize these qualities." What is interesting to A. N. is that the students say that even though they have a lot of writing in the senior year, journal writing is worth the time because they learn much from their reflections. They say that the reflections add meaning to their nursing care.

A. N. has continued to work on using structured journal entry responses for her nursing students. In fact, she and two colleagues have written an article about her work with reflection (Nielsen, Stragnell, & Jester, 2007) that illustrates the guide she uses to help her students reflect on their clinical experiences in the field.

Case 8: Community Health—Using Metaphors

Isabelle has been teaching undergraduate students in the community nursing program in a large public university for 7 years. In addition, she has worked in Ghana as a community nurse. Her rich background in an international setting influences her classroom practice here in the United States.

Students in Isabelle's classes write weekly reflections on experiences in the community clinical nursing settings. She reads all of their reflections. She wants them to make images of their work in these complex and dynamic settings, and therefore asks students to use a metaphor she learned in Ghana: "To feel fulfilled each day, we must cross four rivers: delight, community, love, and challenge." She asks her students to consider this metaphor as they reflect on their actions and interactions in their clinical setting. To do this well, they should sit in stillness and quiet, stop thinking about their experiences, and let an image come to mind that expresses their week in this complex clinical setting. This image and their reflection on it becomes the journal entry. "Journaling is a proxy for the experience. Writing is the only way to capture that experience. Journaling is not a mental process only. When it is true and deep, the journal entry embodies experience with emotional, cognitive, and verbal components. I know you cannot always wrap words around your experience, so I let them draw, write poetry, or use some other form of expression."

How does she assess these entries? "I don't grade them; however, the accountability comes in the written conversation between me and the students about their entries. I may ask them to use another method that might help them express themselves in a fuller way." She notes the need for students to reflect deeply about the context in which they are learning about nursing. They are also learning about themselves and the background knowledge they bring to their work. "In a community setting, they often encounter, for example, Latino women who don't speak English, who may have ridden a bus for an hour with three children to get to the clinic for help. I ask how they can relate to these women and their lives." Isabelle looks for self-awareness and the ability to identify their own assumptions in their reflections.

Isabelle has used this assignment for many years because it seems to help students identify their own biases and assumptions in a very concrete way, and build bridges between their clinical experience and the social context in which they find themselves. She finds that, when they express themselves in their journals this way, they seem to have the ability to understand the perspective of the poor and underserved. Furthermore, they become acquainted with how they respond to others in a totally different and often quite unfamiliar context.

Case 9: Service Learning—Using Student Feedback

Vicki teaches in the Women's Studies department in the College of Liberal Arts and Sciences for a large public university. The bulk of her teaching load involves teaching an undergraduate University Studies class for a 6-credit, senior service learning capstone requirement. The service learning requirement involves students working in multidisciplinary teams with a community partner and culminates in a project completed in collaboration with that community partner. Journals are a critical component of her classes.

Vicki explains that her teaching is informed by her own experience with journals. Having kept a journal since the fourth grade, it is the way she learns. In working to construct her service learning course, it became clear early on that the bulk of the work the students would need to complete involved an extensive reflective piece on what they were experiencing in their field sites as well as their experience of being members in a cross-discipline, collaborative team. She designed her course with this in mind and provides class time for journaling. At the outset of class, Vicki introduces the concept of journaling and provides specific information regarding journaling requirements and expectations in the course syllabus. "It's weighted heavily," Vicki explained. "In some ways my job is to deconstruct what journaling means to students due to students' previous experiences with journaling for other professors. If students have had a negative experience, it will take them a while to build trust in this class's journal-writing expectations."

When it comes to grading, one of the main criteria is that students turn in their journals on time because she uses the journals to craft the direction of the class. She reads the journals to identify student issues and concerns. As she responds to the journals, she also modifies the course to address these issues so that students can be open and unafraid of moving ever more deeply into the course experience.

Students must also complete their journals in a timely manner because they are used as a classroom community-building tool. Vicki asks students to suggest topics they want to explore as a class, and their journal responses provide an avenue for a unique collaboration between student and instructor when it comes to course development and design. Another critical component of the grading experience comes with her explanation to students that she "wants only that piece that that individual student can supply." In explaining this, Vicki compares student journals to Birkenstocks: A student's journal is uniquely molded to his or her own insights and experience. Vicki says that it is her expectation that by as early as the second week of class she should know who the author of a journal is without looking at the student's name.

Vicki explains how journal writing must be distinguished from regular academic writing. She says that many students experience some level of anxiety when they first hear of the requirement. Consequently, Vicki does not dialogue with students about conventions of writing like punctuation, complete sentences, or even organization. Instead, she provides feedback that helps students see themselves in their own writing. This feedback is often interrogative and asks students to engage in a written response dialogue. In this way the journals provide Vicki with a unique way to get to know her students. She reads each journal at least two times, writes in the margins, underlines, and asks key questions that are student centered and conversational as a way to help students notice things they have written. Ultimately, students come away grateful for having the opportunity to engage in writing in an authentic and honest way.

Journals meet a variety of student and faculty interests. Vicki is always trying to figure out how to better meet the needs of students; reflective journals offer another way for her to connect with their issues. Journal writing broadens the possible ways that students can engage and shows students how to develop their critical-thinking skills. Journals are very contextual; that is, their content depends on the course and on what students are specifically doing.

Vicki has students complete a final journal entry as a letter to themselves. They read through their past journals, write a final journal letter, and then put it in an envelope. The students address the envelope to themselves, and put a date on the envelope that indicates when they want the journal letter mailed to them. When the date arrives, Vicki drops the envelope in the mail. This provides students with a rich opportunity to listen to themselves at a future date and reflect on where they have been.

Case 10: Biology—Observing the Natural World

Anna has been teaching biology at a historically black women's liberal arts college for 5 years. She currently teaches Developmental Biology, Botany, and Biology of Women, and uses journals in all three courses. The first journals she tried were nature journals in Developmental Biology. She has students write in these during overnight field trips, while they sit quietly and alone in nature. Because many of these biology majors grew up in urban settings, the journals help them to focus affectionately on the natural world, and to notice real detail. Often students produce "superficial, syrupy stuff" at first, but given time and guidance, will begin writing in their own voices about "real brushes with wonder." She tells of one student who was sitting in the

Okefenokee swamp writing a poem in her nature journal about how silent the wilderness was, when, part way through, the student drew a diagonal line across it all, and wrote in capital letters, "NATURE IS LOUD!"

In botany, the journal is a "constant tool." Anna gives her students at least three prompts per week and students can create their own prompts as well. The journal counts "as much as a test" in this course, or 25% of their grade. She grades on effort in drawing from life, the quality of the entries, and whether students are "focused, curious, and open." Illustrations are an especially important part of the botany journals (see Figure 4.8). A professional scientific illustrator is invited to the class to get the students started with some drawing techniques and a lesson on observation, and all students must purchase a zippered pouch filled with color pencils and art supplies to carry with their journals. The prompts force students to visit, illustrate, and interact with plants around campus and their homes almost every day for a whole semester. Some prompts are experimental, while others are more contemplative.

Anna feels that she is able to model her perspective on biology and says, "There's a lot of me in the prompts I give, and a lot of each student's self in her responses." As the journals fill with drawings, they become "things of beauty." Students tell Anna that they proudly share their journals with others and revisit them after the class is over. For this reason, the product is in some ways as important as the process. The lessons learned are longer-lived and more likely to be associated with good feelings and a sense of mastery. Anna says that getting students to feel this way about plants, when they started out thinking that biology was "all rubber gloves and curing cancer" is a wonderful outcome from the journals. She also believes that the journals help the students to "integrate their career choices with their insides."

In the Biology of Women course, Anna asks students to write daily and turn in brief entries on note cards, as a way of taking roll. In this class, she gives no prompts for the "Body Journals"; all entries are self-generated, and students write on everything from "body image, to nose bleeds, to cramps, to smells after sex." At the end of the course, each student selects two of her entries to record on a white dress (see Figure 5.6). Wearing white dresses is a tradition at the college, and thus has particular symbolism for these women. Over the years, Anna hopes to collect "class body journals" this way, and to display all the white dresses in a show. Although Anna reads all the journal entries from her Developmental Biology and Botany students, and writes back to them, she does not read all the Biology of Women entries. She states that "Biology of Women is a class that just begs for a private journal!"

Anna feels that journals help the students to become more active learners; "PowerPoints can make them passive, whereas writing and drawing are active and private processes." She says, "People don't banter as much in private," and one of her goals is to help her students enjoy more profound thoughts about their bodies and the natural world around them. "I now so believe in using journals in the classroom that I've become an evangelist!" She states, "Journals really help teachers access their students. In one form or another they are my solution to almost any academic ill. More professors should give these wonderful tools a try!"

Conclusion

These cases are examples of how journals are being used by faculty across the country. They are certainly not an exhaustive description of the possibilities, but simply a sampling of the many ways in which journals are used. Surprisingly little has been written across disciplines about the practice of journal keeping in college classrooms. Aside from our own work and a few others (Boud, 2001; Fulwiler, 1987; Hiemstra, 2001; Kerka, 2002; Stevens, Cooper, & Lasater, 2006), most studies of journal writing focus on a single discipline and what the instructor and the students learned from the enterprise (Carter, 1997; Haley & Wesley-Nero, 2002; Kasten, Wright, & Kasten, 1996; Koirala, 2002). The disciplines addressed in these publications include math (Burns & Silbey, 2001; Koirala, 2002), business (Fisher, 1990; Loo, 2002), English (Dickerson, 1987; Graham, 2003; Nelson, 2004; Qualley, 1997), nursing (Craft, 2005; Durgahee, 1998, 2002; Krmpotic, 2003; Penney & Warelow, 1999), English as a Second Language (Suzuki, 2004), and engineering (Hampton & Morrow, 2003), to name a few. Journals are also used quite extensively in the preparation of teachers and administrators in education (Baker & Shahid, 2003; Fenwick, 2001; Gil-Garcia & Cintron, 2002; Ostermann & Kottkamp, 1993; Kraus & Butler, 2000; Peyton, 2000; Tsang, 2003). The use of journals in these courses vary; they might be used as a vehicle to deliver course content, such as math or engineering; as a way to monitor field or clinical experiences, such as in nursing; or as the centerpiece for the course, such as Nelson's class in "Writing and Being." Here the journal writing becomes a way for students to "heal the past, claim the present and chart the future" (2004, p. xvii).

The collection of cases offered in this chapter provides an overview of the possibilities for using journals in college classrooms in a variety of disciplines. The faculty members who teach these courses come from community colleges as well as from 4-year public and private institutions across the country. They have derived a number of fascinating ways to teach with journals, each peculiar to their own disciplines and learning goals. The journals students produce are as varied as their teachers and include annotated drawings in architecture, reflections on clinical work in nursing, analyses of poetry in English, and thoughts on ethical issues in food chemistry. However, they all have several common elements. They are all aimed at encouraging students to think more deeply about their learning and its connections to their "real" lives. The journals are never graded for grammar and punctuation. At the heart of the enterprise, they all spring from a solid belief in the value of reflective practice in the classroom.

One interesting insight here is that the use of journals is instructive to both the students and the faculty who teach those students. We are able to learn from the struggles and mistakes of both the students and their teachers, as these faculty members gladly share what they would do differently. We hope you have found these cases as useful and fascinating as we have.

10

CASE STUDIES: JOURNAL KEEPING IN PROFESSIONAL LIFE

IN CHAPTER 9 WE PRESENTED CASES OF FACULTY who use journals in their classrooms. We now turn to cases from a graduate student, faculty members, and administrators who use a journal in their professional lives. Faculty members use their journals to keep track of the meetings attended, to organize and manage programs, as well as to plan and conduct research projects. Faculty members may also serve as department chairs, blending the faculty and administrative roles of higher education; they use journals to juggle their multiple roles and track the details of their complex lives. Both faculty and administrators often use their journals to record the meetings they attend, make to-do lists, and to plan for the future. In this chapter we also examine the journal-keeping practice of one graduate student who has used journal keeping to manage research projects as well as teaching functions in his role as a teaching assistant.

Some of these professionals keep a single journal to manage their many roles and tasks. For example, Skip, the director of a large research unit and former interim dean, keeps one journal where he logs all the meetings he attends and takes the journal home on weekends to reflect on the future of his organization. Others keep individual journals for each role. Gerry, a department chair, keeps "six active journals," one for his work as chair, one for each of his three research projects, one to record data on all the programs he's loaded onto his computer, and one to deal with a university-wide committee he is currently serving on. Most professionals use their journals in a similar manner, as a very functional and organizational part of their professional lives. Some have found unique ways to use the journal to organize their research agendas, or to engage in critical reflection on their career paths both now and in the future. In many ways these journals are a path to a more reflective and conscious life, a way to mentor oneself, a means for working, as Gerry states, "at a higher level."

This chapter presents you with cases of individuals who have been keeping a journal in their professional lives for many years. They are veterans who have much to teach us and who wisely know that keeping a journal in their work life keeps them organized and efficient, rather than taking their precious time. Often, faculty and administrators in colleges and universities lament that they would love to keep a journal, but simply do not have the time. The experiences of the professionals discussed in this chapter challenge this belief, demonstrating in detail how journal keeping adds to their efficiency rather than robbing them of precious time. No one is telling these journal keepers what to do and none of them would continue to keep a journal if it did not serve them well.

Table 10.1 is a quick reference list of the cases in this chapter with additional information on special journal practices that each case demonstrates.

These cases can teach us about how to lead a saner and more centered professional life. They show you how professionals balance a complex array of roles and tasks through time-tested and individualized journal-keeping practices. These cases also illuminate the practices we described earlier in the book. With these concrete examples, you can find a way to meet your own particular needs and in the process learn how the keeping of a journal actually adds time to your day and enhances your sanity, rather than being an added burden, something you must do or should do. These cases contain the wisdom of seasoned and successful professionals, those who have met the many challenges of their jobs and found creative ways to process their work-life events. Jean, for example, is near the end of her career as a dean and has just started a "transition journal" as she begins her last year in university service. Here she wisely recognizes the need to reflect on the meaning of this major change in her career trajectory. She will no doubt be more aware of her feelings and better equipped to let go as she moves on.

Whether you are coming to the close of your career in higher education, or just beginning, it is our hope that these cases can lead you to new ways to understand your own professional life, as well as to increase your sense of organization and well-being. Certainly if you look across these cases, you will see academics who share their insights about how they grapple with the constant and competing demands of academic life. These demands are woefully familiar to all of us. Here then are some

Table 10.1
Journal Keeping in Professional Life by Discipline and Unique Journal Practices

Case Number/Name	Discipline/Department	Unique Journal Practices
#1 Gerry	Engineering Faculty and Department Chair	Multiple journals for administration and research projects
#2 Kofi	International Studies Faculty and Department Chair	Journals at three "sites" to remember and record events, contacts, and reflections
#3 Micki	Teacher Education Faculty	Three-column method on pages with grids Organize and reflect on teaching, research, writing, and service
#4 Richard	Educational Technology Doctoral Student	Brainstorm and reflect on teaching and future goals
#5 Barbara	Integrated Studies Faculty and Program Chair, College President Emerita	Organize life and reflect on professional/personal experiences Collect observations and write poetry
#6 Skip	Director of a Research Unit	Organization and strategic planning
#7 Louise	Associate Dean	Keep records Reflect on scholarship and leadership
#8 CJ	Community College Board Member	Write "morning pages" Organization Reflect on leadership
#9 Jean	Retiring Dean	Organizational tool and to keep records Document reflections on "transition" to retirement

antidotes to that overwhelmed feeling, as well as new paths to increased organization and fresh understandings of a life that is all too often crazier and busier than we would like it to be.

Case 1: A Department Chair in Engineering

Gerry is a professor of mechanical engineering at a public university and the chair of his department. He began keeping a journal about 26 years ago, when he was a graduate student and began documenting his lab work. At present he keeps "six active journals." He keeps a journal of his administrative activities: meetings with staff, faculty, students and university committees. He says he uses this journal to record things he might otherwise forget. He keeps a separate journal for each research project, and he showed us a new journal for a project that just got funded. He keeps a separate journal about his computers, including programs on each, serial numbers, and activation keys.

Gerry's use of the journal and the number of journals he keeps "grew with my professional responsibilities" and has "really blossomed in the last 5 years." He says, "Right now these are just captures." They are places for him to "unload his mind" so that he doesn't have to remember everything. When it is written in his journal, he knows he won't forget it and can work "without anxiety." He describes these journals as similar to the "pensieve" in the Harry Potter novels, the place where Dumbledore deposits his memories when he pulls them out of his mind. Gerry writes daily in his administrative journal, and weekly in his research journals. He says he doesn't write everything down; only what he feels is important. He describes himself as not rigorous or compulsive about his journal keeping. What he chooses to write in his journal depends on several things: first, if he has strong emotions about something and needs to "unburden" himself from the emotion; second, if he feels a need to describe just what happened; and, finally, if he needs to process something that happened in the past. His journals contain "no half-baked information."

At home and about once every 6 months, Gerry uses a personal journal when something comes up, but "only if I feel like I need to work something out, to talk to myself." He always takes a journal with him when he takes a vacation and this becomes his personal journal.

He values small, leather Moleskine 5" × 8" journals with gridwork pages that he can easily carry to meetings because they have high-quality paper, a small envelope in back to file things, and fine leather covers. He learned about these journals from a Website "for alpha geeks," www.davidco.com, that is like a "personal 12-step program on how to organize your professional life."

Gerry always starts a new entry on the right-hand page of his journal, sometimes leaving the left page blank, in case he needs to go back and add thoughts or events from the previous meeting. The preceding blank page is "spillover space," space for going back and reflecting on what happened. There are also sticky notes in his journal of to-do lists, and these can easily be discarded when the task is done. Or he will create boxes in front of his to-do items, so that he can check off an item when it is completed or put an X through it if he decides not to do it. He keeps extra sticky notes and his business cards in the front of his journal, as well as his address and phone number, in case the journal is lost. He offers a reward of a "negotiable" amount to the person who finds it.

Gerry has been chair of his department for less than a year and has tried during that time to be "accurate, transparent, and complete." He says his professional journals are "not a place for personal venting." Even though he describes himself as a "passionate person," he values the ability to be dispassionate in these work journals, approaching situations with a certain amount of "detachment." For example, he has a group of students that are always pushing the limits, asking for more lab time, and so on. He states, "I cannot let my frustration punish them." He might register that he is annoyed in his journal, "but only briefly." He tries to use restraint and recognizes that his journal might at some point become public. Although he sometimes thinks that the students are acting like "a bunch of flaming bozos," this should not be the place he acts from. "It's not helpful," he says. "It's distracting." The journal allows him time to get perspective and plan an appropriate response to help the students learn from their mistakes.

Gerry has continued to use his journals because he believes the process "positively reinforces itself." He feels relieved when he is able to capture things on paper; it is like a "metaconsciousness." He alludes to Parker Palmer's discussion of how at some point in your life you will find yourself without a mentor (*Courage to Teach,* 2007, pp. 25–26). "Keeping a journal is a way for me to be conscious, a way of mentoring myself. Sometimes you've got to sit with yourself and get clear." His journal helps him to "work at a higher level."

He does not go back and reread entries systematically, although he will look for checked boxes on his to-do lists. He also moves out sticky notes of things he has accomplished. He says, "Sticky notes agitate me." They are merely a place for "temporary unloading." It feels good to discard them when the tasks are completed.

Gerry recommends that his students keep a lab notebook and would recommend his journaling process to colleagues, but "only if somebody asks me." When asked about the amount of time journaling takes, he states, "Managing your life takes time. This is fine for me, but it is not for everybody."

For Gerry, the journaling process is "like brushing your teeth. You don't feel good if you don't brush." This is a form of "personal productivity that just feels better." Yet he states, "I wish I could be more regular." While Gerry believes that keeping a journal is "a way to pay attention, to hone some consciousness," right now he feels the process for him is more about "emergency noting." He says, "I would love to be a more reflective individual." Yet, his journal contains opportunities for "joyful inspiration" within the discipline and the structure, just like playing sports. "I even give myself permission to make a cartoon in my journal."

Case 2: A Professor of International Studies

Kofi is a professor of international studies at a public university. He has been keeping a journal since the early 1960s when he was in graduate school in Ghana. His journal has evolved just as his life has evolved. He is now a department chair, a full professor, and leads groups of students for field site visits to Ghana and Suriname. His journal method grew from his frustration of trying to keep everything that was happening in his life in his weekly planner. He still keeps a weekly planner for appointments; yet he has three other "notebooks," as he calls them, that play an important role in his life. His background is archaeology and he describes himself as a "cultural anthropologist." His journal keeping follows several of the models he has learned from his discipline. Like an archaeologist, Kofi has notebooks in three "sites": in his office in the Black Studies Department, in another office in the International Studies Department, and one at home.

How does he use his journal? His journal is 5" × 8" with a stiff cardboard cover, which is spiral bound so that it lies flat when opened. The pages are lined, but his entries are written in bold script across the lines. His more recent journals have pocket dividers where he can put things that have meaning for him like thank-you notes or newspaper articles. One pocket held an article from the *Chronicle of Higher Education* about a former colleague's work on faculty development at her new job. From a 1997 journal on his shelf, he pulled out a poem he wrote. His journal is a "recording device" as well, a place to record phone calls, names, addresses, brief notes from meetings and encounters, even sticky notes from other important meetings. He notes names, addresses, discussions, recommendations he writes for graduate students, and, if he makes an appointment with someone in the future, he puts it down. If he has an idea about research or his department, he quickly makes a note of it in his "notebook." He staples things into it occasionally. After he records the date at the top of the page, he numbers the first item, then draws a line, numbers, and starts his second item.

Does he go back and reread entries? "Yes, yes, yes, I do that a lot. I take a break, grab an old journal and I look through it to see if there is anything I need to follow up on." He has all of them saved at home on his bookshelves. He looks for information from years ago that may be useful today. For instance, recently he looked at an old journal that recorded a conference in Switzerland, and he flipped through to see with whom he had conversations and where he went during the conference. He keeps the two most recent journals handy as he moves through a new one. Sometimes when he goes through the old ones, he notices something he forgot to do and then he will act on it.

Kofi says, "I am the audience for my journal. However, if I am somewhere and I need the information from the other journal at the other location, I will call my secretary and she can find the date and give it to me. I now see that she is keeping a journal just like mine to help her organize her day." For my home journal, my wife looks at it a lot to see what I am doing and often says, "You do a lot." He records relatives calling, friends calling, and family discussions in his home journal.

Journal keeping has "confirmed my belief in record keeping. It has helped me to be on my toes." "Look, here I have the name and contact information of a guy I met in London last year. It is not like Meeting Maker or Palm Pilots." He noted that to get information from "digital devices, you have to go to the computer. They are slow and you have to scroll up and down to find something."

He is not worried about privacy at all. "I am a very open person. My journal is like a link to my past activities. With my background as an archaeologist, I know that the past is very important in my present. The journal is the historical link to my past. The journal represents life unfolding, days rolling one into the other. All of these journals are links. I look at them. My family, my children, even my nieces and nephews, will see who I am and what I did with my life."

Case 3: A Professor of Teacher Education

Micki, a tenured associate professor at a large public university, has been keeping a journal related to her academic work since 1998. Although she kept one in the past to make daily entries on the growth of her daughter, this is the second journal she has kept related to her work life. She kept the first one in 1993 when she was an administrator outside of academe. She notes, "I could see my work at a glance and I could document for my administrators what I was doing with my time." Today, she teaches, conducts research, and holds several leadership positions in department, state, and national interest groups in her field.

Micki uses a three-column method. She states, "I keep one journal, which I use continuously throughout the day. See where I put down '10:30 Dannelle dropped by and wants to interview me. Meet at 1:00.' I put check boxes in the third column to indicate the need to do an activity or follow-up. The check in the box tells me that I did it. I put flags or 'stickies' on things that I am still working on from previous dates. It is a visual cue. I even add these tabs to indicate the things I have left over from my last journal that I still need to do."

In her three-column journal, the first column contains a running record of the time and the date of the activity. The middle column contains the notes of what happened during that time and the third column is the to-do list that rises out of the meeting or event. She says, "In the middle column, I am listing things discussed, such as a meeting with our department chair. I write about meetings with students or notes on student teaching observations. I record the words that students say when I ask them how things are going in the field. When they walk in the door and their first word is 'surviving,' that goes in my journal and later that may have meaning for me. After a while I realized that what I am doing can be research as well. I may have a history of meetings with a particular student and that is helpful for documentation of a record of problems. I realize that the whole thing is actually data that can be useful later."

The journal has several uses for Micki. "My journal helps balance so many things. I have many things going on at the same time. The only way to keep it all straight is to journal. It is like I have all these plates spinning in the air—some have chips because they have fallen or collided with one another. They collide less often when I have a journal." In fact, her journal plays a central role in her academic life, "I keep my journal with me. I use it all the time. When I don't have it, I am lost. I will have to go back and enter what has happened in my journal so that I can do what I said I will do."

When asked what the journal has taught her, Micki said, "Be selective about what I write. I looked at my old journals and I saw too many details: agenda topics for my classes repeated term after term, group advising notes, the same each time I did it, week after week. After a while I realized I did not have to write it down each week. I now keep an agenda for my classes and reminders to bring things like AV equipment, but not all the details I used to put in my journal." When she goes back to reread her journal, it is usually "on a fact-finding mission to find evidence of something."

Micki uses a personal digital assistant (PDA) to keep track of her schedule. She teaches technology courses to her students, creates curriculum with technology, and even manages the Website of her national special interest group. When asked what role the handwritten journal plays in relation to her PDA, she smiled and said, "I use my [PDA] to identify dates that I did something and then I can go to my journal to find the details and meeting notes. It is like an archive. It is a planning and recollection document. . . . I want to know what happened to my life. I don't have to account to anyone except me. I can re-create my life with my journal."

Some people say, "It takes too much time." Micki's response is, "What takes the time is forgetting it and having to go back to my journal and fill in what I did. It streamlines my activities. For example, six students came to advising today; three had interests in (my area). . . . I know I can use this for data, for research now. I use it for admissions and for recruitment information."

When asked about an apt metaphor for her journal keeping, she thought quietly for a while. Then, she said, "To me it's like planting a garden. The journal has all the seeds. It is their raw form, but they're still seeds. Once planted, they have the potential to do more, for example, GTEP [a departmental program] advising notes, middle level research—in gardening the next thing to know is how far to plant the rows apart. The potential is there. I cannot imagine my life without it. It adds a quality to my life like art adds quality. There is a personal satisfaction to see the garden grow or just to see art. It adds nourishment to my work life."

Case 4: A Doctoral Student

Richard, a doctoral student in curriculum and instruction, regularly keeps a journal. He began keeping a journal when he entered the doctoral program 1 1/2 years ago, on the advice of his doctoral advisor. He writes almost daily on his lunch break, for at least 5 minutes, about his life as a student and his work.

Richard states that keeping a journal has taught him a lot about himself and that his professional decisions are now based on "good evidence." When he first started the doctoral program he didn't know why he was there. He says he met a lot of "smart people" and thought about dropping out of the doctoral program. Then he realized that each student had expertise in "his own study" and that he had expertise in technology that others did not have. He says the process of journaling has been "empowering." He realized that "you know something and you're there for a reason." This process has helped him to prepare for decisions that lie ahead of him. He feels he understands himself better and is able to, he says, "give myself time" through his journal.

Richard has also used his journal to brainstorm ideas for grant projects and course redesign. When money became available, he was ready with ideas and concrete suggestions. He was able to focus on both the implementation process and outcomes for educational projects.

He feels his journal has helped him to become a more competent professional partly because he recognizes when he is becoming less productive. When this happens he takes the next day off. He realizes that he needs a break and that the next day, when he wakes up, the work will still be there.

He writes chiefly about work in his journal, his long-range goals, where he'd like to go with his dissertation, and so on. He doesn't write about his personal life, but keeps the journal strictly to examine and reflect on his professional life. His advice for other doctoral students is to try journal writing for 4 to 5 months, then "look back to see how you've changed." He recommends finding a particular time to write (lunchtime works for him). He believes the process has helped him to "re-find" himself.

Richard states that keeping a professional journal "helps you understand why you are in a doctoral program." He spends time writing "what I wonder about." This is an easy way to move your dissertation topic along and is not as scary as trying to answer the question, "What is your dissertation topic?" He firmly believes all doctoral students should be exposed to journal writing, that it helps you to "think on a daily basis."

Case 5: A Professor of Integrated Studies

Barbara has been keeping a journal for many years. She kept her first journals when she was in sixth grade; "they had pink plastic covers with a little lock." Years later, she keeps a journal to record, organize, celebrate, examine, and reflect on all aspects of her life.

Barbara is a college president emerita and is now a professor and program director. Her journal travels with her everywhere. "Each type of journal I buy depends on where I happen to be at the time. I just check out what is available and what attracts me." Thus she has a variety of journals and each one reflects where she was at that time in her life. "The form and shape of a journal shapes my thoughts, too." The first entry in her new journal is always something about her surroundings and her feelings. "I am conscious of myself as I write. I always record the date and time."

Barbara uses her journal under three different circumstances. The first is when she wants to say something about an experience such as her response to reading a poem or a book. The second circumstance is when she wants to talk to herself and actively listen to what she has to say to herself. "I will write down an idea and then respond to the idea, like a conversation." The third circumstance is when she has an observation she wants to record and not forget. A few weeks before our interview she took her mother to the Huntington Library in Los Angeles. She took notes on the pebble garden. When she met some people there, she put the contact information in her journal. During the interview, she showed me another example of how she records observations in her journal. Because she heard someone sweeping outside her window, she wrote down the words, "swoosh, swoosh" on the page. "I love the sound of sweeping. A few pages later, this sound led me to write a poem on sweeping and the swoosh, swoosh sound. I often sit on my patio and the poems come to me. I do not plan to write them, but they come. All the seeds for these are in my journal."

During the interview, she took me on a "journey" through her journal, showing me the variety of entries: "Here is a meeting of the *Education of Leadership Review* board; here is an appointment with my doctor; here, the university calendar; here, drawings." She also puts cards and memorabilia loosely in her journal. She states, "I have artifacts in my journals: leaves, poems, photos of family." They stay with that journal when she stores it. The journal she showed me was literally bursting at the seams. She said that she was just about finished with this journal and would have to find a new one.

Although her journal is arranged chronologically, when she is not done thinking about something, she leaves a space open to come back to it. She reads her journal writings when she is on the plane. Sometimes she realizes that she does not remember writing something: "That is both a terrible and wonderful feeling because it reminds me of our very human vulnerability. We forget things."

Barbara will not go anywhere without her journal because it plays such an important role in her life. "My journal writing develops and invokes my thinking, to generate, to discover, to find out about me. Writing itself just develops and changes me as I do it. Sometimes I just sit and wonder at the mystery of my own journal entries."

Barbara also uses her journal as a planning tool. "I plan courses and speeches and presentations in my journal. It is an expression and a development of my scholar self. For example, I had a round of trips and speeches from August 6 to October 15. I had to pack for the trips and in my journal I not only worked out my clothes packing list for these various events, board meetings, speeches, classes, family responsibilities at many different locations throughout the United States, but I was able to think about what I was doing at each spot as I made the packing list. In the end, I was able to pack in 5 minutes."

Both reading and writing help Barbara in her professional and personal life. "I read every day. I read many things from physics to history. After I read, I write. If I am writing about it in my journal, I can't avoid thinking about it." Barbara believes that the journal is where her cognitive functioning takes place "broadly and deeply."

Barbara uses the computer to journal occasionally. "Now that I have an electronic journal, I can write faster. I write little essays but it does not do the same thing." The handwritten journal feels more authentic. She feels her mind wrestling with things as she writes them down. "It is like chopping onions with a knife or with a food processor. The journal is the knife. It is a physical thing to keep a journal. . . . There is a physical effort. With the food processor, you do not touch the onion; your experience of the onion is more distant."

Barbara's journal de-stresses and grounds her. "If I am stressing, I start writing to recover myself, to find out who I am. When I want to know what I really think, I write in my journal. It is more than a mirror. It does not reflect me. It is organic, working collaboratively with myself. It is discovery work."

One powerful role the journal plays in her life is to help her as a professional. Because of her leadership roles and the speeches and presentations she makes, she has to develop, connect, and be able to present different ideas. She says, "These ideas for speeches and connections with things, come out of my deepest sense of myself. I ask myself, 'Who is this speech for? What do I know and why?' and then I start writing the speech." Asking herself those questions in her journal and responding to them fosters new connections and new ideas that she did not have before she started interrogating herself in writing.

Some might think that when you have a lot of administrative and leadership responsibilities, it is not possible to keep a journal. There is no time. Not for Barbara. Because her journal nourishes her spirit, it helps her be the most sincere and honest self she can be as a leader. Barbara is grateful that she has the opportunity to work on problems that are important. Yet she could not do this work without her journal. "When I became a college president, I never stopped journaling. I never stopped publishing articles, going to conferences, doing poetry. I never stopped writing in my journal. It is the key to my resilience, my intellectual growth." She told me about a willow tree outside her office when she was a college president; writing about that willow through the seasons allowed her to get a perspective on the human interactions she faced every day. At the second college board meeting, she read from her journal about her hopes and dreams for the college. One board member said that was a breakthrough for them; it opened up the board in a new way. "When we read from [our journals], we are sharing something of the self . . . holding these battered pages and reading. . . . They can see that and know that you are leading from your authentic self." This kind of communication is central to Barbara's leadership style.

The journal provides Barbara with what she calls "that layered consciousness, that awareness of ourselves going deeply into the sources of our own inspiration and thought where we work both halves of our brain. We integrate the limbic emotion and our memory centers. This muscular neural work in my journal is the very heart of growth."

Case 6: A Director of a Research Unit

Skip is the director of a research unit on the campus of a large, urban university in the western United States. He directs the work of 100 to 150 faculty and often puts in 12- to 15-hour days. He has been keeping a journal at work for more than 8 years, both during his appointment as associate dean of the college where he works and in his present position as director of the research unit. He describes his job as one that demands multitasking and believes that his "book" helps him to track the many demands of each day.

Skip uses small, bound composition or lab books with lined paper and carries one with him everywhere he goes. It goes to all his meetings and at home with him at night and on weekends. In it he records the date and time of each meeting he attends, who was present, and the salient events of the meeting. He lists the decisions that were made and the follow-up tasks he must accomplish as a result of that meeting. One book is filled every 3 to 4 months and each book is numbered consecutively. At this point he says he has "several boxes full of them." When first asked about the book he was carrying, he said, "This? This is my life!"

The notes Skip takes are only for him. No one else sees his entries, and he says he uses a kind of shorthand that most people, even his secretary, would not understand. Skip creates extensive to-do lists from the meetings he attends. He tracks his to-do lists, circling items that have not been attended to, and starring those that must be accomplished immediately. When a task is completed, Skip crosses it off the list. If an item has not been completed, but he has taken some action on it, he puts a check mark by it, to indicate that he is working on it. At the end of a book, he reviews the entire book and carries forward those tasks that have not been accomplished, often creating three to four pages of to-do's in the front of his new book. Reviewing his last journal and starting a new one with a to-do list allows Skip to reflect on the scope of his work and plan strategically for the coming months.

When asked what the process has taught him, Skip grins and says, "I've got more work than time!" He sees his journal as a way to manage that time well, to work more efficiently, and to "avoid bottlenecks." For him, the process is one of reflection and planning. He often reviews his entries at the end of the day to digest the events of the day and plan for the next. At this time he asks himself, "What am I working on? What am I procrastinating on?" He says it is easy to attend to the small tasks and avoid the larger more complex issues that really need his attention. This process helps him to face the tasks he might otherwise avoid, tackling their complexity in the quiet of his home during the evenings. He uses long weekends for what he calls "long-range planning," for generating new ideas and attending to unrealized potential in himself and the organization. For Skip, this process keeps him responsible to his colleagues so that he does not keep them from doing their work through his own failure to attend to a particular task. He says his journal helps "to keep him from getting in their way," something that is extremely important to him. Skip's to-do lists help him to keep his promises to colleagues about what he must do to keep a project moving forward.

During meetings Skip notes only the salient events, decisions or tasks. His notes are cryptic and succinct. Sometimes he lists only the date, time, and those in attendance. If nothing important happened, the entry is otherwise blank. In "boring meetings"

Skip will often create to-do lists, flipping back to recent days to review and synthesize. He says it looks like he's working, so no one knows his mind is not on the meeting he is in.

Some meetings that are extremely important are tagged with bright colored tabs. For example, meetings with the chancellor when the unit was under attack were tagged so that he could go back to them again and again. He said his notes on who was there, what was said, and decisions that were made were vital to the survival of the organization. Other notes on personnel issues that are needed for legal documentation are transferred to his official files. His book is "not an official record, but I can create documents from it." He uses his journal in conjunction with his PDA. The PDA lists his schedule for the day and his journal records the events of each meeting. He says there is not enough room to do that on his PDA. Thus it acts like an index for his journal, allowing him to go back and find the details of a meeting that is listed in the PDA.

Skip describes the journal-keeping process as one of self-analysis, or constant self-evaluation. His journal is his conscience, creating a set of checks and balances that help him to maintain a sense of teamwork and camaraderie in his organization. It is a vital part of his work life, a valuable tool, and one that at this point he believes he could not do without.

Case 7: An Associate Dean

Louise has been the associate dean for the last 7 years. She uses beautiful, legal-size books that she purchases from the university bookstore. They are wine colored with gold trim etched in the cover. The pages are numbered and each page is divided by a gold line down the middle. The twenty journals she has filled sit in a row on a shelf in her office, looking organized and scholarly. She says she fills one about every 3 or 4 months. Unfortunately, the bookstore does not carry these legal-size books any more and her latest journal is a spiral-bound pad in a vinyl binder. She says it feels much more "note-takish" and is not as satisfying to use, without the page numbers and the two columns. She is going to search the bookstore again, hoping to find the journals she was using.

She uses the journal's divided page to create a double-entry system. One side contains raw data from her meetings with people and the other side contains her to-do lists and reflections on the meetings that she attends. She has been keeping a journal using this current style since 1999. She began keeping a journal after observing the use of journals by faculty in the college, the dean, and others she knows across campus. Louise uses her journal in meetings she attends, at her desk at work, and at home. She often takes her journal home to reflect on events and plan ahead. She says it is most important to set down fleeting ideas she has about her work before she forgets them.

The contents of Louise's journal are "more than meeting notes" because the pages also contain reflections and plans for moving the organization ahead, as well thoughts on helping individual faculty to grow in their careers. Her journal is private and she also uses it to reflect on her working relationships with the dean and her faculty. She states that it helps her to be more efficient: "My journal is a tool for scholarship and leadership." She feels the main advantage of keeping a journal is the ability it gives her to reflect on her professional life.

Louise states that she wishes that she could be more systematic about her writing. If she could change anything, she would begin to conduct more content analysis of her entries, returning to what she's written, and color-coding the entries according to content. This would be most useful in helping her to understand the work of an associate dean, something she studies and has written about.

Others in the school of education count on her to have notes about what went on in various meetings. They say if anyone has an account of the meeting, it will be Louise. They regard her as very organized. Louise sees herself as an "archivist" for the school and its work. She says the journal is an effective tool to assist her in "forwarding everyone's work, including my own." She sees the process as an active one and regards the term "reflection" as "too passive" for her sense of her journal-keeping process.

Louise's journal-keeping process is evolving. She used to write more than she does now. Through her work as associate dean, she has realized how important eye contact is when meeting with someone, thus she is writing less. She sounds concerned about writing less and says she needs to take the time to go back and recap conversations when she is done with a meeting. This tension, between time to document what is going on and the need to be more actively involved in a meeting may be a concern to other journal keepers, as well. Time is always an issue for busy professionals. When asked about whether this process takes too much of her time, a frequent complaint of those who do not journal, Louise said that she doesn't have enough time in her work day *not* to journal. She is moving into the dean's position next fall, and fully intends to keep using her journal to handle her busy days.

Case 8: A Community-College Board Member

CJ is a retired English professor who ran for the community-college school board after her retirement. She has a Ph.D. in medieval literature and served a 4-year term on the school board, from 2003 to 2007. Previous to that she taught English at the same community college from 1981 to 2001.

She has been keeping a journal since 1979 when she attended a conference that introduced her to Peter Elbow's work *Writing Without Teachers* (1973). Elbow's advice was that freewrites should be written without consideration of audience. Adapting Elbow's idea, she took up journal keeping with the self as audience in mind. Her journal keeping was sporadic until about 10 years ago, when a friend gave her Julia Cameron's *The Artist's Way* (1992), at which point she began to write daily "morning pages." "Morning pages" consist of three pages of freewrites. With what she calls her "bookkeeper's soul" she now faithfully writes for about an hour until she has filled three pages, rarely two or less. She always stops when she has three pages.

She writes in a chair she bought for 99 cents from a friend, with the light over her shoulder and a table next to her. She uses a spiral notebook with dividers and pockets in it. She uses the pockets for letters or cards she wants to keep. She writes "first thing in the morning" with a cup of coffee and nuts or fresh fruit to munch. She then reads informational material and meditates for 15 minutes.

CJ says this process "keeps me sane." She deals with a lot of issues that require confidentiality during her executive sessions with the board of education. Because she describes herself as "pathologically open," she turns to her audience of one and processes these issues in her journal, because she cannot discuss them with anyone else. Her journal keeps her centered, and she says she can tell if she is not writing enough. She gets upset about trifles. In her journal she writes drafts of things as well as writing about what she calls her "obsessions." These include such things as her weight, food, and money or finances. The drafts she writes often address issues that the board is unfamiliar with or that are unpopular. For example, when the board wanted to build a new culinary arts program and building, CJ thought this unwise. She roughed out her presentation to the board in her journal. She spent several mornings laying out her position and timing it until she had a 7- to 10-minute presentation, which she believed was the maximum length of time they would listen.

Her journal was most helpful during the first month after she was elected to the board when she "felt so alien." She knew the rest of the board didn't like or trust her. Her journal is a place where she can tell the secrets from executive sessions, be honest about other board members, rehearse unpopular stands, and note observations about the college president. When the president attacked her in public, she was not able to write about it for several days. When she finally did, her writing helped her find the core of what was upsetting her.

She is also writing her memoirs and often begins a new section in her morning pages. In this way, she makes discoveries about what she is thinking. Lately she has been writing about her childhood neighborhood. Before that she wrote about the inside of her house, where the basement was her hell (the place where she was punished), and the attic her heaven, because that was where her parents' cousin, Helen, stayed on the weekends to attend church with them. Helen was "an elegant, wonderful person" and the attic held Helen's "aura."

CJ uses lists in her journal, lists of what she likes most about her life, or of compliments people have given her. When she was getting ready to retire, she made long lists of things to do upon retirement because she found her self-esteem in her job, and she was anxious about losing her identity. She says she knows now that she will be a teacher for the rest of her life, but her teaching will take different forms than it has in the past. Her journal is where she feels she can be most honest with herself. She turns to her journal when she is angry with someone, when she feels powerless, and when she doesn't know what to do about these issues.

In her journal she can examine her own behavior, and ask herself, "Why did I do this?" She says she has a voice in her that emerges, a nurturing self that says, "Oh, it's OK. Here's what you need to do to take care of yourself." This is also the voice that says to her, "That wasn't very smart!" She describes this voice as "some loving mother who lives in those pages." She says she doesn't write when she's sick, but is beginning to feel that is a mistake. She begins to get slightly depressed and to wonder "Why is life so bleak?" Suddenly it hits her, "You dummy! You're not writing!" She feels better when she is writing, more in control of what happens to her and what she does.

CJ's advice is that people should read Julia Cameron: "She's so permissive." CJ believes that "everyone in the world needs to do this." She cautions that journal keepers must find a way to feel safe, to find the privacy they need. She says that most of what she writes is boring, that it is "mostly babbling drivel, but that's what I need." Journaling helps her to take care of her obsessions.

Finally, CJ uses her journal to keep track of trees she loves. She says there is a tulip tree right outside of her window that she watches bloom in the spring. Then when the petals begin to fall and she is saddened by this, she reminds herself, "Honey, if it bloomed all year, you wouldn't look at it." She also notices, as it looks more and more raggedy, that its leaves are sprouting. The tree is so old that it has grown down the hill in search of light. Someday, with too much rain, it may be uprooted. This tree reminds CJ of the transitory nature of life. She says it gives her "enormous joy and a little bit of sadness."

Case 9: A Retiring Dean

For the past 7 years, Jean has been dean in one of the schools at a comprehensive public university. She has kept both personal and professional journals over the course of her career. She is currently keeping a "transition" journal as she begins the process of retirement from academic life.

Jean states that she has been keeping personal journals "on and off" since the 1960s. She has a box full of them at home and says they are "a place to communicate with myself." She usually writes when she has some problem to address or some issue to work through, calling these journals "a record of difficult times." She describes her personal journal process as "erratic" or "episodic." She often starts in the fall, having grand plans about writing regularly, but finds she writes "as I need to." She writes a lot "on airplanes" or when she has time to reflect, sometimes trying out new methods, such as the process of writing morning pages delineated by Julia Cameron in *The Artist's Way* (1992). The use of a personal journal, for example keeping morning pages, has been "energizing" and "freeing." In her personal journal she can say anything. She states, "The more I write, the easier it is."

Jean began keeping a professional journal during her first deanship at a small, state school in 1975. She used a spiral notebook at first to keep a record of meetings and phone calls. She found that she needed a record of people she met with "because they were going to expect me to remember." Later, she began to use bound, black, lab notebooks when she came to her current institution. She keeps this notebook in a "carrier" or folio so she can also carry loose papers in it. All the contents of these journals are work related, and she describes these journals as "much more systematic and regular" than her personal journals. These professional journals contain dated notes on meetings, as well as lists, outlines for things she's working on, doodling, drafts of letters, and other reflections. She says, "The act of writing things down makes them accessible to me even if I don't look at it again." It is in many ways a memory device for her.

Jean says her journal entries are "not systematic." She may use a double-entry system or boxes and stars to note things she must do. Her journal has given her "a wonderful sense of always knowing where things are." When she was a teacher, someone suggested putting everything in the same place. She states, "I don't naturally come to the orderly management of paper. I'm sort of like Pig Pen when it comes to how to manage the various parts of my life."

Her professional journal also gives her the ability to look back and reflect on events. She has a record to refresh her memory, "particularly around things that become contentious later." She tried a coding system at one time but says, "I'm just not that systematic." Jean believes her journal allows her to shift gears more quickly. With everything in one place, she can move to the next meeting or event, knowing that she has a record of what happened in the last meeting and will "be able to check back in" when necessary. Her notes are sketchy, but she is usually able to bring back a conversation when needed. She is also able to track multiple threads of events more easily this way. She calls her journal a "thinking place" and feels it helps her to make decisions more easily. She says, "It keeps me listening and less distracted in meetings" because she is writing down what happens. "It keeps me from talking too much," she says. She feels the process allows her to just listen and try to understand other's perspectives, as well as to be "more present" or "in the moment" as she moves through her work day.

Jean uses her journal in conjunction with her PDA. She uses this calendar as an index to her journal. She pastes her weekly calendar into her journal so she knows what meetings she has attended, as well as what is ahead for her. She carries the journal at work and takes it home with her to reflect and plan. She says, "It really has been a chronicle of the years." Her professional journal also contains some personal items, such as quotes that she particularly likes, the words to a song she wants to capture, and grocery lists, as well as her notes on her work day. When asked about the time it takes to journal as a dean, Jean states that her work journal saves time because she doesn't have to go back and reconstruct past events. Everything is in one recognizable place.

In the fall, Jean will be retiring and moving back to her home state. She started a transition journal about a year ago, when she realized she would be stepping down from her work as dean. She wanted to chronicle this transition, to remember the last time she did something and to reflect on her feelings as she makes this big change. She feels that the journal will help her to be "more present" with this transition.

Jean chose a spiral notebook with "a stiff cover." The notebook is lined with "college rule." She said she likes how the pages feel. They are easy to write on. In addition to her own reflections, Jean has included clippings of events, quotes from books she has found helpful, poems, and essays in her transition journal. She said this is new for her and she is really enjoying the process. She keeps a "fun" section in the back of her journal with writing ideas and lists. One list she made was of "things I won't miss" as dean. It included having to come to work when "I have a cold and feel groggy and achy," having to keep track of a million details, and "feeling that I regularly leave my office with more undone than I have accomplished."

In trying to capture a sense of her journaling process over the years, Jean describes it as similar to "running intervals" or "bursts of light." Her personal journals have been a conversation with the self, "a place to listen and nurture." Much like a river, her journaling has rapids, places where you drift along, and quiet pools or eddies where you are going nowhere. Her professional journal is much more utilitarian, more "like a net for capturing or holding" things. Jean has spent a lifetime journaling in various forms and is now ending her career using the same mode, to capture or hold the experience of retiring.

Conclusion

This chapter covers a wide variety of people working in higher education and includes the journal-keeping practices of faculty, students, and administrators. These professional educators all use their journals to reflect on their work lives, but also to track their growth or progress and to organize the many tasks they face, keeping track of events and people they encounter in their work. Thus, while their journals are used to reflect on the meaning of their work, they also serve as organizers for their lives. Our research (Cooper & Stevens, 2006) indicates that faculty and administrators in higher education used their journals for four general purposes: for conversation, for organization, to review and reflect on their multiple roles, and to cope with the complex mental demands of their jobs in individualized and unique ways. You see these four purposes reflected in the journal-keeping conventions of our cases. Certainly all contain conversations with the self, but Jean's comment that her journal is "a place to communicate with myself" directly addresses this function. Sometimes these conversations are in truncated form such as Skip's to-do lists, and in other cases appear in more extensive narrative forms such as Richard's reflections on possible research projects and his future career.

Micki, with her spinning plates and notes on meetings with students, is an example of the second function, using the journal to keep herself organized throughout her workday. Skip, too, relies on his journal to help him keep track of his responsibilities to his colleagues and his organization. Louise is even seen as an "archivist" by her colleagues for the work they all do together.

Third, most of these journal keepers use their journals to review and reflect on their work and their roles within their organizations. Micki, for example, uses her journal to keep track of all her responsibilities and as a record of what has gone on. She refers back to her journal when she is "on a fact-finding mission to find evidence of something." Skip takes his journal home and uses it to think about the future direction of his organization. For him, the journal is not only a memory aid, but a tool for strategic planning. Jean is taking the long view on her work by keeping a transition journal in which she reflects on the end of her career, while Richard is at the beginning of his career and looking forward to what might be ahead for him professionally.

Finally, within these cases you see the various journal-keeping styles or methods that reflect individual differences in coping with the complex mental demands of work in higher education. Louise, for example, keeps her journal at work and tracks her work day with it. CJ, on the other hand, keeps her journal at home and uses it chiefly to reflect on her life as a board member, struggling to understand her own complex reactions to board events and rehearsing what she might say at the next meeting. Barbara uses her journal for reflections on her work and her personal life, creating a document filled with poems as well as notes on meetings and speeches she must give.

The research of other scholars on journal keeping in professional life mirrors these functions. Shepherd (2004), for example, while working as a management advisor, used his journal to describe events in his professional life and then asked the following questions: How do I feel? What do I think? What lessons have I learned? What action will I take? After a time, Shepherd would reflect further on the event, asking these follow-up questions: What have I learned from what I have done? What have I done with what I have learned? Shepherd states, "When I reread my entries, I am able to make most sense out of what I have written if I think of the entries as a journey along a path" (p. 228).

In short, these cases provide you, the reader, with a variety of practices and uses for the professional journal. Whether you are a student working toward a future career as a professional, a faculty member working toward tenure, or an administrator attempting to organize your complex tasks and busy days, these examples will provide you with a rich array of possibilities for your own work.

AFTERWORD
Where to From Here?

As this book comes to a close, we reflect on where it might take you in your own life and work. Embedded in our practices, and our students' and colleagues' voices, our work points to possibilities, endless possibilities that range from fostering learning and reflection in your students' writing, to giving voice to your own personal development, to organizing your professional life, and even reflecting on and improving your health. We hope that we have provided you with enough possibilities, whether you are a graduate student, a faculty member, an administrator, or are walking some other professional path. Like Virginia Woolf, we know that the journal is a capacious hold-all and an elastic space. It can support your journey, wherever it leads, in classrooms and professional life. We wish you joy and insight from journal keeping and look forward to hearing from you as you travel the journal-keeping path. Please visit our Website at www.journalkeeping.com.

APPENDIX A
Journal-Writing Techniques

1. Freewriting

What is it?	Freewriting is a process whereby writers write for a specific period of time, say 5 minutes. The topic is not specified in any way. The goal is to write whatever bubbles up in the mind. There are no grammar, content, or topic rules. The basic rule is that the pen hits the page and does not come up for a specified period of time.
What learning objectives does it serve well?	• To build fluency in writing (e.g., the ability to write out ideas without fear of censure or hesitation, or editing while writing) • To develop writing voice • To generate new ideas in developing papers and projects • To gain confidence in writing
Procedures	1. Describe freewriting and the reasons for doing it. 2. Establish the rule: Do not lift your pen for the specified period of time. Tell students there are no other guidelines—no topic rules, no

grammar rules, no sense-making requirements; the only rule is to write.

3. Follow-up: Ask writers to describe how the process of freewriting worked for them.

Example: A student freewrite from Joe	Freewrite on being in class, on being in life, on being under the gun. . . . I have to ask myself why I am so hard on myself. I am stressed about things that shouldn't be stressful. I miss my cat. I miss my parents. I miss the highway. The blue-haired girl hasn't been in touch. Her last communication was cryptic and strange. I sent her a quote from Miro about his attraction to empty spaces. This is where my heart leads me when I let it. . . .
Example: A freewrite from Elsa, a non-native speaker of English	Freewriting, my reflections about my own writing—I'm noticing while I'm reading my free writing two distinct things, one is how amazing is my mind when I have *Áno presi—n o tensi—n!* about spelling or grammar. The second is that most of my writings are in the present tense (*À Por que? . . . no lo se. . . .* I will try to write in past and present tense) my metareflection is teaching me or is giving me information about myself. *Y me hace pensar,* think about my changes. Since I start to write more often about myself in the journal I can see the good and bad day, *Á Los d'as buenos y los malos!* I think I really engage in my reflections in a battle *encontra del miedo a escribir* my feelings. I'm thinking I will write and write and write to vent my emotions, things that I can't say with words and destroy the adversary *"el miedo,"* the fear. *Primero hare una lista de los miedos para analizar uno a uno y luego refleccionar.*

2. Focused Freewriting

What is it?	This is a type of freewrite in which writers focus on a theme or key question and write about it for a specified time.
What learning objectives does it serve well?	• To develop fluency in writing (e.g., the ability to write out ideas without fear of censure) • To encourage authentic response to a subject • To acknowledge what writers already know about a subject • To generate new ideas in developing papers and projects • To identify key questions that might be unanswered

Procedures	1. Write about a theme or topic at the top of a blank journal page. Write for a specified period of time, say 10–15 minutes.
	2. Write down anything that comes to mind about this topic. Ask questions like the following:
	
	  • What do I already know about this topic?
	  • What do I want to know?
	  • What are the problems with this topic?
	  • What are the key words associated with the topic?
	  • What are the advantages in using this topic?
	  • What worries do I have about writing a paper?
	  • Why do I care about the topic?
	  • Why should others care?
	  • What lingering questions do I have about the topic?

Example: Student focused freewrite on topic for action research project from Greg	TOPIC: Building Classroom Community An issue that I have been thinking about in my class for my action research project is building a

class community. How do you build a community where students have voice, yet we can still complete the content? . . . It seems so often much easier to tell the class the "rights" and "wrongs" rather than create a place where they share ideas and work with one another rather than against each other. I wonder if this is because of the competitive nature of many games we play and the incentives given in school. How do I allow (no, really, incorporate) the games that many students seem to like so much without disenfrachising students that are hurt by competition? Does the competition create an environment that fosters "survival of the fittest" attitudes? Another possibility is that the test-taking-crazy education era that we are in creates competition that further separates our students and stimulates these attitudes.

Metareflection: Originally I thought that differentiated instruction was what I wanted to focus on for my action research project. As I talked with others in my group I realized that competition was a major problem in my classroom that needed addressing. Through the freewrite, I was able to narrow down how competition related to student learning. The freewrite also helped me to "open up" the possible negative effects of a competitive classroom. This reflection pushed me to look beyond the classroom as well. This method of getting my ideas on paper was very effective.

3. Lists

What is it?	Listing involves creating a list of words or ideas or phrases that are a response to a particular topic, idea, or phrase.
What learning objectives does it serve well?	• To generate new ideas in developing papers and projects

- To elaborate on one idea
- To brainstorm many possible answers, responses, or ideas related to another idea

Procedures	1. Introduce the idea that adults already possess the ability to make lists. This journal-writing technique is familiar to writers because we are well-practiced list makers.
	2. Note that it is best not to edit while making the list. Writers can edit after the list is made.
	3. It is best to just keep on making the list and only stop when the writer feels that he or she has thoroughly run out of ideas.
Example: A student list from Meg	People keep journals to:

- To learn
- To reflect
- To emote
- To gripe
- To problem-solve
- To whine
- To leave something behind
- Because it is an assignment or assessment that is required of them
- To prove they exist
- To remember important events
- To record things that they might forget
- To celebrate
- To keep track of milestones or journeys
- Because it appeals to them
- Because they need something to do while lounging at the coffee shop
- For health
- As self-therapy

4. Log

What is a log?	A log is a list of dated entries, usually in columns, with brief descriptions of events that have taken place on that date, for example, student observations, field work interactions, out-of-class group meetings, or research conducted in the library.
Why use logs?	• To learn how to be organized and be able to present experiences in a coherent, organized way • To document student field activities • To demonstrate accomplishment of course out-of-class expectations
Procedures	1. Decide on the format you will use for the log. If asking students to keep a log, it will be helpful to have an example of what a completed log looks like. 2. For students, rather than having them turn in their journals, have the students photocopy the log for grading.

Example: A phone log from a professional journal	A log of phone messages from a faculty journal:
	    Wed. 392-4443 Ken or 946-3334
	    Wed. 392-4445 Ken
	    Thurs. x64670 Diane – OSAS
	    Convocation, May 11th, 6:30pm
	    Fri. 521-2288 Ruby, Dr. Hines, 6 mos. Check up
	    Fri. 959-8966 George in Hilo,
	        finalize summer/fall schedule

5. Dialogue

What is dialogue?	A dialogue is a written conversation with two or more clearly defined parts, roles, or people.
What learning objectives does dialogue serve well?	• To understand the perspective of others • To generate good ideas from other "parts" of oneself • To uncover biases and preconceived notions

• To elaborate on and develop sensitivity for different perspectives

Procedures	1. For students, introduce dialogue by asking whom they can have a conversation with. They will name people, pets, and eventually get to things or even emotions and ideas.
	2. Writers can have a dialogue with anything that they spend a lot of time thinking about or something that has an attraction or repulsion for them.
	3. Set up the dialogue on a journal page similar to the way a play is written, with a new line for each speaker:
	Student: _____
	Other speaker: _____
	4. Be sure to debrief the dialogue in class either with other students or with the whole class. Often the dialogue will unveil some hidden fears and misperceptions.

Example: A dialogue with a student's master's thesis from Alyssa	**Me:** What's up Plan B, or can I call you P.B. for short?
	PB: No, my name is Eve.
	Me: Oh, sorry! I made this same mistake before with my coffee mug, Lani. Sorry for being so egocentric.
	Eve: It's okay, you didn't know.
	Me: Why Eve? Why not "The Paper" or even a cool name like "Electra?"
	Eve: That's my middle name. But you know, Eve, like the first woman? I'm about women and tenure policy right? . . .
	Me: Wow . . . you are smart. And you know me pretty well.
	Eve: Duh! I'm a little part of your brain, and I'm waiting to take on a more tangible form. I'm ready and I'm pretty sure you are ready. . . . The time has come, young grasshopper. . . .
	Me: It's time to write!

Eve: Chi-hee! There you go. I expect to be at least five pages by Sunday. Tomorrow finish reading, and outline, and just start the title page. You'll feel better and so will I.

Metareflection: Oh my gosh, I don't think I've ever written something so insightful and helpful before. I don't even know where to begin but I feel like a weight has really been lifted. . . .

I like this exercise because I get to be silly and uncensored. I write the first thing that pops into my head and usually when I reread what I wrote and even read between the lines, my dialogue has a lot to say. . . .

This was a great exercise.

Example: A dialogue with time from Jeff's journal

Me: I never seem to get enough of you.

Time: Why not?

Me: Because it seems that I am always taking on too many tasks.

Time: Why do you do that?

Me: Because I guess I am trying to better my life.

Time: Why?

Me: I guess I must not like where I am at right now and I need to move forward.

Time: Aren't you happy where you are at?

Me: Not really. I feel like I am in a place that sucks out all my energy and I have nothing left of myself. I miss hanging out with you.

Time: It doesn't sound like this conversation is really about me.

Me: Well, I need more of you to accomplish my goals.

Time: What will you do when you reach your goals?

Me: Enjoy more of what I do. Stop feeling like I am constantly swimming upstream.

Time: Will you finally be able to hang out more with me?

Me: That is the idea. I know that we really need each other, but I am afraid that if I hang out with you

now, I won't get to hang out with you later. It is
a bit of a Catch-22.

Time: Well, then you better hurry up and finish.

Me: You are right. I do have to write a paper this
weekend. I guess I won't see you for awhile.

Time: That's okay. I'll always be here, waiting.

Metareflection: I felt like things popped up and took
over the conversation as I wrote. I didn't really
know where I was going, but the conversation
ended on its volition. What I realized from
this brief exercise is that time really isn't my
problem but rather why I take on so many
tasks. Do I really need to be a full-time teacher,
a graduate teaching assistant, a graduate research
assistant, a graduate student representative all
at the same time while I write my dissertation?
Why am I so afraid to create more time
for myself? This is something that I need to
explore further about myself. If only I had
the time. ☺

6. Concept Mapping

What is concept mapping?

A concept map (mindmap, conceptual framework)
contains a set of ideas and indicates the relationship
among the concepts by placing them in a visual
diagram with links between the ideas. Typically,
though not in all cases, the concept map looks
like a series of boxes or bubbles with lines or arrows
among them indicating the relationship between
the concepts.

What learning objectives does concept mapping serve well?

• To visually represent the relationship among core
ideas within a given subject, chapter, term paper,
field experience

• To understand how ideas are organized in a hierarchical system within a given discipline

• To learn how to take a sea of ideas and organize them in a coherent and sensible way
• To see the overall organization of a lecture

Procedures

1. Have students brainstorm and list all the concepts related to a particular topic in one page in their journal that has a blank page on the other half. Some faculty have had students use sticky notes for this activity. Students put one idea per note.

2. Have students reorganize the ideas into logical categories. This is an iterative process in which they might cluster some ideas together but not have a label for the category. After they have done this

Example: A concept map made by a non-tenured faculty member about her work

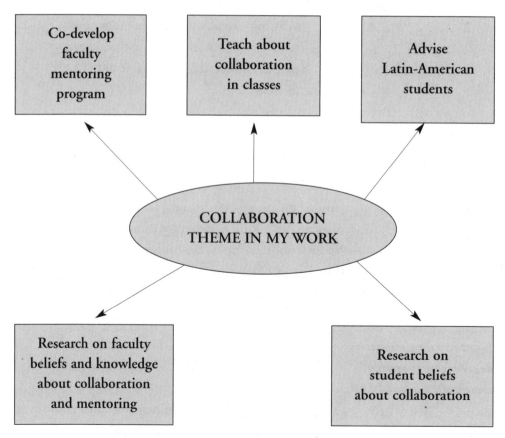

Source: Derived from Stevens & Cooper, 2002.

organization, make a chart on a blank page of the journal with key ideas clustered together with sub-ideas around them. Then, write a sentence that describes this cluster.

7. Metaphor

What is metaphor?	A metaphor is a linguistic device in which one object, part, or person is conceived of as being something else. Metaphor seeks to draw a parallel between concepts. For example, the Internet is an "information superhighway."
What learning objectives does metaphor serve well?	• To build fluency in writing (e.g., the ability to write out ideas without fear of censure) • To generate new ideas in developing papers and projects • To build confidence
Procedures	1. Introduction: Tell students that they are going to use a linguistic device called metaphor to help look more deeply into the journaling experience. Sometimes when we use metaphor it helps us understand the original target word better. 2. List ten activities down the side of the journal page that are not necessarily related to journal writing. 3. Have the student select one that seems to have the most elements that are similar to writing in the journal. 4. Write a list of descriptors for this activity. For example, bicycling requires some physical skill, follows a path but can easily take other paths, can have a goal. There are hills and valleys and each requires a different effort. You don't have to have the knowledge of how a gear works to change speed. You can do it alone or with others. It is affected by the weather. 5. Then write some sentences that describe how journaling is like this activity using the descriptors for the activity. For example, journal writing takes you down different paths. Bicycling and journal writing require that you have some basic physical skills. Sometimes you keep on

riding or writing even though you may not be exactly sure where you are headed. Both bicycling and journal keeping are affected by climate: For the bicyclist, it is the weather, for the journal writer, it is the emotional and intellectual climate.

Example: A metaphor from an athletic trainer, Neil	I think the journal is a great way to dump all of the thoughts and ideas gathered throughout the day. The journal is a punching bag; it just absorbs everything you throw at it, no matter what angle and no matter how hard or soft. It just takes it and does not give you some reason to be mad.

8. Metareflection

What is it?	Metareflection is a process in which journal writers reread their journal entries from prior months or weeks and reflect on those entries. It is a reflection on reflections or journal entries.
What learning objectives does it serve well?	• To develop the habit of reviewing, rereading former entries • To recognize how the writer has grown and changed over time • To develop reflective capacity through practice with the writer's own materials • To see trends and patterns in thinking over the term • To see the value of journal writing • To generate new ideas through combining old ones • To build confidence through observation of thinking over time
Procedures	1. To be able to write a good metareflection, writers need to read old journal entries.

2. As writers are rereading, note entries that catch attention or are meaningful in some way. They can be marked with tabs or photocopied to review later.

3. After writers have selected the attention-getting entries, then ask themselves some questions like these:

• Why did I make this selection?

• Have I changed since then?

• What does it mean to me and to my life in general?

Example: A metareflection from Dannelle's professional journal

I want to think about how my journal writings actually affect my research. How does that really work? Hmmm. . . . Research and journaling—the role, impact, power of journaling in developing, growing, and germinating research ideas. How does a journal germinate ideas? It contains the seeds of thought. The seeds are potentials, lifeless-looking, dry, and shriveled—but when nurtured, watered, cared for, they swell up and burst and grow and bloom. I am thinking of fat pea seeds or zinnia seeds or thin, airy marigold seeds, lifeless at first but plant them in rich soil and add water, there they go with white root threads bursting out of the seed shell.

A journal nurtures the seeds of ideas by holding them like the seed holds the potential for life. The journal holds them as dated entries from conferences, meetings, journal article summaries, and conversations with peers. It surrounds each idea with other ideas from conferences, books, musings, teaching, and research projects. As the journal gets filled up, it allows the free flow of ideas within it, and it also holds all of the other influences in my life to come around and these attach themselves to the initial idea to create a complex network or root system. The white root threads connect the ideas and show how they can work together to nourish larger ideas. When I cull my old journal pages for ideas and then photocopy the pages, I harvest the ideas and put them together in new ways for conference proposals and papers. My journal is a living document.

APPENDIX B
Contributor Contact Information

THE FOLLOWING FACULTY CAN BE CONTACTED regarding their use of journals in their classrooms or professional life.

Name	E-mail	Discipline	Area of Expertise
Anne Nielsen	nielsena@ohsu.edu	Nursing	Reflective journaling to promote thinking and judgment
Micki Caskey	caskeym@pdx.edu	Teacher Education	Use of a journal in professional life
Michael Flower	flowerm@pdx.edu	Philosophy	Use of a blog for student learning
Kofi Agorsah	agorsahe@pdx.edu	International Studies	Journal keeping in international field settings and in professional life
Isabelle Soule	soulei@ohsu.edu	Community Health Nursing	Using metaphor for reflection
L. Rudolph Barton	bartonl@pdx.edu	Architecture	Journaling for seeing and reflecting
Gerry Rechtenwald	gerry@me.pdx.edu	Mechanical Engineering	Journal for multiple responsibilities in professional life
M. B. Ogawa	ogawam@hawaii.edu	Curriculum and Instruction	Journal keeping as a graduate student
Anna Edlund	aedlund@spelman.edu	Biology	Journals in biology class: prompted, nature, body journals
Barbara Mossberg	mossbergb@aol.com	Integrated Studies	Journals to engage students; journals in professional and personal life
Dannelle Stevens	stevensd@pdx.edu	Curriculum and Instruction	Classroom, personal, and professional
Joanne Cooper	jcooper@hawaii.edu	Higher Education	Classroom, personal, and professional

REFERENCES

Adams, K. (1998). *The way of the journal: A journal therapy workbook for healing* (2nd ed.). Towson, MD: Sidran Press.

Ash, S. L., Clayton, P. H., & Atkinson, M. P. (2005). Integrating reflection and assessment to capture and improve student learning. *Michigan Journal of Community Service Learning, 11*(2), 49–60.

Baker, T., & Shahid, J. (2003, April). *Helping preservice teachers focus on success for ALL learners through guided reflection.* Paper presented at the annual meeting of the American Association of Colleges for Teacher Education, New Orleans, LA.

Bandura, A. (1975). Analysis of modeling processes. *School Psychology Digest, 4*(1), 4–10.

Banta, T. (2002). *Building a scholarship of assessment.* San Francisco: Jossey-Bass.

Bargh, J. A., Gollwitzer, P. M., Lee-Chai, A., Barndollar, K., & Trotschel, R. (2001). The automated will: Nonconscious activation and pursuit of behavioral goals. *Journal of Personality and Social Psychology, 81*(6), 1014–1027.

Baxter Magolda, M. B. (1998). Developing self-authorship in graduate school. In M. S. Anderson (Ed.), *The experience of being in graduate school: An exploration: New Directions for Higher Education, #101* (pp. 41–54). Thousand Oaks, CA: Jossey-Bass.

Baxter Magolda, M. B. (1999a). Learning-centered practice is harder than it looks. *About Campus, 4*(4), 2–4.

Baxter Magolda, M. B. (1999b). *The search for meaning in young adulthood: Implications for educational practice.* Paper presented to the Association for the Study of Higher Education, San Antonio, TX.

Baxter Magolda, M. B. (2001). *Making their own way: Narratives for transforming higher education to promote self-development.* Sterling, VA: Stylus.

Baxter Magolda, M. B. (2002, January). Helping students make their way to adulthood. *About Campus, 6,* 2–10.

Baxter Magolda, M. B. (2004). Evolution of a constructivist conceptualization of epistemological reflection. *Educational Psychologist, 39*(1), 31–42.

Belenky, M., Clinchy, B., Goldberger, N., & Tarule, J. (1986). *Women's ways of knowing: The development of self, voice and mind.* New York: Basic Books.

Berman, J. (1994). *Diaries to an English professor: Pain and growth in the classroom.* Amherst, MA: University of Massachusetts Press.

Black, R. S., Sileo, T. W., & Prater, A. (2000). Learning journals, self-reflection, and university students' changing perceptions. *Action in Teacher Education, 21*(4), 71–89.

Blackburn, R., & Lawrence, J. (1995). *Faculty at work: Motivation, expectation and satisfaction.* Baltimore, MD: Johns Hopkins University Press.

Bligh, D. A. (2000). *What's the use of lectures?* San Francisco: Jossey-Bass.

Blood, R. (2002). *The weblog handbook: Practical advice on creating and maintaining your blog.* Cambridge, MA: Perseus.

Boice, R. (1990). *Professors as writers: A self-help guide to productive writing.* Stillwater, OK: New Forums Press.

Boice, R. (2000). *Advice for new faculty members.* Needham Heights, MA: Allyn & Bacon.

Boud, D. (2001). Using journal writing to enhance reflective practice. In L. M. English & M. A. Gillen (Eds.), *Promoting journal writing in adult education: New directions for adult and continuing education, No. 90* (pp. 9–17). San Francisco: Jossey-Bass.

Boud, D., & Walker, D. (1998). Promoting reflection in professional courses: The challenge of context [Electronic version]. *Studies in Higher Education, 23*(2), 191–206.

Boyd, E. M., & Fales, A. W. (1983). Reflective learning: Key to learning from experience. *Journal of Humanistic Psychology, 23*(2), 99–119.

Brookfield, S. (1990). Using critical incidents to explore learner's assumptions. In J. Mezirow (Ed.), *Fostering critical reflection in adulthood* (pp. 177–193). San Francisco, CA: Jossey-Bass.

Brookfield, S. (1991). The development of critical reflection in adulthood. *New Education, 13*(1), 39–48.

Brookfield, S. (1995). *Becoming a critically reflective teacher.* San Francisco, CA: Jossey-Bass.

Brookfield, S. (1998). Critically reflective practice. *Journal of Continuing Education in the Health Professions, 18*(4), 197–205.

Brookfield, S. (2006). *The skillful teacher: On technique, trust and responsiveness in the classroom* (2nd ed.). San Francisco: Jossey-Bass.

Brost, B. D., & Bradley, K. A. (2006). Student compliance with assigned readings: A case study. *Journal of Scholarship of Teaching and Learning, 6*(2), 101–111.

Bruner, J. S. (1969). *On knowing: Essays for the left hand.* London: Oxford University Press.

Bryan, M., Cameron, J., & Allen, C. (1998). *The artist's way at work: Riding the dragon.* New York: Quill/William Morrow.

Burns, M., & Silbey, R. (2001). Math journals boost real learning. *Instructor, 110*(7), 18–21.

Cameron, J. (1992). *The artist's way: A spiritual path to higher creativity.* New York: Tarcher/Putnam.

Carter, C. (1997, April). *The use of journals to promote reflection.* Paper presented at the annual meeting of the American Educational Research Association, Chicago, IL.

Clandinin, J., & Connelly, M. (1998). Stories to live by: Narrative understandings of school reform. *Curriculum Inquiry, 28*(2), 149–164.

Claxton, G. (2006). Thinking at the edge: Developing soft creativity. *Cambridge Journal of Education, 36*(3), 351–362.

Cooper, J., & Dunlap, D. (1991). Journal writing for administrators. *Review of Higher Education, 15*(1), 65–82.

Cooper, J. E., & Stevens, D. D. (Eds.). (2002). *Tenure in the sacred grove: Issues and strategies for women and minorities.* New York: State University of New York Press.

Cooper, J. E., & Stevens, D. D. (2006). Journal writing and academic work: Four cases of higher education professionals. *Reflective Practice: An International Journal, 7,* 349–366.

Cooper, J. E., Stevens, D. D., & Chock, M. (2006). *Journal keeping across disciplinary boundaries: Eight case studies of classroom use.* Paper presented at the annual meeting of the Association for the Study of Higher Education, Anaheim, CA.

Craft, M. (2005). Reflective writing and nursing education. *Journal of Nursing Education, 44*(2), 53–62.

Crème, P., (2005). Should student learning journals be assessed? *Assessment and Evaluation in Higher Education, 30*(3), 287–296.

Crotty, T., & Allyn, D. (2001). *Evaluating student reflections.* River Falls, WI: University of Wisconsin. Retrieved January 2, 2007, from ERIC Document Reproduction Service No. ED459174.

Culley, M. (1985). *A day at a time: The diary literature of American women from 1764 to the present.* New York: Feminist Press.

Davis, T. L. (2002). Voices of gender role conflict: The social construction of college men's identity. *Journal of College Student Development, 43,* 508–521.

Dawson, K. M. (2007, February). Blog overload. *Chronicle of Higher Education, 53*(22), C2–3. Retrieved August 23, 2008, from http://chronicle.com/archive/

Del Toro, G. (2008). *Guillermo Del Toro's sketchbook.* Retrieved August 13, 2008, from http://www.panslabyrinth.com/sketchbook.html

DeSalvo, L. (1999). *Writing as a way of healing.* San Francisco: Harper.

Deshler, D. (1990). Metaphor analysis: Exorcising social ghosts. In J. Mezirow (Ed.), *Fostering critical reflection in adulthood: A guide to transformative and emancipatory learning* (pp. 296–313). San Francisco: Jossey-Bass.

Dewey, J. (1933). *How we think: A restatement of reflective thinking to the educative process.* Boston: D.C. Heath. (Original work published in 1910)

Dewey, J. (1938). *Experience and education.* New York: Collier Books, Macmillan.

Dewey, J. (1944). *Democracy and education.* New York: Free Press. (Original work published in 1916)

Dickerson, M. J. (1987). Exploring the inner landscape: The journal in the writing class. In T. Fulwiler (Ed.), *The Journal Book* (pp. 129–136). Portsmouth, NH: Heinemann.

Diehn, G. (2003). *The decorated page: Journals, scrapbooks and albums made simply beautiful.* New York: Lark Books.

Drago-Severson, E. (2004). *Becoming adult learners: Principles and practices for effective development.* New York: Teachers College Press.

Ducate, L. C., & Lomicka, L. L. (2008). Adventures in the blogosphere: From blog readers to blog writers. *Computer Assisted Language Learning, 21*(1), 9–28.

Durgahee, T. (1997). Reflective practice: Nursing ethics through story telling. *Nursing Ethics, 4*(2), 135–146.

Durgahee, T. (1998). Facilitating reflection: From a sage on the stage to a guide on the side. *Nurse Education Today, 18*(2), 158–164.

Durgahee, T. (2002). Dialogism in action: Talking fact and fiction. *Journal of Psychiatric and Mental Health Nursing, 2,* 419–425.

Elbow, P. (1973). *Writing without teachers.* New York: Oxford University Press.

Elbow, P. (1981). *Writing with power: Techniques for mastering the writing process.* New York: Oxford University Press.

Ellison, N. B., & Wu, Y. (2008). Blogging in the classroom: A preliminary exploration of student attitudes and impact on comprehension. *Journal of Educational Multimedia and Hypermedia, 17*(1), 99–122.

English, L. M., & Gillen, M. A. (2001). *Promoting journal writing in adult education.* San Francisco: Jossey-Bass.

Eyler, J. (2002). Reflecting on service: Helping nursing students get the most from service-learning. *Journal of Nursing Education, 41*(10), 453–456.

Fatton, A., & Eklundh, K. S. (1997, January). *How to support in-process planning in a computer-based writing environment.* Royal Institute of Technology, Sweden. Retrieved June 21, 2008, from http://64.233.179.104/scholar?hl=en&lr=&q=cache:FIj2i-g86VMJ:ftp://ftp.nada.kth.se/pub/documents/IPLab/TechReports/IPLab-119.ps.Z+Ann+Fatton

Fenwick, T. J. (2001). Responding to journals in a learning process. In L. M. English & M. A. Gillen (Eds.), *Promoting journal writing in adult education: New directions for adult and continuing education, No. 90* (pp. 37–47). San Francisco: Jossey-Bass.

Fisher, C. M. (1990). Student journal writing in marketing courses. *Journal of Marketing Education, 12,* 46–51.

Flowerday, T., & Schraw, G. (2003). Effect of choice on cognitive and affective engagement. *Journal of Educational Research, 96*(4), 207–215.

Fox, J., & Morrison, D. (2005). Using concept maps in learning and teaching. In P. Hartley, A. Woods, & M. Pill (Eds.), *Enhancing teaching in higher education: New approaches for improving student learning* (pp. 39–47). London: Routledge.

Frank, A. (1952). *Diary of a young girl: 1929–1945.* Garden City, NY: Doubleday.

Fulwiler, T. (1987). *The journal book.* Portsmouth, NH: Heinemann.

Gee, M. A. (2004). On keeping an academic journal. *Teaching English in a Two-Year College, 32*(1), 26–30.

Ghaye, T., & Lillyman, S. (1997). *Learning journals and critical incidents: Reflective practice for health care professionals.* Wiltshire, UK: Quay Books Division, Mark Allen.

Gil-Garcia, A., & Cintron, Z. (2002). *The reflective journal as a learning and professional development tool for teachers and administrators.* Paper presented at a Conference on Word Association for Case Method Research and Application, Germany.

Glass, R., & Spiegelman, M. (2008). Incorporating blogs into the syllabus: Making their space a learning space. *Journal of Educational Technology Systems, 36*(2), 145–155.

Glaze, J. E. (2001). Reflection as a transforming process: Student advanced nurse practitioners' experiences of developing reflective skills as part of an MSC programme. *Journal of Advanced Nursing, 34*(5), 639–647.

Glaze, J. E. (2002). Ph.D. study and the use of a reflective diary: A dialogue with self [Electronic version]. *Reflective Practice, 3*(2), 154–166.

Graham, L. (2003). Writing journals: An investigation. *Reading Literacy and Language, 37*(1), 39–42.

Grumet, M. (1990). Retrospective: Autobiography and the analysis of educational experience. *Cambridge Journal of Education, 20*(3), 321–326.

Haley, M., & Wesley-Nero, S. (2002). *Dialogic construction and reflective practice: A teacher educator's action research study of teacher as learner.* Paper presented at the TexFlec Conference, Austin, TX.

Hampton, S., & Morrow, C. (2003). Reflective journaling and assessment [Electronic version]. *Journal of Professional Issues in Engineering Education and Practice, 129*(4), 186–189.

Hatcher, J. A., & Bringle, R. G. (1997). Reflection. *College Teaching, 45*(4), 153–159.

Hattie, J., & Timperley, H. (2007). The power of feedback. *Review of Educational Research, 77*(1), 81–112.

Hiatt, G. (2008). Reducing over-complexity in your scholarly writing. *Tomorrow's Professor.* Retrieved February 2, 2008, from http://ctl.stanford.edu/Tomprof/postings.html

Hickman, K. (1987). There's a place for a log in the office. In T. Fulwiler (Ed.), *The journal book* (pp. 391–396). Portsmouth, NH: Heinemann.

Hiemstra, R. (2001). Uses and benefits of journal writing. In L. M. English & M. A. Gillen (Eds.), *Promoting journal writing in adult education: New directions for adult and continuing education, No. 90* (pp. 19–26). San Francisco: Jossey-Bass.

Hoban, G. (2000). Using a reflective framework to study teaching-learning relationships. *Reflective Practice, 1,* 165–183.

Holly, M. L. (1989). *Writing to grow: Keeping a personal-professional journal.* Portsmouth, NH: Heinemann.

Holt, S. (1994). Reflective journal writing and its effects on teaching adults. In *The Year in Review,* Vol. 3. Dayton: Virginia Adult Research Network. Retrieved June 15, 2007, from ERIC Document Reproduction Service No. ED375302.

hooks, b. (1994). Tongues of fire. *Utne Reader, 63,* 136–138.

Hopkins, R. L. (1994). *"Like life itself": Narrative and the revitalization of educational practice.* Paper presented at the annual meeting of the John Dewey Society, New Orleans, LA.

Hubbs, D. L., & Brand, C. F. (2005). The paper mirror: Understanding reflective journaling. *Journal of Experiential Education, 28*(1), 60–71.

Hughes, H., & Others, A. (1997, January 1). Dialogic reflection and journaling. *Clearing House, 70*(4), 187.

Intrator, S. (Ed.). (2005). *Living the questions: Essays inspired by the work and life of Parker J. Palmer.* San Francisco: Jossey-Bass.

Iwaoka, W. T., & Crosetti, L. M. (2008). Using journals to help students learn subject matter content, develop and practice critical reasoning skills, and reflect on personal values in food science and human nutrition classes. *Journal of Food Science Education 7*(2), 19–29.

Jackson, M., & Jackson, R. (2005). The threads we follow. In S. Intrator (Ed.), *Living the questions: Essays inspired by the work and life of Parker J. Palmer* (pp. 183–195). San Francisco: Jossey-Bass.

Jacoby, B. (Ed.). (1996). *Service-learning in higher education: Concepts and practices.* San Francisco: Jossey-Bass.

Janesick, V. J. (1998, April). *Journal writing as a qualitative research technique: History, issues and reflections.* Paper presented at the annual meeting of the American Educational Research Association, San Diego, CA.

Janesick, V. J. (2004). *"Stretching" exercises for qualitative researchers.* Newbury Park, CA: Sage Publications.

Jensen, S. K., & Joy, C. (2005). Exploring a model to evaluate levels of reflection in baccalaureate nursing students' journals. *Journal of Nursing Education, 44*(3), 139–142.

Jones, S., Torres, V., & Arminio, J. (2006). *Negotiating the complexities of qualitative research in higher education.* New York: Routledge.

Journaling after trauma may be beneficial. (2002). *Mental Health Weekly, 12*(35), 8–14.

Kabat-Zinn, J. (2005). *Coming to our senses: Healing ourselves and the world through mindfulness.* New York: Hyperion.

Kajder, S., & Bull, G. (2004). A space for "writing without writing": Blogs in the language arts classroom. *Learning and Leading with Technology, 31*(6), 32–35.

Kalb, C. (1999, April 26). Your health: Pen, paper, power! *Newsweek, 133,* 75–76.

Kaplan, D. S., Rupley, W. H., Sparks, J., & Holcomb, A. (2007). Comparing traditional journal writing shared over e-mail list serve as tools for facilitating reflective thinking: A study of preservice teachers. *Journal of Literacy Research, 39*(3), 357–381.

Kasten, B. J., Wright, J. L., & Kasten, J. A. (1996). *Helping pre-service teachers construct their own philosophies of teaching through reflection.* Paper presented at the annual meeting of the National Association of Early Childhood Teacher Educators, Dallas, TX. Retrieved June 15, 2007, from ERIC Document Reproduction Service No. ED402072.

Kegan, R. (1982). *The evolving self: Problem and process in human development.* Cambridge, MA: Harvard University Press.

Kegan, R. (1994). *In over our heads: The mental demands of modern life.* Cambridge, MA: Harvard University Press.

Kegan, R., & Lahey, L. L. (2001). *How the way we talk can change the way we work: Seven languages for transformation.* San Francisco: Jossey-Bass.

Kerka, S. (2002). *Journal writing as an adult learning tool: Practice application brief.* ERIC Clearinghouse on Adult Career and Vocational Education. Retrieved June 9, 2005, from ERIC Document Reproduction Service No. ED470782.

King, P., & Baxter Magolda, M. B. (2005). A developmental model of intercultural maturity. *Journal of College Student Development, 46*(6), 571–592.

Kitchener, K., & King, P. (1994). *Developing reflective judgment: Understanding and promoting intellectual growth and critical thinking in adolescents and adults.* San Francisco: Jossey-Bass.

Klein, K., & Boals, A. (2001). Expressive writing can increase working memory capacity. *Journal of Experimental Psychology, 130*(3), 520–533.

Kleinman, S., & Copp, M. (1993). *Emotions and fieldwork.* Thousand Oaks, CA: Sage Publications.

Koirala, H. P. (2002, July). *Facilitating student learning through math journals.* Proceedings of the annual meeting of the International Group for the Psychology of Mathematics Education. Retrieved June 9, 2005, from ERIC Document Reproduction Service No. ED476099.

Kolar, K., & Dickson, S. V. (2002). Preservice general educators' perceptions of structured reflective logs as viable learning tools in a university course on inclusionary practices. *Teacher Education and Special Education, 24*(4), 395–406.

Kolb, D. A. (1984). *Experiential learning: Experience as a source of learning and development.* Englewood Cliffs, NJ: Prentice-Hall.

Kraus, S., & Butler, K. (2000). *Reflection is not description: Cultivating reflection with pre-service teachers.* Paper presented at the annual meeting of the American Association of Colleges for Teacher Education, 52nd annual meeting. Retrieved June 9, 2005, from Eric Document Reproduction Service Document ED440079.

Krmpotic, J. (2003). Reflective process in the study of illness stories as experienced by three nurse teachers. *Reflective Practice, 4(1),* 19–33.

Kuzu, A. (2007, July). Views of pre-service teachers on blog use for instruction and social interaction. *Turkish Online Journal of Distance Education, 8*(3), Article 2.

Lakoff, G., & Johnson, M. (1980). *Metaphors we live by.* Chicago: University of Chicago Press.

Lankard, B. A. (1996). *Acquiring self-knowledge for career development: Eric Digest No. 176.* Eric Clearinghouse on Adult Career and Vocational Education. Retrieved June 30, 2006, from ERIC Document Reproduction Service. No. ED399414.

Lepore, S. J. (1997). Expressive writing moderates the relation between intrusive thoughts and depressive symptoms. *Journal of Personal and Social Psychology, 73*(5), 1030–1037.

Lincoln, Y. S., & Guba, E. G. (1985). *Naturalistic inquiry.* Beverly Hills, CA: Sage Publications.

Loo, R. (2002). Journaling: A learning tool for project management training and team-building. *Project Management Journal, 33*(4), 61–66.

Lowenstein, S. (1987). A brief history of journal writing. In T. Fulwiler (Ed.), *The journal book* (pp. 87–97). Portsmouth, NH: Heinemann.

Lu, R., & Bol, L. (2007). A comparison of anonymous versus identifiable e-peer review on college student writing performance and the extent of critical feedback. *Journal of Interactive Online Learning, 6*(2), 100–115.

MacLeod, L. (1999). Computer-aided peer review of writing. *Business Communication Quarterly, 62*(3), 87–95.

Magnusson, D. (1995). Individual development: A holistic, integrated model. In P. Moen, G. Elder, & K. Lusher (Eds.), *Examining lives in context: Perspectives on the ecology of human development.* American Psychological Association: Washington, DC.

Mallon, R. (1984). *A book of one's own: People and their diaries.* New York: Penguin Books.

Martindale, T., & Wiley, D. A. (2005). Using weblogs in scholarship and teaching. *TechTrends, 49*(2), 55–61.

McLeod, S. (2007, May). Professors who blog: Web 2.0 publishing venues don't need to clash with higher education's traditional practices. *Technology and Learning, 27*(10). Retrieved August 23, 2008, from http://www.techlearning.com/

Merriam, S., & Caffarella, R. (1999). *Learning in adulthood: A comprehensive guide* (2nd ed.). San Francisco: Jossey-Bass.

Mezirow, J. (1981). A critical theory of adult learning and education. *Adult Education, 32*(1), 3–24.

Mezirow, J. (Ed.). (2000). *Learning as transformation: Critical perspectives on a theory in progress.* San Francisco: Jossey-Bass.

Miller, D. (2003). Journaling: Telling your professional "story." *Library Media Connection, 22*(2), 32–35.

Moon, J. A. (1999a). *Learning journals: A handbook for academics, students and professional development.* London: Kogan Page.

Moon, J. A. (1999b). *Reflection in learning and professional development: Theory and Practice.* London: Kogan Page.

Moon, J. A. (2006). *Learning journals: A handbook for academics, students and professional development* (2nd ed.). London: Kogan Page.

Morgan, G. (2006). *Images of organization.* Thousand Oaks, CA: Sage Publications.

Moxley, R. S. (2005). It also takes courage to lead. In S. Intrator (Ed.), *Living the questions: Essays inspired by the work and life of Parker J. Palmer* (pp. 256–268). San Francisco: Jossey-Bass.

Murray, D. (1984). *Write to learn.* New York: Holt, Rinehart and Winston.

Nelson, G. L. (2004). *Writing and being: Embracing your life through creative journaling.* San Francisco, CA: Inner Ocean Press.

Nicassio, F. (1992, January/February). SwampLog: A structured journal for reflection-in-action. *The Writing Notebook, 9*(3), 13–18.

Nielsen, A., Stragnell, S., & Jester, P. (2007). Guide for reflection using the Clinical Judgment Model. *Journal of Nursing Education, 46*(11), 513–516.

Noddings, N. (1984). *Caring: A feminine approach to ethics and moral education.* Berkeley, CA: University of California Press.

Novak, J., & Gowan, B. (1984). *Learning how to learn.* New York: Cambridge University Press.

O'Connell, T., & Dyment, J. (2006). Reflections on using journals in higher education: A focus group discussion with faculty. *Assessment & Evaluation in Higher Education, 31*(6), 671–691.

O'Hanlon, C. (1997). The professional journal, genres and personal development in higher education. In S. Hollingsworth (Ed.), *International Action Research: A Casebook of Educational Reform* (pp. 168–178). London: Falmer Press.

Online Education Database. Retrieved August 12, 2008, from http://oedb.org/library/features/top-100-education-blogs

Orem, R. A. (2001). Journal writing in adult ESL: Improving practice through reflective writing. In L. M. English & M. A. Gillen (Eds.), *Promoting journal writing in adult education: New directions for adult and continuing education, No. 90* (pp. 69–78). San Francisco: Jossey-Bass.

Ostermann, K. F., & Kottkamp, R. B. (1993). *Reflective practice for educators.* Newbury Park, CA: Corwin.

Palmer, P. J. (2004). *A hidden wholeness: The journey toward an undivided life.* San Francisco: Jossey-Bass.

Palmer, P. J. (2007). *The courage to teach: Exploring the inner landscape of a teacher's life.* San Francisco: Jossey-Bass.

Park, C. (2003). Engaging students in the learning process: The learning journal. *Journal of Geography in Higher Education, 27*(2), 183–199.

Pennebaker, J. W. (1990). *Opening up: The healing power of expressing emotions.* New York: Guilford Press.

Pennebaker, J. W. (2000). Telling stories: The health benefits of narrative. *Literature and Medicine, 19*(1), 3–18.

Pennebaker, J. W. (2004). *Writing to heal: A guided journal for recovering from trauma and emotional upheaval.* Oakland, CA: New Harbinger Publications.

Pennebaker, J. W., Mayne, T. J., & Francis, M. E. (1997). Linguistic predictors of adaptive bereavement. *Journal of Personality and Social Psychology, 72*(4), 863–871.

Penney, W., & Warelow, J. (1999). Understanding the prattle of praxis. *Nursing Inquiry, 6,* 259–268.

Perry, W. (1999). *Forms of intellectual and ethical development in the college years.* San Francisco: Jossey-Bass.

Peyton, J. K. (2000). *Dialogue journals: Interactive writing to develop language and literacy.* Washington, DC: National Clearinghouse for ESL Literacy Education.

Pipher, M. (2006). *Writing to change the world.* Riverhead: Putnam.

Progoff, I. (1992). *At a journal workshop: Writing to access the power of the unconscious and evoke creative ability.* New York: Tarcher/Putnam.

Qualley, D. (1997). *Turns of thought: Teaching composition on reflexive enquiry.* London: Heinemann.

Rainer, T. (1978). *The new diary: How to use a journal for self-guidance and expanded creativity.* Los Angeles: Tarcher.

Rankin, E. (2001). *The work of writing: Insights and strategies for academics and professionals.* San Francisco: Jossey-Bass.

Read, B. (2006). Think before you share. *Chronicle of Higher Education, 52*(20), 13–19.

Rodriguez, Y. E., & Sjostrom, B. R. (1997). *Cultural moments: A teaching strategy for preparing teachers for cultural diversity.* Paper presented at the annual meeting of the American Association of Colleges for Teacher Education, Phoenix, AZ.

Ruderman, M. N., & Ohlott, P. J. (2002). *Standing at the crossroads: Next steps for high-achieving women.* San Francisco, CA: Jossey-Bass.

Schön, D. A. (1983). *The reflective practitioner: How professionals think in action.* New York: Basic Books.

Schön, D. A. (1987). *Educating the reflective practitioner.* San Francisco: Jossey-Bass.

Schuttloffel, M. J. (2005). Reflective Practice. In S. Tice, N. Jackson, L. Lambert, & P. Englot (Eds.), *University teaching: A reference guide for graduate students and faculty.* New York: Syracuse University Press.

Shapiro, J., Kasman, D., & Shafer, A. (2006). Words and wards: A model of reflective writing and its uses in medical education. *Journal of Medical Humanities, 27*(4), 231–244.

Shepherd, M. (2004). Reflections on developing a reflective journal as a management advisor. *Reflective Practice, 4,* 221–241.

Shonagon, S. (1967). *The pillow book of Sei Shonagon* (I. Morris, Trans.). New York: Columbia University Press.

Silvia, P. J. (2007). *How to write a lot: A practical guide to productive academic writing.* Washington, DC: American Psychological Association.

Slattery, J. M., & Carlson, J. F. (2005). Preparing an effective syllabus: Current best practices. *College Teaching, 53*(4), 157–165.

Smyth, J. (1998). Written emotional expression: Effect sizes, outcome types and moderating variables. *Journal of Consulting and Clinical Psychology, 66*(1), 174–184.

Smyth, J., Stone, A., Hurewitz, A., & Kaell, A. (1999). Effects of writing about stressful experiences on symptom reduction in patients with asthma or rheumatoid arthritis. *Journal of the American Medical Association, 281*(14), 1303–1309.

Sneath, K. N. (2001). *Be a kid again.* Carmel, IN: npower.

Spalding, E., & Wilson, A. (2002). Demystifying reflection: A study of pedagogical strategies that encourage reflective journal writing. *Teachers College Record, 7,* 1393–1421.

Stafford, W. (1964). Writing the Australian crawl: Views on the writers' vocation. *College Composition and Communication, 15*(1), 12–15.

Stevens, D. D. (1996). The ideal, real and surreal in school-university partnerships: Reflections of a boundary spanner. *Teaching and Teacher Education: An International Journal, 15*(3), 287–299.

Stevens, D. D., & Cooper, J. E. (2002). Reflecting on your journey: How to keep a professional/personal journal. In J. E. Cooper & D. D. Stevens (Eds.), *Tenure in the sacred grove: Issues and strategies for women and minorities* (pp. 203–224). Albany: State University of New York Press.

Stevens, D. D., & Cooper, J. E. (2007, April). *Journal writing in the classroom: Effective use and assessment across the professions.* Paper presented to the annual meeting of the American Educational Research Association, Chicago, IL.

Stevens, D. D., Cooper, J. E., & Lasater, K. (2006, April). *Journal keeping in educational settings: Doorway to engaged citizenship, reflective practice and adult development.* Paper presented at the annual meeting of the American Educational Research Association, San Francisco.

Stevens, D. D., Emil, S., & Yamashita, M. (2007, October). *What role does journal keeping play in mentoring international doctoral students?* Paper presented at the annual conference of the Western Washington Regional Research Conference for the Education of Adults, Bellingham, WA.

Stevens, D. D., & Everhart, R. E. (2000). Designing and tailoring school-university partnerships: A straightjacket, security blanket, or just a loose coat? *Professional Educator, 22*(2), 39–49.

Stevens, D. D., & Levi, A. J. (2005). *Introduction to rubrics: An assessment tool to save grading time, convey effective feedback and promote student learning.* Sterling, VA: Stylus Press.

Stiler, G. M., & Philleo, T. (2003). Blogging and blogspots: An alternative format for encouraging reflective practice among preservice teachers. *Education, 123*(4), 789–797.

Stork, A., & Sisson, C. (2005). What! . . . Writing in a science class? In S. Tice, N. Jackson, L. Lambert, & P. Englot (Eds.), *University teaching: A reference guide for graduate students and faculty.* New York: Syracuse University Press.

Suzuki, R. (2004, June). Diaries as introspective research tools: From Ashton-Warner to blogs. *Teaching English as a Second or Foreign Language, 8*(1). Retrieved July 8, 2005, from http://www-writing.berkeley.edu/tesl-ej/ej29/int.html

Swartzlander, S., Pace, D., & Stamler, V. L. (1993, February 17). The ethics of requiring students to write about their personal lives. *The Chronicle of Higher Education,* 130–131.

Tanner, C. A. (2006). Thinking like a nurse: A research-based model of clinical judgment in nursing. *Journal of Nursing Education, 45,* 204–211.

Thompson, B. (2007). The syllabus as a communication document: Constructing and presenting the syllabus. *Communication Education, 56*(1), 54–71.

Thompson, J. (2000). *Making journals by hand.* Glouster, MA: Rockport Publishers.

Thorpe, K. (2004). Reflective learning journals: From concept to practice. *Reflective Practice, 5*(3), 327–344.

Trotter, A. (2007, Fall). Digital divide 2.0. Ed tech experts tackle the question: Is there still a technological divide between the haves and have nots? *Education Week.* Retrieved August 23, 2008, from http://www.edweek.org/dd/toc/2007/09/12/index.html

Tsang, W. K. (2003). Journaling from internship to practice teaching. *Reflective Practice, 4*(2), 221–240.

Valli, L. (1993). Reflection in teacher education programmes. In J. Calderhead & P. Gates (Eds.), *Conceptualizing reflection in teacher education.* London: Falmer Press.

Valli, L. (1997). Listening to other voices: A description of teacher reflection in the United States. *Peabody Journal of Education, 72*(1), 67–88.

van der Rol, R., & Verhoeven, R. (1993). *Anne Frank, beyond the diary: A photographic remembrance* (T. Langham & P. Peters, Trans.). New York: Penguin Group.

Vygotsky, L. S. (1978). *Mind in society.* Cambridge, MA: Harvard University Press.

Walden, P. A. (1988). A learning journal as a tool to promote learning skills. *Feminist Teacher, 3*(2), 14–17, 35.

Wallace, C. C., & Oliver, J. S. (2003). Journaling during a school-based secondary methods course: Exploring a route to teacher reflection. *Journal of Science Teacher Education, 14*(3), 161–176.

Wang, J., & Fang, Y. (2005). *Benefits of cooperative learning in weblog networks.* Retrieved June 15, 2008, from ERIC Document Reproduction Service No. ED490815, http://www.eric.ed.gov:80/ERICDocs/data/ericdocs2sql/content_storage_01/0000019b/80/1b/c4/82.pdf

Wassell, B., & Crouch, C. (2008). Fostering connections between multicultural education and technology: Incorporating weblogs into preservice teacher eduction. *Journal of Technology and Teacher Education, 16*(2), 211–232.

Weimer, M. (2002). *Learner-centered teaching: Five key changes to practice.* San Francisco: Jossey-Bass.

Whyte, D. (2001). *Crossing the unknown sea.* New York: Riverhead Books.

Winningham, M. L., & Preusser, B. A. (2001). *Critical thinking in medical-surgical settings: A case study approach* (2nd ed.). London: Routledge.

Woods, L., & Dinino, K. (2006). *Visual Chronicles.* Cincinnati, OH: North Light Books.

Woolf, V. (1954). *A writer's diary.* New York: Harcourt, Brace. (Date of entry: Easter Sunday, April 20, 1919.)

Yukawa, J. (2006). Co-reflection in online learning: Collaborative critical thinking as narrative. *International Journal of Computer-Supported Collaborative Learning, 1*(2), 203–228.

INDEX

ALSO AVAILABLE FROM STYLUS

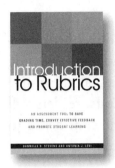

Introduction to Rubrics
An Assessment Tool to Save Grading Time,
Convey Effective Feedback and
Promote Student Learning
Dannelle D. Stevens, Antonia J. Levi

"I have been teaching for 20 years and have always stayed away from rubrics as too mechanical—without ever giving them a fair chance. This summer, desiring to improve my teaching, I read a number of books on teaching in higher ed. in our library, including yours. I found your book very well organized, no longer than it needed to be, and very helpful. This morning I will be working on making two or three rubrics for projects in my Understanding Movies class for fall, and I expect them to improve the quality of student learning and the process of the class."—**Scott Moncrieff,** *Professor of English, Andrews University*

"The authors serve up the seven short chapters of this 128-page book as easy to read, delectable teaching and learning aids that can be adapted and employed with almost any post-secondary course, at any level . . . a handy resource with excellent potential for cultivating interdisciplinary relationships and an aid that extends the location of education beyond the classroom."—**Teaching Theology & Religion**

"*Introduction to Rubrics* offers an excellent guide to those student affairs professionals who have articulated clear intended learning and development outcomes and sought ways to measure the degree to which students are mastering those outcomes."—**Journal of College Student Development**

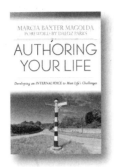

Authoring Your Life

*Developing an Internal Voice to
Navigate Life's Challenges (new subtitle)*
Marcia B. Baxter Magolda
Foreword by Sharon Daloz Parks

A guide to addressing life's challenges and competing demands, to developing self-discovery, and to supporting
others on life's journey. Through reflecting on the stories of thirty-five
adults whom the author has interviewed for over twenty years, readers will
gain important insights about themselves, and develop the confidence to
handle significant transitions and unexpected circumstances.

This book is intended for anyone confronting problems for which they
don't feel adequately prepared. Offering advice on how to be "good com-
pany" for those who have set out on their journey to self-authorship, the
book is also addressed to partners, family members, friends, teachers, student affairs personnel, mentors, and employers who can offer support to
those that face these challenges.

For scholars, this book includes the latest articulation of the author's theory
of self-authorship. It is also suitable as first-year experience/freshman seminar
text.

22883 Quicksilver Drive
Sterling, VA 20166-2102

Subscribe to our e-mail alerts: www.Styluspub.com